AGEING, RITUAL AND S

Ashgate AHRC/ESRC Religion and Society Series

Series Editors:

Linda Woodhead, University of Lancaster, UK
Rebecca Catto, University of Lancaster, UK

This book series emanates from the largest research programme on religion in Europe today – the AHRC/ESRC Religion and Society Programme which has invested in over seventy-five research projects. Thirty-two separate disciplines are represented looking at religion across the world, many with a contemporary and some with an historical focus. This international, multi-disciplinary and interdisciplinary book series will include monographs, paperback textbooks and edited research collections drawn from this leading research programme.

Other titles in the series:

Understanding Muslim Chaplaincy
Sophie Gilliat-Ray, Stephen Pattison and Mansur Ali

Discourses on Religious Diversity
Explorations in an Urban Ecology
Martin D. Stringer

Social Identities Between the Sacred and the Secular
Edited by Abby Day, Giselle Vincett and Christopher R. Cotter

Religion in Consumer Society
Brands, Consumers and Markets
Edited by François Gauthier and Tuomas Martikainen

Contesting Secularism
Comparative Perspectives
Edited by Anders Berg-Sørensen

Religion in the Neoliberal Age
Political Economy and Modes of Governance
Edited by Tuomas Martikainen and François Gauthier

Ageing, Ritual and Social Change

Comparing the Secular and Religious in Eastern and Western Europe

Edited by

PETER COLEMAN
University of Southampton, UK

DANIELA KOLEVA
University of Sofia, Bulgaria

JOANNA BORNAT
Open University, London, UK

ASHGATE

Ageing, Ritual and Social Change

Comparing the Secular and Religious in Eastern and Western Europe

*The stories that have emerged from this endeavour are compelling –
the more so since the individuals in question are allowed to speak
for themselves. This is one reason why I am delighted to commend this
important piece of research to the widest possible range of readers.
There are many others.*

Grace Davie, University of Exeter, UK

*Concern over an ageing society will be a primary issue driving social
policy around the world in the next few decades. This impressive volume
examines the impact of social and specifically religious change on the
experience of ageing in two very different areas of Europe, and should be
required reading for every interested policy maker and researcher.*

Vern L. Bengtson, University of Southern California, USA

Exploring European changes in religious and secular beliefs and practices
related to life passages, this book provides a deeper understanding of the
impacts of social change on personal identity and adjustment across the life
course. According to the latest research, Europeans who consider religious
services appropriate to mark life passages significantly outnumber those
who declare themselves as believers. Drawing on fascinating oral histories
of older people's memories in both Eastern and Western Europe, this book
presents illuminating views on peoples' quests for existential meaning in
later life.

Ageing, Ritual and Social Change presents an invaluable resource for all
those exploring issues of ageing, including those looking from perspectives of
sociology and psychology of religion, social and oral history, and East-Central
European studies.

Published by
Ashgate Publishing Limited
Wey Court East
Union Road
Farnham
Surrey, GU9 7PT
England

Ashgate Publishing Company
110 Cherry Street
Suite 3-1
Burlington, VT 05401-3818
USA

www.ashgate.com

British Library Cataloguing in Publication Data
A catalogue record for this book is available from the British Library

The Library of Congress has cataloged the printed edition as follows:
Coleman, Peter G.
  Ageing, ritual and social change / comparing the secular and religious in Eastern and Western Europe by Peter Coleman, Daniela Koleva, and Joanna Bornat.
      pages cm. -- (Ashgate AHRC/ESRC religion and society series)
  Includes bibliographical references and index.
   ISBN 978-1-4094-5215-7 (pbk.) -- ISBN 978-1-4094-5216-4 (ebook) --
ISBN 978-1-4094-7083-0 (epub) 1. Older people--Religious life. 2. Aging--Religious aspects. 3. Aging--Europe. I. Title.
  BL625.4.C65 2013
  200.84'6--dc23

                                                                        2013008922

ISBN 9781409452140 (hbk)
ISBN 9781409452157 (pbk)
ISBN 9781409452164 (ebk – PDF)
ISBN 9781409470830 (ebk – ePUB)

Printed in the United Kingdom by Henry Ling Limited, at the Dorset Press, Dorchester, DT1 1HD

Contents

PART IV GENDERED AGEING AND RELIGION

PART V REVIEW AND CONCLUSIONS

Notes on Contributors

Simina Bădică is a researcher and curator for the Romanian Peasant Museum in Bucharest, working on memory, oral history and museum representations of Eastern Europe's recent past. Her MA thesis was an oral history of queuing and scarcity in 1980s Romania and she is currently completing her PhD on representations of Communism in Romanian museums. She received fellowships from the Volkswagen Stiftung, New Europe College (Bucharest), Open Society Archives (Budapest) and Central European University (Budapest).

Joanna Bornat is Emeritus Professor of Oral History in the Faculty of Health and Social Care at The Open University (UK). She has degrees in Sociology from the Universities of Leeds and Essex and is Visiting Professor, School of Sociology and Social Policy, University of Leeds. She has a long-standing interest in oral history, ageing and old age and is joint editor of *Oral History*. Her research and publishing has included learning opportunities for older people, reminiscence in care settings, stepfamilies and older people, older people and intergenerational relationships and medical migration and geriatric medicine. She has a particular interest in the methodologies of oral history and in the re-use of archived interview data. She is a founder member of the Centre for Ageing and Biographical Studies and an advisory panel member of Australian Generations: oral history, memory and everyday lives.

Peter G. Coleman is Professor of Psychogerontology at the University of Southampton, England, a joint appointment between the Faculties of Social & Human Sciences and of Medicine. He is also an associate member of the Centre for Research on Ageing at the university. After obtaining a PhD in the psychology of ageing at the University of London in 1972 he worked for five years in the Department of Social Gerontology at the Institute of Applied Psychology (GITP), Nijmegen, the Netherlands, before returning to England. Most of his research relates to the mental health of older people, especially the functions of reminiscence and life review and sources of self-esteem and meaning in later life. He has co-edited textbooks for the British Society of Gerontology, and contributed to Handbooks in the fields of Clinical Psychology, Gerontology and Spirituality. He is a Fellow of the British Psychological Society and an Academician of the Academy of Social Sciences (UK).

Galina Goncharova has a PhD in History of Culture. She is Assistant Professor at the Department of History and Theory of Culture, Sofia University. Her research interests are in the field of oral history, social history of medicine, youth cultures, and religion. She has published on the social role of the Bulgarian Orthodox Church, generational discourses, Bulgarian folk medicine. She has received research fellowships from the Maison des sciences de l'homme et de la société–Sofia and the Centre for Advanced Studies–Sofia. She has participated in a number of collective projects including "The Social Role of Orthodox Priests" (supported by FOROST, LMU München) and MICROCON: A Micro Level Analysis of Violent Conflicts (supported by EU Framework Programme 6).

Sidonia Grama is an independent researcher in social anthropology and oral history. She has a background in Sociology, and received her PhD in the field of History of Mentalities and Oral History from Babes-Bolyai University, Cluj, Romania. Her doctoral thesis examined the 1989 Romanian revolution as reflected in collective memories and social imaginaries, while her fields of interest revolve around the anthropology of memory. Her fieldwork, research and publications include topics such as: the anthropology of the memory of the 1989 Romanian revolution; political mythology and the (non)violence of the 1989 European end(s) of communism; sites of memory and political commemorations, cultural representations of the recent past, oral history as an epistemic project; and genres of memory and oblivion in oral history. She had a doctoral research scholarship at the Institute of Social and Cultural Anthropology (ISCA), Oxford University, and is an alumnus of St. Hugh's College, Oxford, UK. She has also been a member of the Oral History Institute in Cluj.

Teodora Karamelska has a PhD in Philosophy (2005) from Sofia University St Kliment Ohridski, is Assistant Professor in the Philosophy and Sociology Department (New Bulgarian University) and Junior Research Fellow at the Institute for the Study of Societies and Knowledge, Sofia (Bulgarian Academy of Sciences). She has received fellowships from Ludwig-Maximilians-Universität (LMU) Munich, the Institute of European History, Mainz, the Institute of Development Studies, University of Sussex and the Center of Methods in Social Sciences, Göttingen. Since 2009 she has been Assistant Editor of the journal *Sociological Problems* and a member of the Bulgarian Sociological Association. Her research interests are in the fields of sociology of religions and ethnic groups, qualitative social research, especially biographical research.

Daniela Koleva is Associate Professor at the Department for History and Theory of Culture, University of Sofia. Her research interests are in the field of oral history and anthropology of socialism and post-socialism, biographical and cultural memory, biographical methods, social constructivism. She has published a monograph on the 'normal life course' in socialist Bulgaria (2002, in Bulgarian) and a number of book chapters and articles in peer-reviewed international journals. Recently, she has edited *Negotiating Normality: Everyday Lives in Socialist Institutions* (Transaction 2012) and co-edited *20 Years after the Collapse of Communism:*

Expectations, achievements and disillusions of 1989 (Peter Lang 2011). She is a member of the International Editorial Advisory board of *Oral History* and of *L'Homme: Zeitschrift für feministische Geschichtswissenschaft.*

Ignat C. Petrov is a physician with specialties in both Psychiatry and Gerontology & Geriatrics. His PhD thesis was on the mental health and self-evaluation of aged rural people. He worked at the Centre of Gerontology and Geriatrics and the psychiatric clinic at the Medical University in Sofia. Currently, he is a consultant at the Clinical Centre of Endocrinology and Gerontology at the same university. Most of his research relates to mental health in ageing and old age, including self-evaluation, depression, and sources of subjective well-being in later life. He is President of the Bulgarian Association on Ageing, an Honorary Member of the Romanian Association of Gerontology and Geriatrics, and a Member of the Council of the International Association of Gerontology and Geriatrics. He has also recently been nominated as a corresponding member of the Bulgarian Academy of Sciences and Arts.

John H. Spreadbury is a research fellow in the Psychology Academic Unit, Faculty of Social and Human Sciences, at the University of Southampton, United Kingdom. He has research interests in psychogerontology, clinical psychology, and the psychology of religion and spirituality. Following the completion of his PhD in Psychology at the University of Southampton he took up the position of research officer on a collaborative research project, funded by the National Institute for Health Research (NIHR), to evaluate the efficacy of a group psycho-therapeutic intervention for improving quality of life for patients with an early diagnosis of dementia and their caregivers.

Hilary Young is currently Digital Curator at the Museum of London. She completed her PhD from the University of Strathclyde in 2006 which used oral history to explore the representation and reception of gender in British children's periodicals from the 1940s and 1950s. She is interested in identity and memory. Her recent publications include (with Selina Todd) 'Baby-Boomers to "Beanstalkers": Making the Modern Teenager in Post-War Britain' in *Cultural and Social History*, September 2012; 'Whose story counts? Constructing an oral history of the Open University at 40' in *Oral History* Autumn 2011; and 'Hard Man, New Man: Re/Composing Masculinities in Glasgow, c.1950–2000' in *Oral History* Spring 2007.

Preface

My first encounter with the ideas put forward in this book was in the form of a research proposal, which was sent to me for review by the AHRC/ESRC Religion and Society Programme. I was delighted to learn that the Programme had funded the project. At a later stage, I was sent a book proposal by Ashgate, which I endorsed very warmly. I was right. The narrative that has emerged is compelling as the voices of elderly people in very different parts of Europe describe their engagements (or otherwise) with religion at key moments in their lives and the reasons for these.

There are several more specific reasons for commending this volume. For a start, the exceptionally rich data contained in these chapters enhance our knowledge of religion in late modern societies. We learn how a particular section of the population (the elderly) work through the vicissitudes of life and how religion has both helped and hindered this process. Religion, moreover, is related to a whole range of other factors: to the life course, to the family, to ethnic and national identities, to economic and political change and so on. I am also attracted to the methodology, which in itself adds to the richness of the material. The use of oral history enables a degree of reflection that bridges the gap between micro and macro approaches to religion. As a result, we see very clearly what C. Wright Mills in *The Sociological Imagination* revealed as the core of sociology: namely the ways in which 'private troubles' relate to 'public issues'.

Two further factors are important. The first can be found in the inter-disciplinary nature of the work. The team has included scholars trained in gerontology, anthropology, psychiatry, psychology and sociology. The second is the comparative dimension built into research process. The choice of countries – Bulgaria, Romania and the UK – is hardly self-evident, but enables the following comparisons: between East (communist) and West (non-communist) Europe; between Orthodox and non-Orthodox countries; between those parts of Europe with a developed welfare state and those without; and between those countries with relatively high indices of religiousness (Romania) and those where secularisation has taken a greater toll (Bulgaria and the UK), albeit for different reasons.

I warm to inter-disciplinary and comparative ways of working for the following reason: both challenge the taken-for-grantedness that occurs when a single discipline talks to itself, or when the process of (say) secularisation that unfolds in one place rather than another becomes normative. I am well aware, however, that both ways of working are demanding. Inter-disciplinarity, for example, requires very careful preliminary work in order to ensure a shared understanding not only of the key concepts and research methods that will be deployed in the research process, but also of the philosophies of science that lie beneath these. This is all the more the case when the methodologies in question are qualitative rather than quantitative. Add to this the misunderstandings that are likely to arise when scholars from different parts of Europe come together in order to establish a common pool of data – that is, one that is available to all of them. The linguistic challenge is considerable. Even simple terms mean different things in different places, never mind the need to find equivalents in different languages for subtle and deeply personal reflections. I have learnt from the introductory chapters in this book that the technique of oral history has rarely been used comparatively. I can see why.

The stories that have emerged from this endeavour are none the less compelling – the more so since the individuals in question are allowed to speak for themselves. In so doing they fill an important gap in our knowledge, since we know relatively little about the connections between religion and the process of ageing and still less about how this occurs in different European societies. Extended extracts from the interview transcripts introduce us to real people who – by definition – have lived a long time, many of them experiencing radical social changes to which they were obliged to adjust. We learn how they did this and how they were helped, or not, by the rituals of their respective religions. The fact that many of those who no longer declare themselves believers continue to access these rituals becomes an important thread in the story.

For the reasons given above, I fully respect the choice of countries that constitute the comparative nature of this work. I have to say, however, that I read with particular interest the material from Bulgaria and Romania. I was captivated by these accounts, first because the content was relatively new to me: I know less about the Orthodox world than I do about Western Christianity and I found it fascinating. The second reason follows from this: I warmed in particular to the experiential dimensions that stand out in these extracts. The Orthodox tradition enacts its understanding of faith; in the Western tradition – and more especially in its more Protestant articulations – the emphasis lies more on teaching than doing. Despite – or perhaps because of – my familiarity with the latter, I found the first-hand accounts of family celebrations, or of three generations tending the icon lamp as they rose in the morning, extraordinarily vivid.

A third factor relates to the different histories of East and West Europe in the twentieth century. Elderly people in both parts of Europe will, of course, remember the Second World War and the profound dislocations associated with this. Those in the East, however, had more to endure: the war was followed by two generations of communist domination that had immediate implications for religion. The fact that it was experienced differently in Bulgaria and Romania, with contrasting outcomes for the vitality of religion, simply adds to the interest. The crucial point lies in the following. This project captures the recollections of a generation with a unique experience of European history: born for the most part in the 1920s and 1930s, they can recall both the advent and the demise of communism. For some, these recollections include considerable suffering.

It is for this reason that I was so anxious to support the initial application to the Religion and Society Programme. I am delighted now to commend the outcome – a highly significant piece of research – to the widest possible range of readers.

Grace Davie
Professor Emeritus of Sociology
University of Exeter

Acknowledgements

We would like to express our gratitude to the many persons and organizations who have made possible the project on which this publication is based. The research was funded by the Religion and Society Programme, with money received from the UK Arts and Humanities Research Council and Economic and Social Research Council. We thank especially the director and assistant director of the programme, Professor Linda Woodhead and Dr Rebecca Catto, who have provided outstanding support throughout both the duration of the project and the preparation of this publication. We would also like to acknowledge the support of the University of Southampton and the St Kliment Ohridski University of Sofia for material and administrative help provided to us throughout the research.

Above all we wish to thank the study participants in each of our three countries. They were willing to share their remembered experiences of a lifetime. In many cases these experiences involved considerable personal suffering. We hope to have interpreted with sensitivity the lives of those who witnessed both the Second World War and the massive social changes that followed. Yet further social change has occurred in the last quarter of a century, which has affected older people, particularly in Eastern Europe. Many have suffered again, through impoverishment and emigration of younger family members, as a result of the transformation of previous communist societies to Western capitalist models. The declining commitment to the ideal of a welfare state in some Western European countries, including the UK, has also resulted in greater hardship among the older population. We cannot judge whether the lives of future generations of older people will be as challenging as those of the individuals we have interviewed, but we have to be prepared for such an eventuality. We should be fortunate to show ourselves as resilient as the participants in this study.

PART I
Setting the Scene

Chapter 1

Introduction:
Ageing and Ritual in a Changing Europe

Peter G. Coleman, Daniela Koleva and Joanna Bornat

Religion and Ageing

The study of religion and ageing is surprisingly neglected. Although transmission of religion and socialisation into its practices usually occur very early in life, the significance of religion often becomes more important in later years. Indeed it can be argued that, as one of human culture's major products, religion is a major benefactor to age, offering sustenance in the face of biological decline and death (Baltes 1997; Coleman et al. 2011a). These benefits take both psychological and social forms in contributing to a sense of continued meaning and purpose in life, and providing continuity of identity and belief in the face of disruptive social change. In addition, religion often provides tangible physical benefits to older people. Many religions have been at the forefront in creating institutions to cater for older people's care needs. Religious organisations also provide social roles for older people, including the transmission of religious practice and teaching, directly within their own structures and indirectly in their encouragement of intergenerational bonds within the family and wider community.

Thus the steady decline of religious affiliation and attendance that has taken place over the last half-century and more in many Western societies has implications for the future of ageing (Coleman, Mills and Speck 2006). We do not yet know whether the non-religious spiritual and humanist philosophies of life that are becoming more available as lifestyle choices to the new generations of older people will offer the same degree of support in late life as religion has done in the past (Howse 1999). Unfortunately these questions have only recently been asked because the study of religion has been neglected by the social sciences in the greater part of the twentieth century, despite the seminal influence of earlier scholars as Emile Durkheim and William James. The new interdisciplinary field of gerontology that developed after the Second World War has also given relatively little attention to the role that religion and alternative meaning-giving philosophies of life play in older people's daily lives. We need to find answers soon because the first predominantly non-religious generations of older people are almost upon us in the UK and much of Western Europe. Their probably different attitudes to important age-related issues such as life prolongation and control over the moment of death, until recently dominated by religious considerations, will need close attention.

There is no strong evidence to support the oft cited claim (Moberg 2001) that people become more religious as they grow old. A more accurate generalisation seems to be that people tend to remain with the same level of religiosity that they acquired when they were young (Bengtson, with Putney and Harris 2013). As successive generations have become less religious, so both belief and attendance at Christian churches in the West have become more concentrated among older people (Crockett and Voas 2006). This has long been recognised in the UK, where Church of England attendance has come to show an increasingly skewed pattern by age, but it has also been observed in the USA, where church attendance has declined in more recent decades (Putnam and Campbell 2010). If these trends continue, there will come a time, perhaps in as little as 20 years within Western Europe, when there will no longer be an age bias within most church congregations, because only a small minority of all age groups will attend. The Christian Churches have been advised to begin considering new ways of evangelising older people of the future who will no longer have been socialised into Christianity when young (Merchant 2003).

Sociologists of religion have taken care to emphasise that the religious decline of historical Christian Western societies is not representative of World Christianity, let alone of non-Christian societies (Davie 2002). Indeed, with globalisation there is the increased possibility of evangelisation by immigrants to the West from other cultures. What has been less noted in the context of Europe itself, however, is that its own nation-states display a huge variety of religious attitudes. In general the north western countries of Europe, including the UK, show a much lower level of religiosity than the southern and eastern ones, such as Italy, Greece, Poland and Romania, but there is no uniform pattern. Some of the lowest levels of religious allegiance are found in small countries of Central and Eastern Europe, such as the Czech Republic and Estonia (Eurobarometer 2005). These differences undoubtedly reflect many factors, but an important one is likely to be the country's previous religious history, and especially whether religion has been a source of social harmony or division in the formation of the current nation-state.

A recent historical factor of great importance is religious repression by communist governments in large parts of Eastern Europe during the twentieth century. In the case of the countries of the former Soviet Union, persecution of religious practitioners and overt believers was exerted over a period of 70 years or more, the length of an average lifetime. Yet religious organisations survived and since 1989 have recovered much of their former practices and adherence (Froese 2008). This survival has been attributed not only to the tenacity of religious adherence in the Russian and other populations affected, but also to the very brutality of the repression, which created so many religious martyrs. The communist governments of the neighbouring countries that came into the Soviet sphere after the Second World War also followed anti-religious policies ranging from open repression in their first decades in power to more subtle and sophisticated manipulation thereafter.

There has been very little comparative study of religion and ageing in Europe. However, two studies, one in Western Europe and the other in Eastern Europe, support the hypothesis that the mental health of older people is better in countries with stronger religious norms of behaviour (Braam et al. 2001; Coleman et al. 2011b). These results encourage further comparative investigation of religion and ageing in selected European countries with differing levels of religiosity. We have therefore sought, as one of the aims of the studies reported in this book, to better understand how religious beliefs and practices, as well as possible secular alternatives to religion, contribute to mental well-being in later life and allow for better coping with life crises.

Bulgaria, Romania and the UK

This book bases itself on a study undertaken in only three European countries, Bulgaria, Romania and the UK, which limits its generalisability. However, it needs to be stressed at the outset that the choice of these three countries reflects two distinct sets of comparison. The first is that between an increasingly secular (UK) and more traditionally religious societies (Bulgaria, Romania), but also between formerly socialist societies which were very successful in reducing religion to a historical relic (Bulgaria) and those where religious ritual retained an important cultural role, although religious persons, especially in professional life, were often discriminated against and persecuted (Romania). Much could be written about the religious history of each country, and further points will be made in chapters 3 and 4 in particular, but the following should suffice for introducing and explaining the choice made.

Bulgaria and Romania are adjacent countries of similar socio-economic status and potential, both recently (1 January 2007) having been admitted to membership of the European Union. Both are characterised historically by Orthodox Christian culture, four to five centuries of Ottoman rule until national liberation was achieved in the later nineteenth century, periods of war and turmoil in the first half of the twentieth century, and communist dictatorship in the wake of the Second World War up until the revolutions of 1989. Both countries also have significant levels of religious heterogeneity. Bulgaria possesses long-established Muslim populations, whereas Romania has larger numbers of Christian minorities (Roman Catholic, Greek Catholic, Lutheran and other Protestant Christians), as well as Orthodox Christians.

There have been long-standing ties between religion and politics in both Bulgaria and Romania (as in all other Orthodox societies). This tradition goes back to the Byzantine Empire and can be traced all through the Ottoman period, especially in the nineteenth century as part of the nation-building processes and the struggles for independence.

Despite the shared dominance of Orthodox Christianity, Bulgaria today displays a much lower level of religious adherence than Romania (Kanev 2002). Large numbers of Bulgarians indicate attachment to Orthodoxy, but religious practice is in European terms relatively low. The Bulgarian Orthodox Church has received back much of its former symbolic and ceremonial role in the post-communist Bulgarian state, but its social and intellectual influence within society remains weak. Explanations for the Bulgarian situation include the successful subversion by the Bulgarian communist authorities of the previous religious meanings of the annual calendar of feasts and festivals by re-conceptualising their meaning (Koleva 2007). The effect has been to weaken Christian connotations in favour of folklorist and older pagan meanings. Thus religion was successfully integrated into 'cultural heritage', a success largely pre-conditioned by the proximity between religion and nation.

However, it is probably over-simplistic to attribute the success of atheist propaganda to the post-war communist government's policy alone. Other factors need to be explored that may have made the Bulgarian church more vulnerable to subversion into a 'museum piece' of Bulgarian history and culture. These include the long Greek dominance over the Bulgarian church from the time of its inclusion in the Ottoman Empire until it was allowed its own clergy and language later in the nineteenth century, and the resulting strong association of the Bulgarian clergy with nationalistic aspirations rather than spiritual leadership. Certainly doubt has been expressed as to whether the Bulgarians were as religious in the past as their, both Slav and non-Slav, neighbours.

The oft cited intrinsic 'realistic' or 'pragmatic' character of the Bulgarian people may be a shorthand expression for an underlying awareness that religion has often functioned more as a communal source of identity than as a personal source of coping or devotion. These attitudes may have paved the way for the rationalistic arguments of a 'scientific' worldview concordant with communist modernisation. However, it is also true that the communist period and its aftermath witnessed a proliferation of forms of 'popular' (informal) religiosity. These were mostly local cults performed by women in rural regions and centred around a 'sacred' place, icon or other marker, relying on ritual practices rather than on a knowledge of the Orthodox canon.

The Romanian Orthodox Church by contrast has shown a much stronger development since the Second World War. After the initial waves of militant atheism were spent, a strong spiritual renewal movement took place in the late 1950s, and there has been a stream of notable spiritual figures both before and after communism. Indeed the Romanian church has produced one of the most distinguished of modern Orthodox theologians (Dumitru Staniloae). Again historical factors may be at play. The Romanian church had a greater degree of independence than the Bulgarian under Ottoman rule (whereas church bells could be rung in Romania, their use was forbidden in Bulgaria). There was also a lack of consistent suppression of the Romanian Orthodox church by communist authorities. A large number of churches were left open, and monasteries continued to function.

However, particularly cruel was the fate of the Greek Catholic Church, which practises the oriental liturgy while remaining part of the Roman Catholic communion. Its entire patrimony was forcefully transferred to the Romanian Orthodox Church. Those who resisted were obliged to form hidden or 'catacomb' communities. Proper recovery of their patrimony remains a matter of contention in Romania (Verdery 1999, 55–94).

The UK provides a marked contrast with both Bulgaria and Romania. The humanist movement, founded in 1896, has grown in strength and organisation in recent years with over 10,000 members in 2010.[1] However secularism as a system of thought has a long history in the UK, tracing its roots back to the philosophers of the Enlightenment, such as Locke and Paine, and allying with free-thinking and rationalist reform movements of the nineteenth century. Even so, Christian beliefs tended to dominate until the major societal change in religious attitudes that began in the early 1960s, and were not the result of direct government policy but of popular movements against church authority (Brown 2001). According to this view, although the decline in allegiance to Christianity may have begun in the aftermath of the First World War as a reaction to the horrors of that war and the inability of the churches, both Catholic and Protestant, to oppose the mass slaughter that occurred, this did not impose lasting damage on the Christian character of the country. Christian values as a socialising force remained strong both through and after the Second World War. The changes of the 1960s were of an altogether different order. Brown in fact suggests that there is a strong association between the sexual and the religious revolutions. For example, the contraceptive pill changed women's attitude to sexuality and to child rearing. At the same time, part of the basis for the strong support women drew from the churches and gave back to them in return was weakened.

Other Western European countries experienced religious upheaval in this period. The UK's near neighbour the Netherlands underwent even greater changes and over a shorter period, changing from a very religious (and religiously authoritarian) society to a liberal one in a period of little more than 15 years. Affiliation to Christian churches dropped by a third in the last 40 years of the twentieth century (Rooden 2010).

In an intriguing study Houtman and Mascini (2002) have collected and analysed data on various age groups in the Netherlands in order to test the thesis both of 'rationalization' and of 'individualization' as explanations of declining religious belief and practice (Inglehart 1997). The evidence strongly refutes the former, which would suggest that declining religious belief has relatively little to do with an increase in the scientific mindset advocated by atheists such as Richard Dawkins (2006). In fact, an emphasis on scientific and rationalistic thinking as well as on religious belief appears more common in older than younger people (Houtman and Mascini 2002, 468). Faith in both religion and scientific authority appears to have declined. What the evidence does support is an increase in forms of spiritual

---

[1] See http://www.humanism.org.uk/.

belief and non-religiosity in younger generations. This seems to reflect a move on the part of younger generations towards emphasising personal life experience as the touchstone of belief, and a distrust and dislike of external authority, especially relating to moral rules and regulations. Such attitudes have only intensified in recent years as a result of the failures of church authority, demonstrated most of all by the Roman Catholic child abuse scandal, which has affected a number of different European countries as well as the USA.

The evidence from this Dutch study provides strong support for the individualism thesis of British sociologists such as Paul Heelas (1998). Houtman and Mascini also draw interesting parallels between New Age Spirituality, with its emphasis on holism, spiritual transformation and syncreticism, and the Gnosticism of the early Christian era (Ehrman 2005). Religion that emphasises external authority has become distinctly less popular in much of Western Europe. Individuals want to make up their own minds without being overly (or at least consciously) influenced by external sources of persuasion and authority.

No matter how personal religious and spiritual worldviews are formed, in reality they are grounded in dialogue with previous cultural traditions, even though they may revise or depart from them. It is such interactions between the personal and the social, between life course and historical change, that this book aims to explore. In particular, it seeks to examine how ritual, considered as prescribed forms of social behaviour linked to particular events in the life of the individual, family and community, adds meaning to life at key transition points.

Ritual as the Focus of Study

In seeking a focus for our comparative study of the impact of twentieth century religious change on older people in European society, we decided on the topic of ritual for a number of reasons. Ritual is increasingly recognised to be as central to the social phenomenon of religion as belief itself. Indeed it is primarily through shared actions, verbal or non-verbal, that persons express religious beliefs. It is also ritual that marks persons out as belonging to one particular religion and not another, and it is often through elaborate initiation rituals that persons join a religious group. Thus, rituals point to the practical and collective aspects of religion.

Participation in rituals implies physical and emotional involvement. At the same time, their symbolic content is productively ambiguous and open to multiple interpretations (not always relating to the supernatural). This 'non-committed ambiguity' (Furseth and Repstad 2006, 128), while it may suggest an explanation for the continuing popularity of rituals in a time of individualisation of religion, provides a promising entry point into the study of contemporary attitudes to religion and its alternatives. Furthermore, increasing emphasis on aesthetic attitudes, symbolic actions and metaphors, rather than cognitive and dogmatic statements, draws attention to the ritualistic and emotional aspects of religion.

However ritual is not only the preserve of religion. Even in times of growing secularisation, people appear often to need a consensus circumscribed by group membership that helps them identify themselves in terms of belonging and distinction from a cultural, national or political Other. They need ways to transcend themselves that lend a feeling of stability to their lives and of infallibility to their worldviews. Not surprisingly, all ideologies have sought expression in rituals and symbols. Their significance is demonstrated by the fact that the communist governments in Eastern Europe that tried to overturn religious allegiance also sought to produce alternative secular rituals to take their place.

Rituals have been thematised in the social sciences since their onset and from different perspectives: anthropologist Arnold van Gennep (1960 [1908]) has elaborated on the structure of ritual, introducing the key concept of liminality to understand rites of passage; sociologist Emile Durkheim (2001 [1912]) has pointed to the importance of rituals for the solidarity and cohesion of the group through the production of collective emotions ('collective effervescence'); anthropologist Victor Turner (1969) has focused on the 'working' of the symbols in rituals, while Maurice Bloch (1992) has seen ritual as a 'conquest' of the present world by the transcendental, seeking to explain by this 'ritual idiom' actual violence and conflict situations.

In contrast, despite William James's (1982 [1902]) pioneering work on 'religious' (nowadays more appropriately classified as 'spiritual') experience, Sigmund Freud's (1961 [1927]) view of religious behaviour as an inferior form of coping was to have more influence on psychology's attitude to religion. The concept of ritual itself is, in the psychological literature, most closely associated with symptoms of obsessive–compulsive disorder. Only in recent years has this negative perspective been challenged by the increasing evidence for the predominantly positive influence of religious belief and practice on health and well-being (Koenig, McCullough and Larson 2001; Coleman 2010).

Rituals are seen throughout this book as socially standardised behaviour with a symbolic content, performed on specific occasions. However, we are not interested in the institutional maintenance and actualisation of such behaviours, even less in their uses for national and other political mobilisations, but rather in their importance for the individuals who perform them and for whom they are performed. Hence the focus is primarily on life-cycle rituals (rites of passage), although in our study we have collected data on older people's practice and experience of all forms of religious ritual. Births, marriages and deaths are also the most important sites for development of non-religious ritual (Davies 2012), where secular alternatives are most clearly visible. Focusing on them, we see performance of rituals as, amongst other things, a form of agency: they help both the cultivation of selves and the construction of communities.

The emphasis on ritual puts individual religiosity or non-religiosity in the context of social interactions where it is received and practised, and in the context of traditions that have been important for its formulation – whether through dialogue or through opposition. It allows us not to lose from sight the non-religious alternatives to religious rites of passage. Thus the project foregrounds collectively accepted norms about attitudes and behaviours, and the beliefs and values that guide them, rather than spirituality as a personal pursuit of existential meaning. The interest in ritual cannot set aside collective and practical aspects of religion since it is groups and institutions (in the broad sense) that provide the setting of the rituals. Thus – in response to the individualism thesis mentioned above – we see the individual and collective aspects of belief as complementary rather than as alternatives. Focusing on the standardised, performative, non-discursive and social aspects of religious practice, we seek to draw a link between the notions of the aim and meaning of human life and the everyday decisions to which they may refer.

The main questions therefore that have guided the investigation refer to the changes in use of ritual that older people remember and whether they perceive these changes as beneficial or rather as losses. Furthermore, we have been interested in secular forms of ritual that have produced a meaningful sense of occasion for births, marriages and deaths. The emergence of these alternatives has differed in the three countries, as well as their level of acceptance. We have also considered that, in many instances, religious ritual remains attractive even for those who have little or no explicit religious belief and practice, and we have tried to explore why this might be the case.

Methods of Investigation: Oral History

Although our project has had an interdisciplinary character, we decided from the outset to give precedence to oral history methods of investigation. This is because our focus was not on the exact content of belief or the nature of ritual and ceremonies in which people engaged but rather on the recall of expressions of belief and non-belief and the ways in which changing ceremony and ritual have been embedded in every day life, over time. Oral history interviews with people over the age of 75 offered the possibility of gathering testimony that would reveal, and enable the exploration of, personal meaning and knowledge within historical, social and cultural contexts, spoken in the words of those who could recall changing practices and who would articulate their feelings and emotions as they spoke of the religious and the secular in their lives. The attraction of oral history methodology lies in the possibilities it offers for such expressions and for memories to be recorded, shared and interpreted amongst the team members.

In focusing on individual lives the Religious and Secular Ceremonies (RASC) project's interviewers and analysts were seeking what was personally expressed, often hidden, perhaps for political reasons, but most often because it was unremarked or considered unremarkable. As Thompson (2000, 20) points out, these 'hidden spheres of social life' provide evidence of the nature of the resistances, compromises and originalities in people's thoughts and the symbolic and practical cultural and social resources they draw on. The result not only adds to what we know of the past, but it may also challenge and revise what we thought we knew (Frisch, 1990). The ability of oral history as a method to focus on the less public aspects of a life is appropriate for a study of belief and non-belief. Being asked to talk about the events of a life not only encourages people to speak with authority, about what they know best, but it also frames what they tell within generational and historical temporalities which, for a cross-national project like RASC, provides a valuable basis for comparison.

To elicit memories of the everyday, of minority experience, of childhood and young adulthood, of migrant or working lives, of leisure, or of forms of subjugation or alternative lifestyles by means of interview or dialogue is, as Portelli (2011, 10) explains, 'the telling of historical narratives in oral form'. There is much to be elaborated from that simple statement. Telling is a social experience, a relationship between two or more people at a certain point in time. The time told may extend over a few or many decades and may include times beyond the experience of the narrator, when myths and traditions are woven into an account. The means of telling, memory, is also no simple act of retrieval. Subjectivity and vulnerability to the effects of time, situation and reputation may all affect what is told. Nevertheless oral historians see these variabilities as adding value because, 'What people believe and what they forget is as significant as what people recall accurately' (Portelli 2011, 11).

Talk about the past may often bring people to a new realisation of the implications of their actions or it may mean that the context of the telling has changed, politically and socially. Managing accounts that may have involved conflict or subterfuge, or which describe events that have changed meaning and value over time, may mean that an interviewee seeks composure, accepting a life and memories of times lived through (Thomson 1994). Awareness of the intersubjectivities, misrememberings and compromises that are a part of the process of recall and remembering is essential to an oral history approach, never more so than in the case of religious and secular ceremonies where involvement is likely to have had both personal and public meanings during changing political, historical and social contexts, which at times will have put people at odds with prevailing ideologies and conventions.

The richness and immediacy of oral testimony have led to a large and ever-expanding literature where 'voice' is given centre stage. This means people using their own language, as far as possible without mediation, in such ways that authenticity will be guaranteed through the narrator's or speaker's own individual form of expression and use of language. Spoken words, when captured by a recording machine, have a compelling effect, but transcription solidifies and fixes their meaning once they are transformed into text. Adding translation inevitably increases distance from the original. This was unavoidable in a project that was working with three distinctly different languages, Bulgarian, English and Romanian. Translation was essential if we were to be able to absorb and understand the interviews and if we were to share our analyses and, of course, produce this book. Comparative studies that cross language boundaries are bound to result in compromises with commitments towards internationalism and individual self-expression (discussed in Chapter 2), and this we acknowledge as a team; however, without a lingua franca, even one as historically tainted as the English language, the project could not have achieved its objectives. We took steps to enhance our understanding, by working closely with transcribers and translators and by constantly checking and assessing meanings at both individual and public levels and with constant reference to historical and political change. In such ways we aimed to preserve the original orality of the data collected but at the same time we remain mindful of the limitations imposed by the method we have chosen.

Research Team

The three editors of this volume shared responsibility for the direction of the research study. One of their first tasks was to recruit experienced and qualified interviewers in the three countries. The result was a rich mix of scholars and researchers with contrasting but also complementary backgrounds in the study of anthropology, history, psychiatry, psychology and sociology, with a particular emphasis on gerontology and oral history. The complete list of the team is given in Appendix I.

Of the total team of 13 persons employed on the project, 10 authors have contributed chapters to this volume. At the team's second meeting in Cluj-Napoca, Romania in 2010, we invited colleagues to contribute a chapter to an envisaged book on the general theme of our research and to propose a theme of particular interest to them individually. We were fortunate that their response was both enthusiastic and varied so that the end result is a book that is not only interdisciplinary but also wide-ranging in its themes. Each author was encouraged to read across the interviews and to conduct some measure of comparative analysis. We have been delighted by their response.

It is important to note that the team reflects the varied background of the study directors themselves in attitudes to the topic of religion as well as in terms of disciplinary training. Thus the team includes persons across a whole continuum of religious to non-religious affiliation and commitment. Although it is unusual to comment on the personal attitudes of researchers to the subject matter of their investigation, we consider variation of attitudes a merit in the case of studying a controversial topic such as religion. Because we were able to listen to each others' presentations at the final project conference in Southampton in 2011 and to read and comment on draft chapters for this book, we have hopefully removed at least some of the major instances of unhelpful bias in interpretation.

A terminological inconsistency throughout the book reflects another aspect of the authors' self-positionings towards the subject matter of research: the terms 'communism' and 'socialism' are used interchangeably to denote the recent past of Bulgaria and Romania. Each of them is linked to theoretical, disciplinary and national contexts. The former refers to the so-called 'totalitarian' paradigm, dating back to Hannah Arendt and Cold War Western theorising, while the latter is associated with the more recent 'revisionist' paradigm. Furthermore, 'communism' is more often used in political philosophy and political science while 'socialism' is preferred in social anthropology and history of everyday life. Finally, terminology is suggestive of national memory cultures as well. Thus 'communism' is preferred in Romania while in Bulgaria, where the recent past has been addressed more hesitantly, both terms are used, with 'communism' connoting a negative attitude and 'socialism' considered more neutral or sometimes even nostalgic. The use of both terms therefore is a fair reflection of the complexity of the discourses about the recent past in the two countries.

Content of the Present Book

We have ordered the chapters into five sections. Following on from what has been written in this introductory chapter, Joanna Bornat elaborates further in Chapter 2 on our methods of investigation and in particular on comparative oral history and its applications to the study of belief and non-belief in late life. A comparative approach to oral history research is not a common strategy adopted amongst oral historians, nor has religion been a topic much researched using this method. In her chapter she considers why this is the case and what can be learned from examples in oral history and from the RASC project to develop research linking narratives of remembering across historical and national boundaries.

The second and largest section of the book (chapters 3–6) provides analysis and exploration of the major questions underlying our project: the emergence of religiosity and non-religiosity in people's lives; personal explanations for engagement in ritual practice; and continuing commitment to religious ritual in otherwise non-religious people.

In Chapter 3 Simina Bădică considers the high levels of religiosity in Romania, comparing these against lower levels in Bulgaria within the context of overlapping national and religious identities. Drawing on interviews from both countries, she argues that, whereas religious identity was incorporated into national identity in Romania during the communist period, this was not the case in Bulgaria. She focuses on funeral rites, identifying the commitment to 'dying Orthodox' in both countries. In suggesting that this declaration is made by both religious and non-religious people, she concludes that religious identity is embedded in national identity and that enforced secularisation and its accompanying rituals were less important than the continuity of tradition.

Hilary Young's focus in Chapter 4 is the discourse of non-religious people and how this is developed in the oral history interview. Her chapter begins with a discussion of current debates on secularisation in the UK and then discusses approaches to interviewing about religious practices within the context of secularisation, suggesting that the trend towards secularisation presents a framework for people to understand their religious past as well as their non-religious present. Having drawn on the testimonies from all three countries, she concludes that the stories which emerge are examples of a search for composure as people find ways to tell which they feel comfortable with in the context of their own lives and the times they have lived through.

In Chapter 5 Sidonia Grama examines religious discourse, analysing the depth of meanings conveyed by what people say and do not say in answer to questioning about their beliefs and practices, paying particular attention to the meaning of silences. She draws attention to the importance of the dialogical experience on the course of the interview, of shared attitudes and views to the subject matter. In the latter part of the chapter she provides detailed analyses of interviews with some of the Romanian participants she herself interviewed who suffered greatly under communism, in part because of their religious convictions and the actions these convictions led them to take in the course of their lives.

In Chapter 6 Daniela Koleva considers the social and psychological dimensions of rituals.[2] She focuses on a seeming paradox: the continuing adherence to religious rites of passage even by non-religious individuals. She is interested in participants' motives to engage in symbolic practices that have obviously lost for them their original meaning of relating to a divine power (or have never had such a meaning). Her hypothesis is of a diffuse social normativity that takes the forms of conformity as an unreflected ethos, of a conscious ethics of solidarity with the immediate we-group, and of an ideology linking religious experience to a cultural tradition.

The next two sections are of particular gerontological interest. They examine topics of importance to understanding the role of religion and functional alternatives to religion in promoting adjustment to ageing. Part III focuses on death and bereavement. In Chapter 7 Galina Goncharova explores ideas about death and their articulation through religious and secular humanist rituals. Starting with a comparison of the models of bereavement and care for the dead in the three countries, she goes on to demonstrate how personal visions of the end of life are grounded in dynamic constellations of cultural practices, social networks and religious or secular worldviews. This allows her to compare the grief systems influenced by different secularisation scenarios, especially those imposed by communist regimes, and to suggest a perspective on funerary and commemorative rituals as expressions of a community of the dead and the living.

Chapter 8 provides a psychological analysis of the value of religious ritual to the bereaved person. John Spreadbury draws on cases from the three countries in examining the role of religious belief and ritual in the context of bereavement. He argues that religious beliefs and practices have potential therapeutic effects in a number of ways, most importantly through a belief in a life after death where reunion with the deceased would be possible, and a belief in a personal relationship with

---

[2]   Sometimes, the term 'ceremony' is used as a synonym to 'ritual'. While in certain contexts the former may be preferred to refer to more formal, public and not necessarily recurrent events, the authors of this book have not found it useful to distinguish between the two terms.

God providing support and protection. Individual and group rituals as enactments of these beliefs seem to be important psychological resources for coping with the loss of loved ones and for the mental well-being of the bereaved.

Part IV provides separate perspectives on adjustment in older men and women. In Chapter 9 Ignat Petrov and Peter Coleman build on their previous studies of the impact of social change on mental health and subjective well-being of older persons. Explicit comparisons are drawn between those men who remained religious through their lives according to their initial socialisation and those who developed a secular frame of mind during the communist period. In general both groups have adapted well to ageing, with those of humanist and specifically socialist outlook showing equivalent levels of well-being to the more religious men interviewed. The chapter includes a number of cases of Muslims, who remain an important minority in modern Bulgaria.

In Chapter 10 Teodora Karamelska considers the role of religion in relation to women's ageing, seeking to understand the experience of the lives of women born between the two world wars. She takes her examples from across the three countries to illustrate different emerging themes, including biographical turning points, the function of rituals and the development of expertise in its application, the interpretation of suffering in life, and the tension between religious authority and autonomy in personal spirituality. She illustrates how, as these women have aged, religion has become integrated into their everyday life and interpreted so as to best deal with their particular situations. Clerical authority can be questioned and personal spiritual experience becomes the primary source of trust.

The final section of the book considers what broad conclusions can be drawn from our project about the role of ritual in later life and the value of conducting comparative analysis in this area. In Chapter 11 Peter Coleman, Sidonia Grama and Ignat Petrov consider the oldest and frailest cases in our samples in each country, those mainly over the age of 85 years. In all three countries the oldest old tend to have been brought up more religiously and to have remained more religious than younger age groups. Religious ritual, including especially prayer, does indeed appear to provide tangible social and psychological benefits to them. However, the lack of comparative material on non-religious very old people makes it hard to draw firm conclusions. The authors consider one of the major findings of the research, the greater respect for religious ritual evident in Bulgaria and Romania as contrasted with the UK, and explore possible explanations, historical, educational and cultural.

In Chapter 12 Joanna Bornat and Daniela Koleva reflect on the process of conducting this research project. They consider what has been learned from attempting to study comparative oral history in the area of religion, and what might be the implications for future research of this kind. They also address the difficult issue of competing interpretations of controversial material, and especially, in regard to conducting research on religion, reconciling the sometimes diverse perspectives of religious and non-religious researchers.

References

Baltes, Paul B. 1997. 'On the Incomplete Architecture of Human Ontogeny: Selection, Optimization and Compensation as Foundation of Developmental Theory'. *American Psychologist* 52: 366–80.

Bengtson, Vern L., with Norella M. Putney and Susan C. Harris. 2013. *Families and Faith: Generations and the Transmission of Religion*. New York: Oxford University Press.

Bloch, Maurice. 1992. *Prey into Hunter. The Politics of Religious Experience*. Cambridge: Cambridge University Press.

Braam, Arjan W., P. Van Den Eeden, M.J. Prince, et al. 2001. 'Religion as a Cross-cultural Determinant of Depression in Elderly Europeans: Results from the EURODEP Collaboration'. *Psychological Medicine* 31: 803–14.

Brown, Callum G. 2001 *The Death of Christian Britain*. London: Routledge.

Coleman, Peter G. 2010. 'Religion and Age'. In *International Handbook of Social Gerontology*, edited by Dale Dannefer and Chris Phillipson, 164–76. London: Sage.

Coleman, Peter G. et al. 2011a. *Belief and Ageing. Spiritual Pathways in Later Life*. Bristol: The Policy Press.

Coleman, Peter G., Marie A. Mills and Peter Speck. 2006. 'Ageing and Belief – Between Tradition and Change'. In *The Future of Old Age*, edited by John Vincent, Chris Phillipson and Murna Downs, 131–40. London: Sage.

Coleman, Peter G., Roxana O. Carare, Ignat C. Petrov, et al. 2011b. 'Spiritual Belief, Social Support, Physical Functioning and Depression among Older People in Bulgaria and Romania'. *Aging and Mental Health* 15: 327–33.

Crockett, A. and David Voas. 2006 'Generations of Decline: Religious Change in 20th Century Britain'. *Journal for the Scientific Study of Religion* 45: 567–84.

Davie, G. 2002. *Europe: The Exceptional Case. Parameters of Faith in the Modern World*. London: Darton, Longman and Todd.

Davies, Douglas J. 2012. 'Changing British Ritualization'. In *Religion and Change in Modern Britain*, edited by Linda Woodhead and Rebecca Catto, 203–18. London: Routledge.

Dawkins, Richard. 2006. *The God Delusion*. London: Bantam Books.

Durkheim, Emile. 2001 [1912]. *The Elementary Forms of Religious Life*. Oxford: Oxford University Press.

Ehrman, Bart D. 2005. *Lost Christianities. The Battles for Scripture and the Faiths We Never Knew*. New York: Oxford University Press.

Eurobarometer. 2005. *Social Values, Science and Technology. Report 225*. Brussels: European Commission.

Freud, Sigmund. 1961 [1927]. *The Future of an Illusion*. New York: Norton.

Frisch, Michael. 1990. *A Shared Authority: Essays on the Craft and Meaning of Oral and Public History*. New York: State University of New York Press.

Froese, P. 2008. *The Plot to Kill God. Findings from the Soviet Experiment in Secularization*. Berkeley, CA: University of California Press.

Furseth, Inger and Pal Repstad. 2006. *An Introduction to the Sociology of Religion*. Farnham: Ashgate.

Heelas, Paul. 1998. *The New Age Movement*. Oxford: Blackwell.

Houtman, Dick and Peter Mascini. 2002. 'Why Do Churches Become Empty, While New Age Grows? Secularization and Religious Change in the Netherlands'. *Journal for the Scientific Study of Religion* 41: 455–73.

Howse, Kenneth. 1999. *Religion and Spirituality in Later Life: A Review*. London: Centre for Policy on Ageing.

Inglehart, R. 1997. *Modernization and Postmodernization: Cultural, Economic, and Political Changes in 43 Countries*. Princeton, NJ: Princeton University Press.

James, William. 1982 [1902]. *The Varieties of Religious Experience*. London: Penguin Classics.

Kanev, P. 2002. 'Religion in Bulgaria after 1989: Historical and Socio-Cultural Aspects'. *South East Europe Review* 5: 75–96.

Koenig, Harold G., M.E. McCullough and D.B. Larson. 2001. *Handbook of Religion and Health*. New York: Oxford University Press.

Koleva, Daniela. 2007. 'The Memory of Socialist Public Holidays: Between Colonization and Autonomy'. In *Zwischen Amnesie und Nostalgie. Die Erinnerung an den Kommunismus in Südosteuropa*, edited by Ulf Brunnbauer and Stefan Troebst, 185–98. Köln: Böhlau.

Merchant, Robert. 2003. *Pioneering the Third Age. The Church in an Ageing Population*. Carlisle: Paternoster Press.

Moberg, David O. 2001. 'Research on Spirituality'. In *Aging and Spirituality. Spiritual Dimensions of Aging Theory, Research, Practice and Policy*, edited by David O. Moberg, 55–69. Binghampton, NY: The Haworth Press.

Portelli, Alessandro, 2011. *They Say in Harlan County: An Oral History*. Oxford: Oxford University Press.

Putnam, Robert D. and David Campbell. 2010. *American Grace: How Religion Divides and Unites Us*. New York: Simon and Schuster.

Rooden, Peter van. 2010 'The Strange Death of Dutch Christendom'. In *Secularisation in the Christian World*, edited by Callum B. Brown and Michael Snape, 175–95. Farnham: Ashgate.

Thompson, Paul. 2000. *The Voice of the Past*, 3rd edn. Oxford: Oxford University.

Thomson, Alistair. 1994. *Anzac Memories: Living with the Legend*. Melbourne: Oxford University Press.

Turner, Victor. 1969. *The Ritual Process: Structure and Anti-Structure*. New York: Aldine de Gruyter.

Van Gennep, Arnold. 1960 [1908]. *The Rites of Passage*. Chicago, IL: University of Chicago Press.

Verdery, Katherine. 1999. *The Political Lives of Dead Bodies: Reburial and Postsocialist Change*. New York: Columbia University Press.

Chapter 2

The Challenge of Difference:
Approaching Comparative Oral History

Joanna Bornat

An exploration of changes in religious and secular ceremonies, beliefs and practices, carried out by interviewing a generation of people whose memories go back over several decades of social and political change in Eastern and Western Europe, and which draws on the expertise of psychologists, oral historians, sociologists and ethnographers, was inevitably going to pose challenges. From the start, striking a balance between detail, difference and universalising generalisation, the RASC research group looked for ways to record, share and analyse interview data which encouraged comparison without losing what was unique or possibly conflicting. The team had drawn up a series of research questions with which to lead their investigation. These related to changes in ritual and ceremony and how these are viewed from late in life; the significance of ritual in the lives of older people; to what extent religious ritual has any attraction for those who have no explicit religious belief and practice; and the nature of secular alternatives.

In this chapter I locate RASC methodologically, beginning with an overview of cross-national comparative studies, moving on to comparison in oral history, I consider why this approach is so rare, pointing additionally to the scarcity of approaches to understanding religion and religious belief in oral history. I then outline the methods adopted by RASC and conclude by illustrating the complexity of working with memory across national and linguistic boundaries by drawing on two examples from the interview data.

Cross-national Comparative Research Projects

Searching for examples of cross-national qualitative research in an attempt to position RASC as a comparative study led to two literatures that are cognate methodologically, oral history and more generally social science. Interestingly, neither appears to be replete nor expanding. I begin with an exploration of social scientists' contributions to debates about comparative work.

Cross-national Approaches in the Social Sciences

Cross-national research projects using qualitative approaches are not as common as might be supposed. Although Rose (1991) points out that comparative political analysis is as old as Aristotle and that the comparative method was a feature in work by Comte and Spencer and the later founders of sociology, Durkheim and Weber (see also Hantrais 1999), more recent divisions in how best to approach cross-national comparative work have tended to undermine confidence and to raise questions about methods and results claimed (Miller and Taylor 2009). The discussions that have arisen are, however, helpful as they draw on experience that is useful to others, such as ourselves.

Hantrais takes a historical look at the evolution of comparative work and in so doing highlights the tensions in an approach that seeks to tackle the complexity of national differences. She points out how the search for generalisations meant that sociologists in the mid twentieth century were searching for characteristics that could be identified as shared across political boundaries or that could be used to classify (Esping and Andersen 1990). This search for universals played down differences, especially those based in culture, in order to be able to construct theories that offered the possibility of generalisation. A contrasting development emerged with research that focused on differences and highlighted cultural relativism, using ethnographic data and basing explanations on the actions and values of individuals. A mid-way position, the 'societal' approach, was followed by researchers who identified patterns or subsets of societies in such a way as to allow for individuality in the social construction of the phenomenon under observation (Hantrais 1999, 94–7).

Large-scale survey-based studies have been the most typical approach to dealing with cross-national comparison in Europe. Some of these have included qualitative methods as a part of their design; the Eurobarometer studies are an example of cross-national studies that have operated at country level since 1973, funded by the European Commission. The Commission has also funded studies that have sought to identify a set of contextual variables that allow for comparison within and between countries, as in the seven-country project, 'Social Strategies in Risk Society', which used a 'socio-biographic method' to consider 'precarity', while Chamberlayne and King used a biographical approach to explore the lives of carers (SOSTRIS 2004; Chamberlayne and King 2000).

Chamberlayne and King were both bi-lingual in English and German and each was familiar with the three countries where they interviewed their 75 respondents. This was to be a great aid to their powers of comparison. Others have pointed out how language can be problematic, first, at the level of meaning where, for example, Ungerson shows that even such basic terms as 'work' and 'education' may be understood quite differently. Also, translation may lead to the 'corruption of data', with publication imposing a 'lock' on the cultural specificity of meanings once they have been rendered into a different linguistic representation (Ungerson 1996, 64; see also Miller and Taylor 2009). For Mangen (1999, 111), the 'ultimate challenge is to make sense of cognitive, connotational and functional meanings', but Mangen argues that, whatever strategies are adopted, an assessment of a project's findings should be linked to what was planned initially given that issues relating to language are likely to force compromises on the research process.

Researchers who have undertaken cross-national comparative projects raise issues about ways of managing contextual complexity, the advantages and disadvantages of discerned difference, the interplay of individual and social/ national structural trajectories, the contribution of shared concepts and the limitations which language difference may impose. All agree that comparisons across national boundaries are challenging while producing unique methodological insights and potentially original theorising. However, working with history and memory adds dimensions that generate even greater complexity and challenge for comparison, a challenge which a few oral historians have taken up.

Oral History and Cross-national Studies

Since the 1970s, oral historians have sought to establish and maintain links between each other with frequent conferences and published collections displaying the interconnections, debates and fruitful themes that demonstrate an intrinsic internationalism. Given this history, it would be reasonable to assume that there must be a substantial body of work to inform studies like RASC. Surprisingly this is not the case, although edited collections and journals include voices from all continents and many countries, as the archives of *Oral History* and *Oral History Review* and two oral history series published by Palgrave Macmillan and Oxford University Press[1] demonstrate. The pioneers of oral history in the UK, US and Europe set out to build networks and provide opportunities for speakers to present accounts drawing on individual, community and national memory at the first International Conference hosted by the UK Oral History Society in 1979 (Ritchie 2011, 9). In the introduction to an edited collection that followed, Thompson points to the disciplinary diversity of the contributors and to individual oral history pioneering roles in the 10 European countries they write from, arguing that there is 'much more of a shared European past than we can imagine'. Concealed behind the particularism of national histories and language differences are, 'grand themes' which are 'cross-continental' (Thompson with Burchardt 1982, 10).

Themed edited collections, significantly those in the *International Yearbook of Oral History and Life Stories* series, encouraged this broad perspective, taking in national differences and drawing out themes with studies which focused on family, migration, totalitarianism and gender (see for example, Bertaux and Thompson 1993). However, although they shared much, the contributors were not working together on a shared project, nor were they comparative. More typically they

---

[1]   See http://us.macmillan.com/series/PalgraveStudiesinOralHistory (accessed 30 May 2012) and http://ukcatalogue.oup.com/category/academic/series/history/orhis.do#.T8XBg Y58vtU (accessed 30 May 2012).

tended to work towards the generalising model which Hantrais (1999) identified, fitting individual national differences into historical sweeps and generational movements. Two examples that have taken a comparative approach, Villanova's interviews with 'illiterate workers' in Barcelona, Baltimore and Nazi death camps (Villanova 2011) and van Boeschoten's, study of wartime massacres in a Greek and an Italian village (van Boeschoten 2007), even so use data collected for different projects at different times. By contrast, perhaps the most notable and extensive international oral history project is Steven Spielberg's 'Survivors of the Shoah Visual History Foundation', which began in 1994 and collected video testimonies from 52,000 Holocaust survivors, interviewed in 56 countries in 32 languages, before expanding to include testimonies from survivors of other genocides and mass slaughters (USC Shoah Foundation Institute n.d.). This is a truly cross-national project, but is restricted to collection and preservation of interview. We were thus left with very few examples to draw on, and indeed the search for examples of cross-national comparative oral history projects narrows down to only three examples previous to RASC.

Of the three international oral history projects that offer a fit with what RASC set out to do, two focus on the same topic, the student movements of 1968. The first, chronologically, is Ronald Fraser's *1968 A Student Generation in Revolt* (1988). This drew on interviews carried out in six countries: the USA, West Germany, France, Italy, the UK and Northern Ireland. In his introduction Fraser asserts that the collaboration between nine oral historians was 'The first large-scale international oral history of its kind'. He identifies their 'point of departure' as a shared view of the internationalism of the 1968 student movement and that 'national specificities would take second place' (Fraser 1988, 4). The latter point they were to modify as the project progressed. The oral historians he lists in his introduction to the book include three who were already influential in the field, in addition to himself: Ronald Grele, Daniel Bertaux and Luisa Passerini (Fraser 1988, 6). Altogether 230 people were interviewed through a network of interviewer contacts.

Fraser outlines how the team worked and maintained contact (this was of course long before email). The interviews were collected between 1984 and 1985 and were 'based on an agenda of questions – though not a joint questionnaire', with questions related chronologically to the movement's events. How people were selected for interview is not explained, although the pen portraits of each interviewee, included at the end of the book, suggest that these were people who were mainly key figures on the political left. The collaborators then wrote drafts, having carried out the interviews, which gave an account of each stage of the movement in their country. These were sent to Fraser, who edited and revised the contributions, a process which he says took over two years and which included 'collective as well as bilateral consultations' (Fraser 1988, 6). From Fraser's introduction we are not given information as to how language differences were managed, although it seems that all but one of the collaborators were fluent in English. The book is divided into sections that offer a chronology, based in the different national locations but with thematic cross-national links drawn from accounts of the events to show the broader political and social analysis that Fraser develops. It was not easily accomplished; indeed the project depended on Fraser's record as a writer for its funding and continuing survival. Grele, a member of the collaborating group, recalls that support came from the publisher's advances and that several of the collaborators were working for free, although others were supported by their employing institutions (Ron Grele 2012, personal communication).

There are a number of obvious differences from RASC. For a start, the time lapsed since the events of 1968, less than 20 years, was much shorter than the lifespan our interviewees were asked to recall. Linked to that is the comparative youthfulness of the interviewees; most would have been under 50 in the mid 1980s, some younger – all at a different life stage than the 75 year olds and over interviewed for our project. However, in terms of history and memory, there are similarities between the two projects. Fraser's aim, and that of his collaborators, was to rescue the 1968 student and worker movements from subsequent interpretations. Grele recalls even so that 'We never really came to grips with one overarching theme to hold everything together. We did talk about this endlessly whenever we met as a group or whenever we met each other informally (and Ronnie at one time travelled to each of us to discuss the progress of the book) but it never really gelled … Even twenty years after '68 it was too early to come to any conclusions' (Ron Grele 2012, personal communication).

Twenty years later again, Robert Gildea and colleagues returned to the events of 1968 with a similarly international oral history project, interviewing activists from 100groups and networks in 14 countries, 'from Spain to the USSR and from Iceland to Greece' (Gildea 2010, 71). They completed 500 life history interviews for a project titled 'Around 1968', during 2007–10 (Gildea 2013, 3). They preferred the term 'networks' as in their opinion it more accurately reflects the swiftly changing grouping and re-grouping that marked 1968. From the networks they identified people 'whose contribution to the events around 1968 was particularly significant or interesting or who were particularly marked by those events' (Gildea 2013, 3). This approach enabled a rather different approach to that of Fraser and his colleagues. For one thing, their 14 countries breached earlier divides and included Eastern Europe, Poland, Czechoslovakia, Hungary, the German Democratic Republic and the Soviet Union as well as Franco's Spanish dictatorship and the Greece of the Colonels. In this way they spread their net further than the 'epicentre of revolt' to a wider geography of action and interconnections (Gildea 2013, 13). Across the project, leaders were sought for interview as well as people not so well known. Apart from scope, another difference from Fraser and his group's approach was their aim to look at the activists' whole lives, with interviews covering 'family, education, political and private choices … friends and contacts and their trajectories through 1965–75 and subsequently'(Gildea 2010, 71). The edited collection published from the project follows the trajectory of activism, taking themes such as revolutions, space, faith, sexuality and violence as well as accounts from those who dropped out, while giving weight to the significance and influence of family relationships as well as traditions of resistance. In contrast with Fraser and his group, public funding meant that they had the advantage of a study that was fully costed and with institutional support for all group members.

The third example of a cross-national oral history project that I consider is no less ambitious, in terms of both scale and historical impact. The International Forced Labourers Documentation Project led by Alexander von Plato completed almost 600 interviews between 2004 and 2007 in 24 European countries and in Israel, South Africa and the USA. The project was funded by the German Foundation, Remembrance, Responsibility and Future (Stiftung Erinnerung, Verantwortung und Zukunft) (Thonfeld 2011, 33) and followed the Foundation's programme of payments to forced labourers between 2001 to 2007, which came after a national process of debate and international negotiation. Forced or slave labour played a significant role in the German war economy. Conscripted in occupied countries into agriculture and factories, these workers had no contract of employment and no opportunity to determine their employment or living conditions (Thonfeld 2011, 34). The interviews were biographical, drawing on people's experiences from their earliest childhood memories, through their experience of forced labour. Project members were interested in people's memories of 'homecoming' and how this affected their memories, as well as how 'the Germans' were regarded (von Plato, Almut and Thonfeld 2008, 14). The interviewing team was assembled by advertising through the International Oral History Association and other contacts, including the International Mauthausen Documentation Project. In response there were applications from 50 groups in 29 countries and in the end 32 groups were chosen to interview in 27 countries and these, with about 72 members of staff, remained with the project to the end, attending briefing seminars and using a set of training materials that were translated into various languages. Interviewees were recruited with the aim of including equal numbers of men and women, working in various occupations and living in a range of types of accommodation, including private homes, farms, concentration camps and detention camps (von Plato et al. 2008, 11).

Apart from collecting accounts of different experiences of enslavement in Germany and occupied areas and of recognition in the various homelands of former slave labourers in the years following the ending of the Second World War, the project leaders were interested to consider the interplay of individual and collective remembering and forgetting. Significantly, these experiences had not played a part in postwar narratives in most countries. The lapse of time and the traumatic nature of many of these memories meant that a cross-national project on this scale would be confronting many difficult and potentially unresolved questions at an individual and a national level. The project's structure and organisation with its contributing national papers and overall management and editorial team is similar to Fraser's 1968 project as members of the central team drew on the data to write about particular themes (see for example Thonfeld's 'national cultures of remembrance; Thonfeld 2011, 34).

So far as oral history is concerned, there are various reasons for the paucity of completed projects, apart from the obvious question of cost and organisational complexity. The identification of a shareable focus was clearly helpful to the three projects described. Without that identified focus, finding an operational moral and political perspective, cross-national comparison maybe problematic. However there is another reason why oral historians have shied away from working comparatively. Oral history's defining characteristic, the recording of voiced memories, could have worked against the very internationalism that proponents espouse, for three reasons. First, the historical dominance of English as a lingua franca has the tendency to discourage internationalism given the association of that language with hegemony and empire. To facilitate a more bilateral approach is costly for projects when both interpretation and translation are required at all stages.

The second reason is that working through translation can only be a very approximate way for oral historians to access original meanings and feelings (see for example discussions by Andrews 1995; Burton 2003; Wheeler 2008) and, although it can reveal unexpected insights, translation goes against the genre's central and defining principles of individual self-expression and empowerment (Thompson 2000; Abrams 2010, 154–61). Translation also raises problems for sustaining a shared authority (Frisch 1990) from the start to finish of a project, if interviewees are not able to read the final product in translation. Archiving too becomes an issue, if interviews or audio files are dispersed into nationally located holdings.

English was the lingua franca for the RASC team with translation from Romanian and Bulgarian taking place after the interviews had taken place. Although undoubtedly this gave native English team members an advantage in some respects, they were relatively disadvantaged in that none was familiar with either of the other two other languages, in contrast with their colleagues from Romania and Bulgaria, who all possessed an excellent standard of English, although they did not speak each other's language. Issues of meaning and understanding are most relevant at the stage of data analysis and interpretation when working in a cross-national group and are evident in the historical, linguistic and cultural complexities that occur when memory is used as the way to access the past, and this is perhaps the third reason why so few comparative projects have emerged from oral history, despite a commitment to a spirit of internationalism. To take note of this is to point out that what RASC set out to do, in a very short time, 12 months, was ambitious and with only these few and rare sightings providing models to be learned from when it came to project development and collaboration. However, what has contributed to RASC's even more exceptional ambition has been the focus on religion and secular ceremonies. If there are few examples of cross-national oral history projects to consult, there are even fewer oral historians who have looked at religion and remembering. In the next section I consider why this is the case before going on to look at how RASC set out to deal with a comparative study of religion and secularism in the lives of three groups of older Europeans, in Bulgaria, Romania and the UK.

Oral History and Religion: A Story of Neglect

A lack of comparative cross-national oral historical studies is matched by oral historians' neglect of religious belief. A search through the oral history literature reveals very few studies making religion a central focus. Religion appears in accounts of interviews with Native Americans, Nigerians, participants in the US Civil Rights movement, in urban and in rural settings, in relation to community membership, ethnicity and family history, and for the part it has played in the lives of people affected by conflict, persecution and rapid modernisation over most of the twentieth century (see for example, Gudziak and Susak 1996; Ilyasoglu 1996). As is evident from a search of the two journals *Oral History Review* and *Oral History*, the term 'religion' commonly appears in project design, indicating topics to be covered, and in published accounts it certainly appears as an aspect of people's lives, sometimes as an indicator of generational change or ethnic or community solidarity (see for example Koleva 2009; Ester; 2008). However, as a phenomenon, a set of practices, a shared experience, religious belief has gained little attention from oral historians, and secularism or non-religious belief has by default experienced even greater neglect.

There have been oral history approaches to studies of specific religious communities and memberships, for example Angrosino (1991) interviewed members of a monastic community, Gerrard (1996) talked to women entering a religious order, Yates (1996) interviewed women priests approaching ordination and Johnston and McFarland (2010) interviewed industrial chaplains in Scotland. Williams in the themed issue of *Oral History*, 'Religion and Belief', argues the case for oral history as the most appropriate method to research popular belief, and is critical of studies that result in religion being 'narrowly defined in relation to its institutional manifestations' and that give 'precedence ... to the analysis of socio-structural change over and above the examination of the actual content of religious ideas'. She expresses her interest as understanding 'the character and content of the beliefs of working people who lived their lives on the edges of the institutional church within the sphere of popular culture' (Williams 1996, 27). In pursuing this she used oral history interviews in a study of working class lives in the London Borough of Southwark, looking back to the period 1880 to 1939 alongside autobiographies, ephemera, local newspapers, music hall songs, folklore and Booth's survey of Londoners conducted between 1866 and 1903.[2] From this she argues, 'It became clear ... that the inhabitants of Southwark were exposed to a range of religious idioms which combined in their understanding to form

---

2   Charles Booth's *Inquiry into the Life and Labour of the People of London* (1886–1903) is archived online at: http://booth.lse.ac.uk/static/a/3.html.

a distinct repertoire of belief. Folk and christian or orthodox elements of belief combined in people's descriptions of life' (Williams,1996, 30). Significantly, her approach was not to ask interviewees directly about belief or formal practices, but to generate responses that expressed feelings and beliefs in a 'distinct language in which beliefs were formulated and conveyed' (Williams 1996, 29). She shows how in interviews various beliefs combined, as for example with Mrs Ivy, who when asked if there was a Bible in her family answered: 'Oh yes, you had to have a Bible, otherwise you would be unlucky if you didn't have a Bible' (Williams 1996, 30).

This approach is developed more fully by Brown (2001) in a monograph that looks at the secularisation of 'Christian Britain' over two centuries. Using written texts for the nineteenth century, he draws on archived oral history interviews for the later period to argue for a 'discursive Christianity' (Brown 2001, 13) that recognises a need to understand belief and non-belief as spoken expressions, described behaviours and reflections on expected Christian activity and institutions. Even so, he is critical of the first wave of oral historians, interviewing in the 1960s and 1970s who, he argues, engaged with interviewees' religiosity in terms of formal practices to explain class differences, thus relegating religious belief to the status of marker or variable. He welcomes the more reflective and subjective approaches of the 1980s and 1990s, which he feels open up possibilities to use the interaction between the worlds of the interviewer and interviewee[3] as having their own intrinsic worth (Brown 2001, 116–17).

Williams' and Brown's work might have been expected to have been followed up by oral historians interested in community and social history, but surprisingly this has not been the case. Two recent publications include religion and belief as aspects of broader discussions, in each case highlighting the role of emotion in recall. Moodie suggests that moments of religious joy may be seen as evidence of emotional expression and a key to feelings about wider social issues and the strength of personal commitment to controversial views (Moodie 2010). The other work re-uses data from an earlier study to explore the significance of a religious experience in the life of a child. Revisiting the data suggests that an opportunity was missed for considering the role of the social workings of religion in a working-class industrial community (Bornat 2010). In both cases, a focus on religion was secondary to the initial enquiry, suggesting that there is scope for oral historians who take a more socio-cultural approach to include beliefs as they interview on a wide range of topics.

Such an approach may be helpful in developing a focus on belief, and on non-belief, given that, as a movement in the UK at least, oral history has neglected religion. Oral history's origins in the UK are within the secular tradition of radical politics which, although recognising the affiliations and attachments of key figures in relation to such movements as Christian Socialism, for example, placed greater emphasis on the significance of institutions and activities that were independent of

---

[3]   Further discussed in Chapter 4.

the established church and religious leaders generally. Yeo, with a richly illustrated argument, offers a corrective to this tendency. In a study of the origins of British socialism in the 1890s he suggests a need to recognise the place of feeling and emotion and also the forms and traditions that such expressions took (Yeo 1977).

Disregard has of course also been a reaction to the role of religion in supporting damaging communitarianism in Northern Ireland and Scotland. From this perspective religious belief has been viewed as historically divisive and the institutions of religious observance as traditionally diverting attention from the realities of working lives (Thompson 1963). Marx's judgement that 'Religion is the sigh of the oppressed creature, the heart of a heartless world, and the soul of soulless conditions. It is the opium of the people' (Marx, 1844) continues to inform historians working within a tradition which focuses on understanding conditions of oppression and inequality in whatever century.

With these precedents, how was the RASC study carried out and achieved?

Designing and Carrying out the Study

In Chapter 1, the case for an oral history approach was presented. Here I go on to outline the methods developed by RASC for working across three countries.

The four research questions which the RASC team devised were designed to deal with differences generated by very great political change as well as the individually unique life experiences of older people in Bulgaria, Romania and the UK over the last 60 years or more, and to encompass both religious and secular perspectives. They are listed in Box 1.

Box 1 RASC research questions

What have been the changes in use of ritual that older people themselves remember and how were they experienced?

What are the consequent benefits as well as losses perceived by those who have witnessed the changing trends in ritual?

What is the character of alternative secular forms of ritual which have produced a meaningful sense of occasion for births, marriages and deaths?

What is the remaining attraction of religious ritual for those who have little or no explicit religious belief and practice?

Working in three countries, with an agreed focus of interest, our aim was not to be statistically representative but to generate and document processes rather than incidences from which generalisation may be drawn and comparisons made (Gobo 2004, 453). The budget allowed for 20 participants in each of the three countries. We therefore aimed to produce three reliable cross-section purposive samples in the three countries each comprising 20 men and women over the age of 75, including people born before 1935 who would have clear memories of the postwar social changes in each of their countries, both religious and non-religious people, living in urban settings. So far as religious affiliation was concerned, each sample was to include followers of the dominant religion, Orthodox in Bulgaria and Romania and Church of England in the UK, and also other religious affiliations including Catholics, Jews and Muslims. Non-believers were to be approached in a way appropriate to their country.

Recruitment was mainly conducted by word of mouth, in part drawing on networks previously established in each of the three countries. In Bulgaria these included churches in Sofia and north-east Bulgaria (Varna and the neighbouring towns of Shumen and Targovishte with a significant Turkish population) as well as Pensioners' clubs; in Romania, interviews were conducted in Bucharest and Cluj-Napoca. In the UK publicity was sought through local religious and secular networks together with visits to local churches and other institutions in two areas, the London Borough of Hackney and Southampton. Where local religious leaders or places of worship were contacted, some snowballing ensued with varied success. In the UK, two additional networks included the local branches of the British Humanist Association and the Jewish museum in London. The interviewees are listed in Appendix II, showing age, gender, occupation, marital status, living circumstances and religious affiliation. Their real names have been replaced by pseudonyms throughout the text.

The interviews were designed to follow a life history structure (see Appendix III) and were drafted in English with careful discussion in the Bulgarian and Romanian teams in relation to language and culture, questions that might be problematic to ask and how to re-phrase them, as well as the best way to introduce certain topics. Interviewees were to be provided with opportunities to talk about their earliest memories, but focusing on the role of religious or secular ceremonies and rituals at key points in their lives. These included first experience of death, being a godparent, graduation and initiation, marriage ceremonies, seasonal festivals, children's baptism and partner's or parents' deaths. On the way people were to be asked about their beliefs and if, how and why these might have changed during their lifetimes. The interview schedule was guided, encouraging open-ended and discursive responses together with opportunities for reflection. Special care was taken against 'priming' the interviewees. For example, there was no mention of 'communist repression' against religion but interviewees were encouraged to talk about their experiences at different times and in different situations. At an initial project meeting in Sofia, members of the research group were familiarised with key features of religious and non-religious activity in the three countries. In particular the changes wrought by the secularisation policies following the Second World War in Romania and Bulgaria and the impact of democracy in 1989–90, were set against a general trend towards secularisation in Western Europe during the same period. This provided an invaluable basis for discussion and comparison.

This discussion was informed by data from the European Values Study (2012) and a decision was made to include eight questions from the Study as a way to link to quantitative cross-national survey data. The European Values Study, which began in 1981, has been repeated at nine-year intervals since then, with Bulgaria and Romania being included respectively in 1991 and 1993 amongst a 2008 total of 47 countries. Religion is only one amongst several topics covered by the Study. Results overall suggest a decline in the number of people taking part in organised religion, but with differences between the West, where secularisation has become the dominant trend and Eastern Europe where participation has increased, although with differences between countries, the Czech Republic being perhaps the least religious. In terms of the three countries in our study, Bulgaria and the UK appear to be most similar in terms of secularisation.

Also included in the schedule was a final self-evaluation test devised by one of the Bulgarian team members, Ignat Petrov. This has been designed for use with older people, having been included in previous studies in Bulgaria. More of an activity than a formal test, participants were invited to make their own estimates of health, intellect, others' attitudes and happiness with an assessment marked on a vertical line drawn on a blank sheet of paper (see also Chapter 9). During the exercise the recording machine was left on with the agreement of participants so that comments could be captured.

The inclusion of the European Values Study questions and the self-evaluation test provided additional dimensions to the open-ended life history interview data and were to prove helpful in relation to points where individual cases were discussed in greater depth. The European Values Study data included helpful contextualisation while the self-evaluation test data provided evidence as to emotional states at the time of the interview.[4]

Within the research team there was little exclusivity as to role. Of the 13, only three members were not also interviewers. This combining of interviewer and analyser roles was to prove a particular strength when it came to working cross-nationally and comparatively. The interviews were all recorded on digital recording machines, then transcribed and translated into English where appropriate. They varied in length; some extended over more than one session but most lasted up to two hours and were completed on one occasion. All of the interviewees signed a consent form in their own language and, in the case of the UK interviews, the audio files and interview transcripts were prepared for deposit in an archive.

The team met on three occasions as a whole group. After the Sofia meeting, the group met five months later at Cluj-Napoca in Romania at a point when about a quarter of the interviews had been completed, transcribed and circulated. At

---

[4]   A more detailed discussion of the self-evaluation test data is developed in Chapter 9.

that meeting the interview guide and the sample were adjusted, some key themes for analysis were identified based on the interviews and a strategy for analysing the translated and transcribed interviews was drawn up. The final meeting, in Southampton in the UK, took the form of an end-of-project seminar and tentative comparative analysis. Various themes were identified during discussion and allocated from the list in Box 2 to members of the group with the aim that each should present a paper on a topic drawn from the themes at the final meeting in Southampton.

Box 2 RASC analytical themes

(Re)invention of ceremonies
Separation of formal and informal ritual as a way of signalling control
Being religious as a personal choice (religion as 'lifestyle'?)
Religion/ritual as tradition
Ritual practices as providing a sense of continuity
Religious identity (family identity; political identity; (quasi)ethnic identity)
Religious education: formal (school) and informal (family)
Belonging: political and social coercion
Belonging, network of support; community – role of local priest
Gender, generation and religious practices
Spiritual capital, its management and investment
Alternative meanings (change of meaning of rituals)
Change in rituals – a result of younger generation's inexperience?
Religious role models established in early life
Space/temporal location of belief/ritual in persons' lives on a day to-day basis
Private (family) and public (national, political) dimensions of religion
Communist state and religion
Methodological issues of comparative oral history
Doubts, questioning

Eight substantive and methodological topics, each an amalgam drawn from these 19 themes, were then developed as shown in Box 3. The eight topics were separately developed from a joint analysis which had the benefit of both religious and secular viewpoints and with contributions from those present which drew on a wide range of disciplines.

Box 3 RASC substantive and methodological topics

1. Personal ideology of death; death-related rituals as expressions of the imagined community of the living and the dead; aspects of grief.
2. Religious rituals from a gender perspective; gender roles, transmission etc.; loneliness – religious and secular forms of consolation and coping.
3. Cognitive and emotional personal significance of rituals; sense of self, self-esteem, attachment, psychological well-being.
4. Re-invention of ceremonies.
5. Methodological aspects of comparative oral history.
6. Religious practices during communism; religious and secular rituals; being inside and outside at the same time.
7. Key points in life; life crises and ways of coping; if religion is taken for granted when do doubts arise; do crises or does trauma encourage a turn to religion?
8. Ageing, belief, and psychological well-being; does religiosity help face the challenges of later life?

In the final part of this chapter I identify two aspects of comparative work which could have presented challenges to sustaining a collective analytical perspective, but which were turned into an advantage in each case: contextual complexity and distance from the original research question.

Gaining from Contextual Complexity

Earlier I suggested that concern about managing contextual complexity has been a deterrent to the pursuit of cross-national comparative research and that oral history's commitment to individual testimony and voice has made international work problematic. The experience of RASC suggests that contextual complexity can be played up as a positive analytic strategy, particularly where differences in interpretation are acknowledged.

To illustrate this point I use an excerpt from an interview with Aurelian Ghelasie who, born in 1914, was one of the oldest RASC interviewees. Trained as an economist, although without much opportunity to practise this profession, he is someone with a strongly Orthodox Christian belief, married and without children. He was imprisoned both before and during the communist era in Romania because of his Legionnaire (Iron Guard) affiliation and his strongly held religious views. In answer to questions about how people, like him, survived prison during communism he replied:

> but I'm telling you, you may accept being shot, but you can't bear with a terror, being subjected to it incessantly, 'cause you're going to lose even your moral sense and lose your wits and lose what … you're lost! And that's the worst

calamity! 'Cause after you come back to your senses, you feel that you should have stayed the first time … not confess … I've told you that once … I was having moral classes, 'cause the legionnaires were raised like that, in the spirit of honour. Honour, no matter what! No matter what, honour … and faith! And … 'cause I never said that that one, or the other one …

… dishonouring …

I said that the sense of honour was above … (silence).

The cultural 'habitus' of any researcher (Hammersley 1997, 138–9) is elusive and, working cross-nationally and cross-culturally, unknowable in its totality. What a researcher brings to a project and to the interpretation of evidence is a complex intertwining of personal biography, which inevitably includes a theorising that will have developed over time, within particular academic environments and in response to past and continuing debates as well as a personal philosophy and outlook that will have their own cultural and historical determinants (Bornat 2010). The knowledge that is included in a researcher's habitus may be explicitly presented in an interview and in the ensuing analysis; it will also have been produced through the unique relationship of an interview and may be unspoken or assumed.

Add to this complexity the public standing of a particular interviewee and the prospect for sharing through comparison appears yet more elusive. Within his home environment, the account of his life that Aurelian gives links to themes of religious persecution, persistence of belief under duress and commitment to the highest principles of honour to a cause and to companions. Within the context of post-communism his story becomes part of the public account of the recovery of democracy and freedom of expression. However, to widen that context and include an outsider's European perspective risks that reputation once Aurelian's beliefs are understood in a broader historical context. The Romanian Legionnaires were noted in the 1930s for a unique form of fascism that linked nationalism to Orthodox Christian beliefs (Ioanid 2004). Viewed within that longer historical trajectory, the language of his account, his adherence to 'honour' and religion, comes across rather differently. This interpretation that runs counter to the image of someone who is a much revered very old man and a victim of religious persecution presents a challenge to the comparative cross-national coherence of a project whose method, oral history, is rooted in notions of empowerment and the value of personal experience. Aurelian's personal and political history has gone through different valuations as political contexts have succeeded one another. To revive his earlier reputation risks not only his standing today but possibly also highlights aspects of religious affiliation that might not be a part of the Romanian post-communist national narrative.[5]

The project team included people who spoke different languages and who had lived through very different political epochs at the opposite ends of Europe. It also, as was pointed out in the introduction, included people with counter-posed understandings and attitudes towards religion and religious practices. In this way we differed strongly from the three comparative oral history projects described earlier. Making sense of these differences and also making use of them as we came to analyse the data presented some of us with personal and political challenges.

For the research team such a dilemma could represent a threat to its coherence and comparative potential, not just at the level of interpersonal collaboration, but also in relation to the range and scope of comparisons that could be made. However, the case of Aurelian suggests that comparative cross-national oral history can operate in different ways, nationally, historically, culturally and generationally. His account may be viewed in terms of each of these categories without necessarily compromising what he advances as evidential truth or personal belief. Add to this the differing and questioning perspectives of research team members and comparison becomes a multi-faceted process with the potential for new interpretations and evaluation from all perspectives. Indeed his account, when explored within the team, helpfully revealed differences that had not been in evidence at the start of the project. These counter-interpretations contributed to the deconstruction and historicisation of concepts such as belief, honour and nation, which otherwise might have remained unquestioned within their specific originating context. This can work both ways, for as Back suggests when explaining his interview and investigation into the extremely right-wing and racist British National Party:

> Critical thinking can play a modest part … in the commitment to see at the intersection of horizons and contrasting values. It involves critical judgement while remaining open to counter-intuitive possibilities that challenge both our interpretations and our political beliefs. (Back 2004, 273)

In such ways contextual complexity, although challenging and sometimes provoking, is to be valued for its potential to be both illuminating and rewarding.

Keeping the Research Questions in View

When a project like RASC crosses so many boundaries, national, cultural, belief-based, linguistic and disciplinary, to name but a few, creating and sustaining the wording of the research questions is of critical importance. The RASC questions

---

[5]   See Chapter 3 for a discussion of the links between religion and nationalism in Romania.

were designed to be inclusive of as wide a range of experience as possible and to be usable by a team of researchers with varied backgrounds in terms of discipline and individual biography. Coupled with a careful approach to recruitment in each country, the aim was to gather accounts that, although not statistically representative, would be indicative of experience and that would be suggestive of generalisations. In presenting findings from accounts that have proved to be quite disparate, links to the original questions are therefore important. The question 'What is the remaining attraction of religious ritual for those who have little or no explicit religious belief and practice?' has an apparent straightforwardness to it that was challenged by some responses. However, if the project was to cohere and also generate new ideas and evidence, the question would have to be maintained as a totality, intrinsic to joint interpretation.

I draw on an example from one of the UK interviews to illustrate how the question might have been challenged yet still enables generalisations to be drawn from the data. Evelyn Everett was born in 1925 and describes herself as a Jewish non-believer. She had a career in university administration after coming to England as a teenage refugee from Germany in the late 1930s. At the time of her interview she was married and her husband was an invalid, needing full-time care at their home. Asked why she prefers the idea of cremation for herself and what kind of ceremony she would like, she gave a lengthy reply including the following where she begins by talking about her cousin's funeral:

> Anyway his ashes are in my, in her son's house, and I said "Well aren't you? When are they going to be buried?" because I think that's terrible they're not to have, either you scatter them, ok, but to – they have, he's got the urn in his house. And so, his sister's the same. She had a, he had a cremation and his daughter's got the urn in her house. That I don't understand and I think it's wrong.

Why do you think it's wrong?

> You don't have your relation – the ashes in your house. I mean I don't mind if they decide to scatter them, ok, that's all right. You have some memory of the scattering. Or you have like my parents have got, a plant, and they have got their name in the book. And Otto – this Professor [inaudible] also cremated, he's got a plaque in Golders Green.[6] [Laughing] So that satisfies me. You must have something.

Like a memorial of some sort?

> Yeah. And my friend now whose husband died last week, she's going to scatter the ashes and she doesn't want to do it herself. So I said "If you pay somebody

---

6   Golders Green crematorium in North London, where many Jewish and non-Jewish secular funeral ceremonies are held.

it would be quite easy". So I think she's having them scattered by somebody at Golders Green and I've promised to go to the funeral. But she says – his sister lives in Southport I think – and she's not in good health, and she said "What would she think?" because all she's going to have is some music, no sermons at all …

Would you have music at your funeral?

Yes, yes I'm picking, I've already picked one tune for a funeral but the other I haven't got, it was, you know on a tape, not on a CD, and I'm not entirely sure. I've just bought a new CD when I went to the, that exhibition in, you know, about Venice, and I bought the CD there. In fact I played it, it's lying there, I played it once and it got stuck. I've just took it back and I think there's something suitable on there. Mozart. Not Mozart but baroque music, which we like. Both my husband and I have always liked baroque music so I would, I am going to pick something from there.

Evelyn has clear and definite views about death and cremation. For her there is no after-life and her insistence on cremation has meant that she says she has come into conflict with other members of her community who say that no Jew should consider cremation given the history of the death camps. Neither cremation, nor a ceremony to mark her death nor the content, which should include music personal to her, are religious. She is however firm in her views about the need for ceremony, a ritual of some kind to mark her life and her passing and for this to involve other people. The example of her cousin's son who has kept his father's ashes in his house seems to disgust and annoy her. It could be that her response is explained by beliefs which, though often embedded in religious practice, may be explained in terms of cultural categorisations of pollution and purity. In her original and influential study of rituals, Douglas argues that rules that classify certain acts or rituals as pure or impure are ways in which members of society are controlled, but also show how they respond to fundamentally existential questions. In such ways, ideas about pollution may be both 'instrumental and expressive' (Douglas 2003, 3). Evelyn's reactions may not be rooted in anything as strong as fear of pollution; however, she may be influenced by the feeling that to keep someone's ashes in a house is somehow improper or evidence of disorder or disrespect. To restore order, a ceremony or recognisable ritual is needed, a scattering, a tree, a name in a book, acts that instil a memory of a person, 'you must have something'. In Evelyn's case, if we apply the research question we see that religious ritual has no 'remaining attraction', but it also shows us that the performance of some kind of special act after death has importance socially and biographically, linking past, present and future through the life of an individual.

The question wording is challenged by responses such as Evelyn's, but using an open inductive process as we analyse allows for individual and subjectively expressed views to be included. This provides a helpful way to check any tendency towards rigidity in interpretation, important for a comparative cross-national project. Interestingly, her account illustrates how religious ceremony and ritual can be both present and absent in the way that someone prepares for death – present in parallel ceremonial practices that she is aware of and rejects, yet absent in what she has planned for herself. The question encourages an exploration of the data that allows for such conscious deliberations, products of individual biography, to be expressed, understood and compared as processes within broader social and cultural structures and practices.

Conclusion

The RASC project was presented with all of the challenges attached to comparative cross-national oral history research in relation to project design, data generation, drawing out evidence and sharing the analysis of the data. Difference was embedded throughout, from the perspectives of the group members to the lives of the 60 people interviewed in three countries which have experienced and continue to experience quite distinct forms of engagement with religious belief during the last 60 or more years. As I have tried to show, those differences have been acknowledged and taken on as positive aspects of the research process rather than obstacles to co-operation and shared analyses. Drawing on the experience of previous approaches, RASC has avoided over-generalisation while not being swayed too close to a relativism that ignores significant difference. By choosing what Hantrais (1999) describes as a 'subset' of the three societies, religious belief and secularism as demonstrated in ceremony and ritual, the group has been able to share data relating to a definable set of social relationships and practices.

Religious and secular ceremonies and rituals are not immutable; as RASC shows, they are cultural and social products manifested through the discursive practices and subjective meanings (Brown 2001) of people who have experienced and who continue to live in particular national historical and political contexts. Following the example of Chamberlayne and King (2000), RASC has drawn on personal memory to generate biographical accounts to link with broader structures and thus compare how belief and non-belief are explained and understood through descriptions of everyday cultural practices and individual philosophies of life. Williams (1996) similarly argues that religious belief and descriptions of ceremonies and rituals need to be understood literally and symbolically in relation to ordinary people's words and their accounts of their lives, using an oral history approach.

Oral history uniquely engages voice and memory to understand the past. When those voices require translation then inevitably something will be lost, emotions may be muted, ideas mediated and the particular linguistics of dialect and culture contained. Any transcription, whether or not it involves translation, will inevitably be less than the sound of an originally recorded voice. On this oral historians agree. While translation adds to this opacity, it also opens up possibilities to explore and discuss language, memory and biographies and to work collectively. Together with a shared conceptual and methodological framework, the RASC researchers have managed to transcend many boundaries with the result that there now exists an addition to the few examples of oral history comparative work and also original substantive contributions to what is known of day-to-day religious and secular practices in three European countries.

References

Abrams, Lynn. 2010. *Oral History Theory*. London: Routledge.

Andrews, Molly. 1995. 'A Monoglot Working Abroad: Working Through Problems of Translation'. *Oral History* 23(2): 47–50.

Angrosino, Michael V. 1991. 'Conversations in a Monastery'. *Oral History Review* 19(1–2): 55–63.

Back, Les. 2004. 'Politics, Research and Understanding'. In *Qualitative Research Practice*, edited by Clive Seale, Giampietro Gobo, Jaber F. Gubrium and David Silverman. London: Sage.

Bertaux, Daniel and Paul Thompson. 1993. *Between Generations: Family Models, Myths and Memories*. Oxford: Oxford University Press. [Revised edition 2005. New Brunswick, NJ: Transaction.]

Bornat, Joanna. 2010. 'Remembering and Reworking Emotions. The Reanalysis of Emotion in an Interview'. *Oral History* 38(2): 43–52.

Brown, Callum. 2001. *The Death of Christian Britain: Understanding Secularisation 1800–2000*. London: Routledge.

Burton, Susan, K. 2003. 'Issues in Cross-cultural Interviewing: Japanese Women in England'. *Oral History* 31(1): 38–46.

Chamberlayne, Prue and Annette King. 2000. *Cultures of Care: Biographies of care in Britain and the two Germanies*. Bristol: The Policy Press.

Douglas, Mary. 2003. *Purity and Danger: An Analysis of Concept of Pollution and Taboo*. London: Taylor and Francis.

Esping-Anderson, Gøsta. 1990. *The Three Worlds of Welfare Capitalism*. Oxford: Polity Press.

Ester, Peter. 2008. '"It was Very, Very Churchy": Recollections of older Dutch-Americans on Growing up in Holland, Michigan'. *Oral History Review* 35(2): 117–38.

European Values Study. Available at: http://www.europeanvaluesstudy.eu/ (accessed 6 February 2012).

Fraser, Ronald. 1988. *1968 A Student Generation in Revolt*. London: Chatto and Windus.

Frisch, Michael. 1990. *A Shared Authority: Essays on the Craft and Meaning of Oral and Public History*. New York: SUNY.

Gerrard, Paul. 1996. '"The Lord said 'Come'": Why Women Enter a Religious Order'. *Oral History* 24(2): 54–58.

Gildea, Robert. 2010. 'The Long March of Oral History: Around 1968 in France'. *Oral History* 38(1): 68–80.

Gildea, Robert, Mark, James and Warring, Anette (eds) 2013. *Europe's 1968: Voices of Revolt*. Oxford: Oxford University Press.

Gobo, Giampetro. 2004. 'Sampling, representativeness and generalizability'. In *Qualitative Research Practice*, edited by Clive Seale, Giampietro Gobo, Jaber F. Gubrium and David Silverman. London: Sage.

Gudziak, Boris and Viktor Susak. 1996. 'Becoming a Priest in the Underground: The Clandestine Life of the Ukrainian Greco-Catholic Church'. *Oral History* 24(2): 42–8.

Hammersley, Martin. 1997. 'Qualitative Data Archiving: Some Reflections on its Prospects and Problems'. *Sociology* 31(1): 131–42.

Hantrais, Linda. 1999. 'Contextualization in Cross-national Comparative Research'. *International Journal of Social Research Methodology* 2(2): 93–108.

Ioanid, Radu. 2004. 'The Sacralised Politics of the Romanian Iron Guard'. *Totalitarian Movements and Political Religions* 5(3): 419–53.

Ilyasoglu, Aynur. 1996. 'Religion and Women During the Course of Modernization'. *Oral History* 24(2): 49–53.

Johnston, Ronnie and Elaine McFarland. 2010. 'With God in the Workplace: Industrial Chaplains in Scottish Heavy Industry. 1970s–1990'. *Oral History* 38(1): 55–67.

Koleva, Daniela. 2009. 'Daughters' Stories: Family Memory and Generational Amnesia'. *Oral History Review* 36(2): 188–206.

Mangen, Steen. 1999. 'Qualitative Research Methods in Cross-national Settings'. *International Journal of Social Research Methodology* 2(2): 109–24.

Marx, Karl. 1844. *A Contribution to the Critique of Hegel's Philosophy of Right*. Paris: Deutsche-Französische Jahrbücher, 7 and 10 February.

Miller, C. and M. Taylor. 2009. 'The Realities of Comparative Research: Reflections from a Cross-national Study of Non-governmental Public Action'. *21st Century Society* 4(2): 215–77.

Moodie, Jane. 2010. '"Surprised by joy": A Case History Exploring the Expression of Spiritual Joy in Oral History'. *Oral History* 38(2): 75–84.

Ritchie, Donald A. 2011. 'Introduction: The Evolution of Oral History'. In *The Oxford Handbook of Oral History*, edited by Donald A. Ritchie. New York: Oxford University Press.

Rose, Richard. 1991. 'Comparing Forms of Comparative Analysis'. *Political Studies* XXXIX: 446–62.

SOSTRIS. 2004. '*Social Strategies in Risk Societies' From Biography to Social Policy. Final Report*. SOE2963010, TSER Area 3.

Thompson, Edward P. 1963. *The Making of the English Working Class*. London: Gollancz.

Thompson, Paul. 2000. *The Voice of the Past*, 3rd edn. Oxford: Oxford University Press.

Thompson, Paul with Natasha Burchardt (eds) 1982. *Our Common History: The Transformation of Europe*. London: Pluto.

Thonfeld, Christoph. 2011. 'Memories of World War Two Forced Labourers – an International Comparison'. *Oral History* 39(2): 33–48.

Ungerson, Clare. 1996. 'Part Two: Qualitative Methods'. In *Cross-National Research Methods in the Social Sciences*, edited by Linda Hantrais and Steen Mangen. London: Pinter.

USC Shoah Foundation Institute. n.d. Available at: http://dornsife.usc.edu/vhi/; http://cordis.europa.eu/documents/documentlibrary/76095551EN6.pdf (accessed 17 January 2012).

Van Boeschoten, R. 2007. 'Broken Bonds and Divided Memories: Wartime Massacres Reconsidered in a Comparative Perspective'. *Oral History* 35(1): 39–48.

Villanova, Mercedes. 2011. 'Case Study: Oral History and Democracy, in *The Oxford Handbook of Oral History*, edited by Donald A. Ritchie. New York: Oxford University Press.

Von Plato, Alexander, Almut Leh and Christoph Thonfeld (eds) 2008. *Hitler's Slaves: Life Stories of Forced Labourers in Nazi-Occupied Europe*. Oxford: Berghahn Books.

Wheeler, Norton. 2008. 'Cross-lingual Oral History Interviewing in China: Confronting the Methodological Challenges'. *Oral History* 36(1): 56–68.

Williams, Sarah C. 1996. 'The Problem of Belief: The Place of Oral History in the Study of Popular Religion'. *Oral History* 24(2): 27–34.

Yates, Paul. 1996. 'The Priesthood of Women: Resourcing identity in the Anglican Church', *Oral History* 24(2): 59–65.

Yeo, Stephen. 1977. 'A New Life: The Religion of Socialism in Britain, 1883–1896'. *History Workshop* 4(1): 5–56.

PART II
Ritual and Story in Bulgaria, Romania and the UK

Chapter 3

'I Will Die Orthodox':
Religion and Belonging in Life Stories of
the Socialist Era in Romania and Bulgaria

Simina Bădică

The Romanian nation was born Christian.[1]

Everybody in our family was an Orthodox, and I will also die an Orthodox.
(Florina Campeanu, 83 years old, Bucharest)

This chapter[2] analyses registered high levels of religiosity in Romania, and lower
levels in Bulgaria, in the context of overlapping national and religious identities.
It argues that the incorporation of religious identity into national identity was
discouraged in socialist Bulgaria, but reinforced in socialist Romania[3] starting
with the 1960s. Oral history evidence is used to track personal religiosity and
the spontaneous connections made with national/family identity, and to propose
a model of 'belonging without believing' as opposed to the West European
'believing without belonging' (Davie 1994). Choosing and organising religious
or secular ceremonies to mark important moments in life is an ideal indicator for
assessing levels of commitment to (religious) traditions in different historical and
personal moments in a life story. Special attention is granted to funeral rites as the
importance of dying Orthodox seems to have resisted attempts by the socialist state

---

[1]   Consultative Council of Denominations in the Socialist Republic of Romania
(1987, p. 12).

[2]   Writing this chapter would not have been possible without the intense and fruitful
discussions of our research group. I have also benefitted from discussions with Maria Falina,
Anca Şincan and Cristian Vasile, whose suggestions and ideas influenced the argument of
this chapter.

[3]   Everyday speech in Romania uses the term *communism* to signify the regime
spanning between 1945 and 1989. As a historian, I prefer *socialism*, *state socialism* and
similar variants (even in the Romanian case, the regime never claimed to have reached the
stage of communism and the country was called the Romanian Socialist Republic), but as
an oral historian I am also inclined to use the terms my interviewees are using. Bulgarian
everyday speech, on the contrary, prefers *socialism* as a general term for the 1945–1989
regime. I shall thus mostly use *socialism* when speaking in the author/historian voice,
although when I am paraphrasing my Romanian interviewees *communism* will also be used
interchangeably with socialism.

to secularise this life passage, especially in the Romanian case. Intriguing cases of declared non-religious persons still claiming to be Orthodox and requesting Orthodox funeral rites are discussed in the context of their life stories. The chapter also highlights, through oral history sources, negotiating practices in performing religious rituals during the supposedly laic communist regime in both Romania and Bulgaria.

As already explained in Chapter 1, Bulgaria and Romania display quite different and divergent levels of commitment to religious values and rituals. In this chapter I explore this surprising difference in two countries with apparently similar histories. The fact that so many historical variables are similar for both Romania and Bulgaria makes the comparison[4] even more significant as it brings the analysis to the universal questions: what brings people close to religion? What finally makes the appeal of religious denominations and religious rituals?

The thesis of 'believing without belonging', meaning high levels of belief with low levels of practice, put forward by Davie (1994) with reference to Britain, and later on extended to the larger situation in Europe, has been intensely discussed and challenged (Voas and Crockett 2005). For this chapter's interest, the importance of Davie's thesis lies in bringing together believing and belonging and pointing out their interconnectedness. Based on the life stories I am exploring in this chapter, I argue that religiousness in Eastern Europe is rather a case of 'belonging without believing', as religious identity is strongly affirmed and connected to national and kin identity, while the same interviewees often confess to having serious doubts about their actual faith. This study is not the first proposing to reverse Davie's famous phrase, from 'believing without belonging' to 'belonging without believing'. The claim has already been made about American Jews (Cohen and Blitzer 2008), Catholic Italians (Marchisio and Pisati 1999) and even Anglican adolescents (Francis and Robbins 2004).

Based on this hypothesis, I argue that lower levels of religiosity in Bulgaria, as compared with Romania, are due to lower levels of symbiosis between national and religious identity. Further, I argue that the overlapping of Orthodox and national identity inherited from the interwar period was reinforced in socialist Romania, quite the contrary to what might be assumed, but discouraged in socialist Bulgaria.

In line with this, I discuss the policies of socialist states towards religion, to support the argument that socialist secularisation and repression of religion were not as aggressive and successful as the Western side of the Iron Curtain has been led to believe. The life stories I analyse provide a subjective narrative of religious life inside the socialist camp in which memories of negotiation and keeping

---

[4]   As a Romanian historian, my analysis is biased in this direction, as I am much more familiar with Romanian historical narratives and sources. Unfamiliar with the Bulgarian language, I could only access an English language bibliography on the subject (these were not very rich) and the interviews translated for this project. The comparison with the Bulgarian situation is mainly used to address new questions and propose fresh perspectives on the Romanian religious question.

family traditions, including religious ones, are much *more* powerful than those of religious repression or atheist alternatives. As the interviewees were socialised in the interwar period, but lived their adult lives in the socialist world, they had to adapt to the dramatic political changes.

Margareta, a Romanian Orthodox Atheist

The specificities and peculiarities of the socialist religious context are best to be seen in the life story of Margareta Calinescu. Margareta is an 82-year-old, very talkative, Romanian woman, an atheist claiming to 'have lived Orthodox' all her life. She is a mixture of traditions and denominations: her parents were Orthodox yet she was baptised Catholic and was married to a Greek-Catholic. Her family observed the Orthodox traditions, although, from what she says, in a loose manner. Both her parents died when she was 18 years old. The moment her mother passed away is also the moment when she remembers losing her faith in God:

> We sat there at the gate of the hospital together [with her sister] and it was then that I first wondered [she holds back her tears], This God, why doesn't he look upon us? And I think that was the moment when I became an atheist.

She finished her university studies in the USSR and became an engineer. She married in the 1950s according to the Greek-Catholic ceremony, although at the time the Greek-Catholic Church had been abolished by the communist state.[5] Her husband, a priest's son, turned out to have a gambling addiction and they finally divorced. During the interview she discussed her own death, explaining that she has chosen to be cremated with a pseudo-religious ceremony, a rare choice among Romania's elders. Yet when she was asked whether she considers herself to be Orthodox, she answered:

> I consider myself an Orthodox, all my life I had been an Orthodox.

> *Well, you just said that you are baptised in the Catholic ritual, and married as a Greek-Catholic.*

> Yes, but I lived as an Orthodox all my life.

---

[5]   In 1948, the Romanian communist government abolished the Greek-Orthodox Church, the second largest church in Romania and incorporated it, churches, priests, believers and possessions, into the Orthodox Church. The official discourse presented this as repairing a historical wrong, a 'reunification' of the Orthodox Church. Historians have emphasised the brutality of this measure and the crucial political gains for both the Communist Party (RWP) and the Orthodox Church, and the strengthening of their relationship after the violent implementation of this abusive decision. See Vasile (2003a, b).

What is it in Orthodoxy that might make an acknowledged atheist declare herself Orthodox? What does being Orthodox mean in the Romanian and Bulgarian context? Is Orthodoxy perceived as a choice or rather as given, a family tradition, an innate condition one is born into?

Socialist Politics and Religious Ceremonies: The Myth of Secularised Socialist Societies

On 7 July 1977 a Christian Orthodox funeral of impressive proportions was taking place in Scorniceşti, a village in Southern Romania. The religious ceremony was anything but unusual for the Romanian rural landscape, even during the communist regime, but the proportion of and protagonists in the funeral rite might have seemed puzzling to a foreign observer. The mother of Nicolae Ceauşescu, Romania's last communist dictator, was being taken on her last road by her son with all the necessary Orthodox ceremony.

It was not the first time a religious ceremony of such proportions had been organised at the highest levels of the communist nomenklatura. In 1972, Nicolae Ceauşescu had already buried his father with the same religious ceremony (Stan and Turcescu 2007, 24), while in January 1958, the prime minister of the first communist government, Petru Groza, was given a state funeral with Orthodox rituals and the most senior clergy attending.

It is already widely accepted that the secularisation attempted by socialist governments all over Eastern Europe was not a success story. Recent scholarly research is more and more inclined to argue that religion was instead used for propaganda purposes and integrated into the socialist state in order to grant national cohesion and support nationalist policies (Ramet 2004; Leustean 2007, 491–521; Sincan 2010, 191–216). Stan and Turcescu thus explain Ceauşescu's contradictory relationship with the church:

> He sought to strengthen his position domestically by appealing to nationalism, which the church considered its turf. In 1968, Ceauşescu acknowledged the role of the Orthodox Church in the development of modern Romania, and in April 1972, he allowed his father's funeral to be conducted according to Orthodox ritual and be broadcast live on national radio. Ceauşescu also tacitly tolerated the use of baptism, marriage, and burial services by communist officials who privately considered themselves Orthodox Christians. (Stan and Turcescu 2007, 192)

As Leustean shows, this trend was not initiated by Nicolae Ceauşescu, but it was already established in the early 1960s, by his predecessor, Gheorghe Gheorghiu-Dej, in his attempts to distance the Romanian Popular Republic from the Soviet Union and to take Romanian communism on a national path. This was a win–win situation for both the socialist state and the Orthodox Church: 'In the following years, with the growth of national Communism and the dictatorship of Ceauşescu, the regime would benefit from the nationalist discourse of the church, while, at the same time, the church would take advantage of the nationalist posture of Ceauşescu' (Leustean 2007, 520).

While contemplating this peculiar political context, a presumably atheistic and internationalist ideology-based state meeting the Orthodox Church in a nationalistic discourse, it becomes less puzzling that religious ceremonies were not only tolerated but were the social norm in late socialist Romania. Compared with the late 1940s and 1950s, when the Stalinist model of church–state relations was enforced (Sincan 2010, 92) and religious ceremonies were indeed discouraged and most of the time hidden from public view, the 1970s and 1980s saw religious ceremonies for weddings, baptisms and funerals flourishing in plain view, thus becoming a well documented reality in the Romanian life stories collected for our research project (RASC).

In 1987 a booklet issued by the Consultative Council of Denominations in the Socialist Republic of Romania stated: 'Respecting traditions, including the religious ones, is characteristic to Romanian reality. For baptism, marriage and funeral, one resorts to religious services' (Consultative Council of Denominations 1987, 13). The booklet, entitled *Religious Life in Romania*, was a response to growing international discontent at the violation of neo-Protestant human rights and was trying to prove that religious freedom was enjoyed by all Romanian citizens. The hidden agenda includes promoting the Romanian Orthodox Church as the national church:

> The Romanian nation [*popor*] was born Christian. Ever since its creation from Dacians and Romans, it was Christian. Romanians were not christened by others[6] and their Christianity is affirmed in the Orthodox Church. There is archaeological proof of existing Christianity all over Romanian territory ever since the 1st century A.D. It is almost a postulate to say that talking of religion in Romania, the Orthodox Church is to be first and most taken into account. This was and this is the Church of the Romanian people.[7] (Consultative Council of Denominations 1987, 12)

---

[6]   This is a reference to the historiographical theory that Christianity was brought to Romanians by already christened Bulgarians, which was not an acceptable theory for Ceauşescu's already, in the 1980s, ultra-nationalistic regime.

[7]   This is how the relationship between the Orthodox Church and other denominations was viewed during the socialist regime: 'Throughout history, starting with the 10th century, besides the Romanian people other population came to inhabit the country's territory: Hungarians, Germans, Serbs, Ukrainians, Jews and so on, kept their traditions, including the religious ones. As a consequence of these historical circumstances, in Romania, alongside the ancestral Orthodox Church, there are other confessions' (Consultative Council of Denominations 1987, 17).

Such positionings result in puzzling formulations for anyone searching for a secular official communist discourse.

Grounds for Comparison across Borders (Romania/Bulgaria)

If the situation in socialist countries might have seemed similar when looked at from the other side of the Iron Curtain, inside the socialist camp the differences were quite significant with regard to religious life. Some of the reasons for the large discrepancies recorded by the European Values Study 2008[8] and earlier studies are to be found in experiences of religious life during socialism and in its relationship with national identity and nationalistic discourse.

This is correlated, in my opinion, with the organic connection constructed between the Romanian Orthodox Church and the Romanian nation in the interwar period, a connection that was not destroyed but, on the contrary, was enhanced during the communist regime. The Bulgarian situation is different. The Bulgarian Orthodox Church did not or could not perform this symbiosis, thus remaining an apolitical institution, a fact that (not so) paradoxically diminished its credibility and the number of its members.

Twenty years after the collapse of communism, this is how two young scholars assess the situation of the respective churches in their countries. In Romania, Sincan states:

> Throughout the communist period, religious life continued. Places of worship were built, though not at the same rate as during the interwar period; the training of priests continued; and several theologians of the period were educated in institutes abroad (Oxford, Geneva, Athens, Regensburg). Furthermore, continuing the tradition of the interwar period, the state's building of national ideology during the 1960s took into consideration religious motifs and the pantheon of Romanian saints, and figures of Romanian church history made their way into the national canon. (Sincan 2010, 192)

In Bulgaria, Metodiev draws very different conclusions:

> Traumatised by its communist experience, the Bulgarian Orthodox Church is persistent in asserting its apolitical attitude, to the extent that it cannot even communicate its own agenda to the state. This apolitical attitude is why the Church (so far) successfully has resisted the temptation to become an exponent and defender of nationalist causes, a syndrome that has not been avoided by other post-communist Orthodox churches. (Metodiev 2010, 650)

---

[8]   See Chapter 1.

While both Orthodox churches are considered a model of co-option of the church by the socialist regime (Ramet 2004, 275–6), the degree to which religious life continued in these two countries in the second half of the twentieth century differed considerably. For example, the number of Orthodox priests is recorded to have decreased in Bulgaria from the 1940s to the 1980s (Metodiev 2010, 649), while in the Romanian case it remained steady throughout this period (Sincan 2010, 196).

Thus, the question of religious revival in Eastern Europe after the fall of communism has already been challenged; indeed some researchers claim that religiosity never actually decreased. One of the few sociological studies on religiousness in post-communist Romania claims religion was only publicly renounced during communism, the personal commitment to religion remaining more or less the same (Gog 2007, 791–801). Gog explains increased religiosity in Eastern Europe after 1989 by the sudden disappearance of public restrictions, talking of 'predictable religious euphoria' after 1989 (Gog 2007, 795).

Secular and Religious Ceremonies in the Public Sphere

An important indicator to be taken into consideration when assessing the vivacity of religious life in the socialist camp is the performance of religious ceremonies. Further, what is to be assessed is not the general increase or decrease in such events for the whole socialist regime, but the variations in different decades of socialism in both countries. We now know that the socialist regime, its policies and its everyday life was considerably different in the 1950s from the 1980s. In as much as religious life is concerned, these time frames are confirmed. In the Romanian case, if the 1950s was a period of repression for religious activities, and even religious ceremonies (more ceremonies were performed in secret, behind closed doors or in faraway places), the 1970s and 1980s saw the return to the public sphere of church weddings and funerals. These became mainstream and common practice even among the non-religious (Consultative Council of Denominations 1987, 13).

The Bulgarian situation is different in this respect, as it includes the successful introduction of secular ceremonies for baptism, marriage and death.[9] If the 1950s are similar in both countries, at least in terms of state policy towards the church and in the church's more or less obedient compromise with the newly established communist power, the 1980s could not be more different. According to the Bulgarian historian Metodiev, the 1980s were 'the most traumatic experience of the policy of enforcement of civil rituals' for the Bulgarian Orthodox Church (Metodiev 2010, 639). According to the same historian, this policy was quite successful as, according to state statistics, the number of religious rituals performed in Bulgaria indeed decreased during the 1980s:

---

[9]   See chapters 6 and 7 for discussion of Bulgarian rituals and ceremonies.

In 1962, the state commissioned a large-scale survey of Bulgarians' attitudes towards religion. The results were published as late as 1968 under the title "The Process of Overcoming Religion in Bulgaria" and they were a genuine surprise. Only 35 per cent of the population described themselves as religious, mainly from the less educated, elderly, rural, and female population. At the same time, the survey revealed that more than 80 per cent of funerals were held with religious rites, more than 52 per cent of newborns were baptised, and religious weddings amounted to 36 per cent. ... This campaign had mixed results. In 1980 the Committee for Church Affairs reported that 40.7 per cent of all newborns were baptised, while only 4.52 per cent of marriages were religious. Religious funerals remained the most popular religious ritual, but in the same year they dropped to 47.9 per cent of all funerals. (Metodiev 2010, 639–40)

Table 3.1　　　Religious ceremonies (percentage) in socialist Bulgaria

Bulgaria	1962	1980
Newborn baptised	52%	40.7%
Religious marriages	36%	4.5%
Religious funerals	80%	47.9%

Source: Metodiev 2010, 639–40.

Another important point is that, although similar statistics are not available for Romania,[10] the interviews conducted in Romania seem to present a contrast with the Bulgarian trend registered in these statistics. That is, while Bulgarian religious ceremonies were decreasing in the 1970s and 1980s, in Romania their number was increasing. For example if an interviewee did not marry religiously in the 1950s, or did it secretly, their children, who got married in the 1970s or 1980s, would have a religious ceremony by default as part of the socially accepted public practice for a wedding. This is best seen in Florina Campeanu's (Bucharest) life story, which will be detailed further on in the text.

The reasons for the sharp discrepancies between two politically similar neighbouring countries are always multiple and intertwined. In addition to the above-discussed overlay between Orthodoxy and national identity, the Romanian case lacks an important component. There was never a strong state policy of promoting civil ceremonies in socialist Romania. Of course, high-ranking communist officials were cremated and their ashes deposited with secular state

---

[10]　　The Romanian state did not conduct surveys on religious practices or beliefs, relying for administrative issues on the internal statistics of the churches. For example, the Orthodox Church declared a number of adherents according to which it was subsidised, churches were built, etc. See Sincan (2010, 196).

ceremonies at the Monument of Communist Heroes[11] (with the notable exception of Petru Groza, who was given an Orthodox funeral in 1958). Similarly, there were no religious marriages or baptisms of children among communist nomenklatura, at least not in public.[12] For example, the Romanian socialist administration never proposed a civil ceremony to replace baptism, as in Bulgaria. Civil marriage was a reality and an obligation even before the Second World War, but not for the other two major life events, birth and death. Even those few who chose cremation instead of burial were faced with the presence of a former priest (*preot raspopit*) who would perform a shortened version of the Orthodox funeral ceremony.

There is no information so far from researchers into church history on whether this option was discussed and rejected by the Communist Party or whether it was ever taken into consideration. Whatever the case, the consequences of not proposing a Romanian secular alternative to religious ceremonies are to be seen in the current still high attachment to churches among Romanian citizens. If there is truth in the often cited joke, 'Orthodox Romanians visit the church three times in their lives: for baptism, marriage, and feet first before being buried' (Stan and Turcescu 2007, 16), then the socialist state did very little to disturb this traditional and minimal form of religious life in Romania. On the other hand, whatever their participation in religious life, 85 per cent of Romanians are still driven to declare themselves religious (according to European Values Survey 1999[13]).

On (not) Remembering Religious Persecution in the Socialist Camp

The degree to which the secularisation attempted during socialism succeeded is still a matter of academic debate. Persecution for religious activity and for religious belief, with some denominations suffering more than others, was a reality in socialist states, especially in the period of establishing communist rule in the late 1940s and 1950s.[14] However, some of the interviewees, even among the religious, claimed that there was no religious persecution during the communist regime in Romania. They were quite eager to argue that religious life went on undisturbed, and even if they heard of persecutions on religious grounds, they personally did not remember anyone who was persecuted for being religious.

In the interviews I conducted, I introduced the question of religious persecution the moment the interviewees mentioned some sort of hidden or forbidden

---

[11] The Monument of Communist Heroes was inaugurated in December 1963 in Liberty Park, Bucharest.

[12] During his visit to Romania in 1963 'Canon Satterthwaite noted that public attendance at churches in Romania was higher than in Moscow and in private meetings he discovered that priests were going to party officials to carry out baptisms and funerals' (Leustean 2007, 178).

[13] http://www.europeanvaluesstudy.eu/.

[14] For a discussion on memories of religious persecution see Chapter 5.

ceremony. We had already decided, when establishing the interview guide, not to use words like 'persecution' or 'repression' in interviews in order to prevent certain types of response. Even so, when talking about hidden ceremonies some of the interviewees denied knowing of people who had had to suffer because of their religious beliefs.

Mirela Dinescu, born in 1930 in Bucharest, was a dressmaker who used to be married to an army employee. She considered herself religious, although not a practising Christian. She spoke definitely when asked:

> *During the communist regime, have you felt somehow or have you heard about people who suffered because of their religion views?*

> No, no, no, the only ones were those who worked in the army and had high positions, but even those were making hidden ceremonies, religious ones.

Ioana Georgescu, born in 1924, admits she is a religious person; her family is very important for her and has observed many religious and popular traditions over the years:

> *During communism how did you celebrate religious Holy Days, did you follow the custom still?*

> Of course I did! Like always!

> *Did something special happen for Christmas and Easter?*

> No, no, like always, the same celebration. I mean we prepared everything in the same way and we would go to church ... You see, when it came to this, we weren't afraid to go to church. There were people in certain areas that were oppressed for that, but that depends ... It depends.

Ion Cotescu, born in 1924, is a retired engineer, living alone in Bucharest after the death of his wife 13 years previously. He comes from a religious family and he was the conductor of a church choir for many years, yet he claimed to be non-religious. When asked about the interference of the socialist state in religious life he said he did not know of such cases and that he himself never felt hindered in attending religious services:

> *Have you ever felt you might be in trouble for going to church, I mean during the communist period?*

> No, no ... not by far, I used to sing [in the church choir] in those years, all this time ...

I know, this is why I am asking.

No, no, it never happened. The only thing, once, when Stalin died, in '53 I think. I was singing in the church, with the choir, of course and the priest mentioned Stalin. And the boys kind of burst into laughter. "Shut up, you, or else they'll take us away! Keep quiet" I said, …

Have you heard of people who had to suffer because of this?

No, no, I don't know, why should I say I do? I don't have any acquaintance who did. I heard there were some who had difficulties. No.

The insistence that there was no persecution for church attendance during the communist regime puzzled me during the interviews. As it can be seen in the transcript, the interviewees were emphatic ('No, no, no'). These subjective memories of religious life during socialism are pregnant with multiple meanings. On the one hand, after the official condemnation of the communist regime in Romania in 2006, public discourse relating to the communist past has become increasingly criminalising, portraying the socialist decades as, in the words of president Traian Băsescu, 'a regime of oppression, which expropriated five decades of modern history from the Romanian people, which trampled law underfoot and forced citizens to live in lies and fear' (Băsescu 2006). Paradoxically, one of the reactions to the official condemnation of communism might be a normalising attempt at a personal level by those who have spent all of their adult life in this 'regime of oppression'.

On the other hand, those interviewed for this oral history project did not consciously reflect on the differences between different decades of the socialist regime when assessing the freedom or restrictions of religious life. They speak of communism as a continuum, trying to defend their lives in front of a younger interviewer who presumably knows nothing of life during state socialism. Thus, they argue at one moment that there was no repression, while at another they admit that they were not allowed to go to church or to have a religious ceremony for a certain event. I think this ambiguity is also due to the socialist regime's long time span and accompanying political changes. During a lifetime the same person might have felt reluctant to enter a church in the 1950s but unhindered to do the same in the 1980s. Thus, their answers are dependent on the period they are recalling under the general term 'communism' in Romania or 'socialism' in Bulgaria.

Florina's Choices[15]

The choices in Florina's life are revealing for the ambiguities of life in (and the memory of) a socialist society. She was born in 1928 in an Orthodox family living in a multicultural small city on the Danube. Although her family observed the main Orthodox ceremonies and feasts, she claims it was mainly out of a concern for tradition and not out of genuine faith:

> And we kept Easter, Christmas, I mean all the traditions in the house. Always, we would cook what we had to, what the tradition was, it was respected. These were always respected. And the Holy Days. There was Saint Elias or some other saint when we had a free day. They would keep these. But somehow formally, it seemed to us. But we knew we had to respect those. We knew it. That's how it was.

When she got married in the 1950s, although not a believer, she chose to have a religious wedding; however, the ceremony was performed on a fasting day when the church normally would not agree to perform weddings. It was a small wedding, no more than 12 or 13, guests, but Florina remembers her mother in law:

> I will never forget this, when we left, going towards the gate, I can see her even now, my mother in law, took Ion by the sleeve and told him, "Do not touch her until you have the religious wedding!"

In a traditional perspective, still powerful in today's Romania, a wedding without a religious ceremony is not a proper wedding. Florina remembers the first wedding she attended as an adolescent in her hometown:

> *Did they also go to church?*
>
> Well, it was a wedding with all the customs. The civil ceremony, the church, everything.
>
> *Were there weddings then [the 1930s] without the religious ceremony?*
>
> No, there was no such thing.
>
> *When did it become possible to have a wedding without the religious ceremony?*
>
> After communism was installed. Although, Simina, you should know that even then the majority of weddings were done with a religious ceremony. That they did it secretly ... I do not remember any wedding, even if it was done by high-

---

[15]   For specific aspects of her case, see chapters 6 and 7.

rank party members … for them to suffer because they married their children religiously.

Florina is ambivalent about whether religious marriage was actually widespread in the 1950s or whether it was avoided. Right after claiming that 'the majority of weddings were done with a religious ceremony', she remembers that her own religious wedding was rather the exception and not the rule:

> I was not a believer. But it was a custom. I mean I cared for respecting these customs. There were some colleagues of mine who got married before, but I think we were the only one who had the religious ceremony.

The reason for these contradictory memories may also lie in the confusion of decades and different periods inside the communist regime. While it may be true for the communist regime as a whole that even high-rank party members got married, or married their children religiously, it is also true that in the 1950s young couples tended to avoid a religious ceremony, by-passing it alltogether or performing it secretly without guests.

Florina herself remembers a wedding where they were godparents. It is in the context of this particular story that she uses for the first time the word 'fear' in relation to attending religious ceremonies, a feeling that she did not talk about in her general discourse on the communist regime:

> We were godparents to Adrian B. And the wedding was in this big church … So in 1950, one or two years afterwards, the priest closed the doors of the church out of fear that someone might come and see he is doing a religious wedding. And he had the ceremony with closed doors.

As her life story unfolds and we reach the time when her daughter got married in the late 1970s, the situation is considerably different:

> *Was it something usual for that period of time, a religious wedding? That was the ritual?*
>
> Yes, everybody was doing it.
>
> *Everybody?*
>
> Yes. Everybody.

As for baptising the children, her daughter and her nephews were all baptised according to the Orthodox custom, but in a ceremony at home performed by the Orthodox priest, a common practice in that period.

She is vocal about wanting to be buried, 'the proper way' with all the Orthodox ritual, 'I was baptised, wed. They will bury me with an Orthodox priest'. Yet, when she is asked, towards the end of the interview, if she is or is not a believer, she repeatedly claims she is unsure, 'Even I don't know if I have or not faith. I can't say. I don't know, I don't know'. When I asked her why she chose to perform religious ceremonies attached to these life transitions she went back to the argument of tradition, or something even stronger than tradition, something that 'runs in your blood':

> because we knew that all of our children, in our family, they were baptised also. Never, you know … There are some things, I don't know, that run in your blood, you know? You can't, how could you? In the end, I say that you can't go without a religious wedding either. In the end. That you go with one or another, that's something else. But a marriage that will result in having children, it seems only normal to have a religious wedding, without being a religious person.

I chose Florina as a case-study as she is a good example of the power and pressure of tradition in the Romanian context. Even though not religious, and unsure about her beliefs, her discourse breaths certainty when she explains what must be done, what is the proper and normal thing to do at life's turning points. I believe this is a pressure that sometimes collided with the rules of the communist state and gave birth to hybrid types of ceremonies bringing together religious traditions with the requirements of the new socialist society.

Negotiating Ceremonies: Secular Ceremonies as Non-ceremonies

Many aspects of everyday life in socialist regimes were subject to negotiation (Koleva 2012). In Romania, the ceremonies accompanying important life transitions like birth, marriage and death were traditionally celebrated with a religious ritual and their religious meaning adapted so as to avoid disturbing the new socialist order. Surprisingly, it was perhaps in the rigid 1950s that the idea of choosing a ceremony first appeared, so that suddenly, even if reacting to political pressure and feelings of fear, there were different scenarios to choose from when deciding on one's marriage or funeral. The main negotiating period was indeed the 1950s and 1960s, as from the 1970s and the development of national communism in Romania the pressure against attending church and performing religious ceremonies almost disappeared. In a brief enumeration, all through socialism, one could opt for:

- performing baptism and marriage at home;
- going to remote churches without guests;
- performing religious ceremonies behind closed doors; and

- celebrating religious holidays, but on different dates (for example, celebrating Christmas on New Year's eve).

Memories of secular ceremonies are helpful in developing an understanding of the importance of religious ritual in the traditional societies our interviewees were brought up in. Some interviewees claimed never to have attended secular ceremonies for birth, marriage or death. However, on closer scrutiny it appears that most of them did attend such ceremonies but, unless unpleasantly shocked by them, did not retain their memories of the moment as a proper ceremony.

Florina recalls the only secular funeral she attended:

Did you ever attend a funeral that did not have a religious ritual? No matter what faith?

Yes, I think I did. I did attend once a funeral, that went without priest almost the entire day.

What do you mean by almost?

Well, the priest was more of an assistant. There were some friends of ours, that, I don't know why, they were afraid to call the priest. It was back in the fifties or the late fifties I think. I attended, once. It seemed pointless to me. But that was the situation. That's what they decided. (Florina, Bucharest)

It was the funeral of a young girl and the grieving father, a convinced communist, decided to have a secular ceremony although his wife was a priest's daughter. Later on in his life, in the 1980s, having felt betrayed by the communist regime, he buried his wife in the Orthodox ritual. Another interviewee, Ion, claims he does not remember any such secular ceremony:

No, no. I know everybody had them. Now I cannot … If they didn't, I did not know of it! I only know those who did … Some would do the baptism at home. He would come with this baptism font, warm up some water, you always have to heat the water when it's a child, you have to …

Why were they doing the baptism at home?

I couldn't say. Maybe also because some were hiding it. What do I know, they were something with the Party or I don't know where and they were hesitant to stay in the church. It was for the better … but they never forgot to do it! Yes.

Why do you think they did it?

Maybe out of tradition, especially, or the family tradition they could not forget ... this is what I think. What do I know, maybe also from some sort of faith ... maybe, actually. (Ion, Bucharest)

In a Bulgarian interview, the couple explain that they did not have a religious wedding yet they took the risk and baptised their children:

Did you and your wife get married in church?

No, she's got a communist background. Her uncle was a political prisoner, her father was a party secretary ...

What about your children, are they baptised?

Yes. We might have got into a lot of trouble with the older son. We got him baptised when he was in first form. And we are travelling to a village called Kochevo. While we are travelling, there's a priest on the bus and my son starts shouting, "Daddy, daddy, this is the priest that baptised me!" Everybody stared at us. So I say to myself, "Oh, we got lucky today!" But we got away with it ... My wife became a god-mother of a lot of children. Not many people were willing to be god-parents at that time. (Zahari Zaimov, Shumen, Bulgaria)

In the Bulgarian sample, recollections of non-religious weddings are more common, even among religious interviewees who would immediately compensate for their non-religious marriage by taking the trouble to baptise their children:

The rituals – it was difficult to have a marriage ceremony in a church, but all my children are baptised, using connections – seemingly without my knowledge, without the knowledge of the mother, only very close friends, because these things were persecuted at that time. (Evlogi Anastasov, Sofia)

The Secret Everyone Knew: Hidden Religious Ceremonies

Baptising children was indeed a matter of choice, some would not conceive of not baptising a child while others would not observe the ceremony. Having an un-baptised member of the family came as a shock to these interviewees. Viorel Ionescu (b. 1927, Bucharest) and his wife told me about the secret baptism of their children; however, their niece intervened to tell them that their son-in-law, her father, is not baptised:

Niece: For example, my father is not baptised.

Grandma: I do not think so, I don't believe it.

Niece: Why can't you believe it? I'm telling you, my father is not baptised!

Grandma: I don't believe it. Maybe they did not want to tell him.

Niece: You want to say that he might be secretly baptised?

Grandma: Well, maybe, what does he know, he was little …

Niece: Well, Grandma and grandpa told him, he is not baptised.

Grandma: Did they?

Niece: They were in the high ranks of the communist party in F.[16]

Grandma: Yes, and it was a small town, people would find out immediately.

Niece: Exactly, you could not go to Ploiesti to baptise your kid.

Grandma [in disbelief]: Well, that's something … I … (Viorel, Bucharest)

If the couple wanted to have a religious wedding, a common choice was sometimes to relocate the whole event to a remote place, away from the everyday environment and acquaintances of the couple as in this story from the Bulgarian 1950s:

The wedding, wait a minute, I'll tell you. It was in 195 … [she wonders]

So, it was after the 9th of September [1944].

Yes, it was after that.

Weren't you worried?

Why should I worry? Even the Party Secretary was wed in church. Do you know what we did? We were clever and we went to Dryanovo. We have cousins there. We went to have our wedding in the church there.

Not in Targovishte?

Do you know what might have happened in Targovishte? He would have been removed immediately. (Milena Chakalova, Targovishte)

---

[16]   Small size town in the region of Moldova, Romania.

Baptisms were performed in a similar manner; the children were taken to other cities or to isolated churches:

> *When the children were born, did you baptise them? The kids?*
>
> Of course ...
>
> *And did you baptise them in church, or at home?*
>
> In church, of course, how could we not?
>
> Wife intervenes: No, they were baptised in church, but in a discrete manner ... we took Adrian to Ploiesti, and Nusa, yes we went to a little church that was hidden. (Viorel, Bucharest)

Sometimes, the search for a more 'discrete' location produced amusing moments, like this Resurrection liturgy in 1950s Romania recalled by Florina:

> And we were thinking where to go. There was the Trei Ierarhi Church, the Patriarchy where they made services really worth attending. But we were afraid to go there. We thought, if they see us, nobody knows us yet ... There behind the Administrative Palace there is a small church. So we went there. The church was full [*emphasis*] with all the Polytechnics, all those coming from Bucharest, foreigners, and students. And, mind you, a lot of Jewish students. I even asked them afterwards, "What were you doing there?" They said the Resurrection is a spectacle. This is what one of the Jews told us. (Florina, Bucharest)

Florina tells this story as a funny event, with everyone trying to hide their presence at the Resurrection service, yet all of them meeting in what they thought was a hidden location. For the historian, this story speaks of common techniques of by-passing official regulations and ordinary people's successful attempts to continue a way of life that had been passed on to them by older generations, a way of life that was not necessarily religious but traditional, and further, national (as her puzzle at the presence of Jews testifies[17]).

Celebrating Christmas was an equally important point for negotiation. The Christmas tree and the tradition of giving gifts to children was kept, yet officially moved towards New Years Eve in order to symbolise the secular celebration of New Year and not the religious celebration of the birth of Christ:

> The Christmas tree, for example we never made it on Christmas day. We would make it closer to New Years Eve. So she [their child] couldn't be asked and tell.

---

[17]   The presence of the Jews might also be interpreted as an argument for the 'national' character of Orthodox celebrations like Easter.

And everybody made it like this. I mean everybody kept the holidays, respected the rituals, but slightly moved them, a bit ahead or a bit behind. (Florina, Bucharest)

Was it difficult to celebrate Christmas and Easter during the communist regime?

Yes, because you had to celebrate it secretly. Within family. Family and nothing else. Didn't go to church, no. (Miron Popescu, Bucharest)

Frequent references to family tradition, to kin, to performing religious ceremonies for the family and within the family seem to suggest that religiosity is very much connected to family life and a sense of community as an extended family (sometimes extended to the national level). In the Romanian sample, even those interviewees who questioned their religiosity, speak of religious traditions that 'run in your blood' (Florina) and of the importance of 'living as an Orthodox' (Margareta). The Bulgarian sample differs in this respect, in the sense that observance of religious ceremonies is more often correlated with the interviewee's conscious decision to be religious or not. The next section dwells on the subjective meanings of being Orthodox for Romanian and Bulgarian elders.

Orthodoxy as Identity: The Importance of Dying Orthodox

Until not so long ago, one could hear in Romanian villages the word 'Christian' used as a synonym for 'human being'. Although this synonymy is already out of use, I want to argue that a new synonymy has emerged in Romanian culture: between the words Orthodox and Romanian. This cultural and political synonymy may account for the high numbers of those who declare themselves to be Orthodox in sociological surveys as well as the persistence of religious rituals even among declared atheists. For these non-religious Orthodox, as I call them, Orthodoxy is yet another form of being Romanian, of being who you are, who you were born and together with those born with the same *blood*.

My argument is that, for the Romanian elders interviewed, being Orthodox seems easier to accept as an identity marker than being religious. Religiousness is associated with being a practising believer, at the least taking part in the Sunday liturgy, while Orthodoxy is something you were born or baptised into, a family inheritance that you cannot actually renounce. For example, one interviewee (Ion, Bucharest) who sang for many years in the church choir and who believes in the Christian God, rejected the label 'religious person'. For him, being religious is often paired with being *too* religious while the only person he definitely describes as being Christian Orthodox is his late father.

Being Orthodox is not a choice, the Romanian sample seems to point out, it is innate. One does not have to do anything to be Orthodox, except maybe observe important ceremonies, baptism, marriage and funeral according to Orthodox ritual, although variations can even be found here (Margareta was baptised Catholic, married according to Greek-Catholic ritual and wants to be cremated, yet she calls herself Orthodox). However, even among these ceremonies one stands out as being of the most important for the Orthodox: the funeral.

Dying Orthodox appears in our interviews to be in direct correlation with Orthodoxy as an identity marker. The connections are automatic. For the elders we were interviewing the funeral remains the last Orthodox rite to perform. 'I was born in Orthodoxy, I will die in this' (Mirela, Bucharest).

The same unquestioned association can be seen in this Bulgarian interview excerpt:

How would you define yourself? Would you say you are Orthodox Christian?

Absolutely. I'm Christian; I'll die Christian. I've told my children that when I die, they'll have to bury me according to Christian rites – with a priest, in my mother's grave. (Evlogi, Sofia)

Another significant association is between being Orthodox and never changing one's religion. Even though the interview guide did not include a question about changing one's religious denomination, some of the interviewees spontaneously declared they would never consider this:

You see, if someone would ask me to change my religion. In fact, I never thought, I never tried or discussed it with someone. Everybody in our family [or people – "neam"] was an Orthodox, and I will also die an Orthodox. That was very clear to me. I will never accept another religion. Or any other name you want to call it. (Florina, Bucharest)

This only adds to my argument that Orthodoxy, and more broadly one's religious denomination, is not considered a matter of choice in these parts of Europe, but rather a genetic trait, similar to having blue eyes or dark hair. Similarly, performing the religious ceremonies for birth, marriage and death, especially death, is equally a matter of custom, of what must be done than a matter of choice.[18] As Florina recalls her parents' funerals, I ask her:

Before their death, did you speak with them, about their wishes, how would they liked to be buried, what ritual to follow?

Not a single moment.

Like, it was understood?

---

[18]   For a discussion on the role played by religion in the context of coping and adjusting to significant bereavement, see Chapter 8.

We did what we believed was right for a Christian to do. Orthodox, like all of my family. But they never said anything.

Conclusions: Belonging without Believing

The ceremonies discussed in this chapter have a particular role in almost any traditional society as a means of introducing the person into the community. Thus performing a baptism or a marriage within the church was equivalent to introducing and accepting a new member or a new couple into the bigger community. Such ceremonies have maintained this role in both Romanian and Bulgarian society, but while Bulgarians and other Europeans for that matter might often replace the religious ceremony with a secular one, Romanians are still socially constrained to perform the religious variant.

'Believing without belonging' (Davie 1994) is a catchy phrase describing a reality where levels of belief are much higher than levels of religious practice. Some researchers maintain that this trend can also be observed in the Romanian situation, as religiousness is becoming more and more deinstitutionalised (Gog 2007). However, the results of this research show an important level of religious practice, performing religious ceremonies at key moments in life, such as birth, marriage and death, paired with a strong reluctance to declare oneself a believer and with disregard for other forms of religious practice. I propose to describe this phenomenon as 'belonging without believing'. As this chapter suggests, it is the particular symbiosis of religious and national identity with a strong respect for tradition that makes Romanian elders one of the most 'religious' groups in Europe. Belonging to the nation, belonging to the family goes together with belonging to the same religious denomination, which, for southern Romania, is almost always the Orthodox Church.

As our research shows, many of the interviewees confess to great personal doubts concerning their faith and some are reluctant to declare themselves religious (as expectations relating to religious practice are still very high in Eastern Europe). However, the Romanian elders interviewed appear to feel on the safe side every time they acknowledge being Orthodox. Within their age cohort the question of looking ahead towards death is crucial and their almost unconditional acceptance of the Orthodox rite as the appropriate one for their funeral testifies more to a life-long commitment to a national and family-related Orthodox tradition than to genuine Christian convictions.

One of the issues this research tackled was the influence and memory of socialist secularisation on religious ceremonies, thus challenging the theory of a religious revival in Eastern Europe after 1989. As a general conclusion, in as much as ceremonies are concerned, our interviewees did not focus on the changes and differences in ceremonies across their lives. On the contrary, most of them suggested that these ceremonies remained the same, no matter in which political regime they were performed and I would argue that it is precisely the unchanging, seemingly immutable character of these religious ceremonies that accounts for much of the attachment and appreciation these ceremonies still have among the elders, and more generally in Romanian society. The comfort of participating in the same ceremony witnessed as a child, performed for one's parents or grandparents is not to be underestimated ('Everybody in our family was an Orthodox, and I will also die an Orthodox').

An important factor that was not taken into account, neither in the interviews nor, because of space limitations, in this chapter either, is the fact that Romanian Orthodoxy is known for having integrated numerous pagan rituals over the centuries. The survival of these pagan rituals, even though transformed so as to appear Christian, could give us a hint in explaining the extraordinary resilience of traditional, religious ceremonies in Romania today.

Socialist secularisation remains a debated subject, although I would suggest that its importance has been over-emphasised when discussing religiosity in Eastern Europe. For the purpose of this analysis, accounting for the differences in religiosity between Romania and Bulgaria, I have argued that socialist secularisation meant different things in different countries. The distinct policies implemented by each state in the secularisation process were more influential than the general atheistic discourse of socialist regimes. What seems to have made the difference in secularisation was a particular measure implemented by the Bulgarian socialist state and not by the Romanian one: the introduction of secular ceremonies for birth and death. However, of still greater importance in both cases is the embeddedness of religious identity in other significant identities and the greater or lesser role assigned to tradition in each society and age cohort.

References

Băsescu, Traian. 2006. *The Speech given by the President of Romania, Traian Basescu, on the occasion of the Presentation of the Report by the Presidential Commission for the Analysis of the Communist Dictatorship in Romania* (The Parliament of Romania, 18 December 2006). Available at: http://cpcadcr. presidency.ro/upload/8288_en.pdf in English (accessed 12 November 2012).

Cohen, Steven M. and Lauren Blitzer. 2008. *Belonging Without Believing. Jews and their Distinctive Patterns of Religiosity – and Secularity. Selected Results from the 2008 Pew Forum U.S. Religious Landscape Survey.* FGH/JCC Association Research Center. Available at: http://www.jewishdatabank.org/ archive/n-pew-2007-report_belonging_without_believing_cohen_2008.pdf (accessed 12 November 2012).

Comisia Prezidentiala pentru Analiza Dictaturii Comuniste din Romania. 2007. *Raport Final.* Bucharest: Humanitas.

Consultative Council of Denominations in the Socialist Republic of Romania. 1987. *Viata religioasa in Romania. Prezentare sintetica.* [Religious Life in Romania. A Synthetic Presentation.] Bucharest.

Davie, Grace. 1994. *Religion in Britain since 1945: Believing without Belonging*. Oxford: Blackwell.

Francis, Leslie J. and Mandy Robbins. 2004. 'Belonging without Believing: A Study in the Social Significance of Anglican Identity and Implicit Religion among 13–15 Year-old Males'. *Implicit Religion* 7(1): 37–54.

Gog, Sorin. 2007. 'Individualizarea experienţei religioase şi erodarea funcţiilor eclesiale în România postsocialistă'. *Romanian Political Science Review (Biserici şi politică în România secolului al XX-lea)* VII(3): 791–801.

Koleva, Daniela (ed.) 2012. *Negotiating Normality: Everyday Lives in Socialist Institution*. New Jersey: Transaction Publishers.

Leustean, Lucian N. 2007. 'Between Moscow and London: Romanian Orthodoxy and National Communism, 1960–1965'. *The Slavonic and East European Review* 85(3): 491–521.

Marchisio, Roberto and Maurizio Pisati. 1999. 'Belonging without Believing: Catholics in Contemporary Italy'. *Journal of Modern Italian Studies* 4(2): 236–55.

Metodiev, Momchil. 2010. *Between Faith and Compromise. The Orthodox Church and the Communist Regime in Bulgaria (1944–1989)*. Sofia: Siela.

Ramet, Pedro. 1987. *Cross and Commissar: The Politics of Religion in Eastern Europe and the USSR*. Bloomington, IN: Indiana University Press.

Ramet, Sabrina P. 2004. 'Church and State in Romania before and after 1989'. In *Romania since 1989: Politics, Economics, and Society*, edited by Henry F. Carey. Lanham, MD: Lexington Books, 275–96.

Sincan, Anca. 2010. 'From Bottom to the Top and Back. On How to Build a Church in Communist Romania'. In *Christianity and Modernity in Eastern Europe*, edited by Bruce Berglund and Brian Porter Szucs. Budapest: CEU Press, 191–216.

Stan, Lavinia and Lucian Turcescu. 2007. *Religion and Politics in Post-Communist Romania*. Oxford: Oxford University Press.

Vasile, Cristian. 2003a. *Intre Vatican si Kremlin. Biserica Greco-Catolica in timpul regimului comunist*. Bucharest: Curtea Veche.

Vasile, Cristian. 2003b. *Istoria Bisericii Greco-Catolice sub regimul communist, 1945–1989. Documente si marturii*. Iasi: Polirom.

Voas, David and Alasdair Crockett. 2005. 'Religion in Britain: Neither Believing nor Belonging'. *Sociology* 39(11): 11–28.

Chapter 4

'God Can Wait':
Composing Non-Religious Narratives in
Secular and Post-Communist Societies

Hilary Young

'The things religious people get from religion – awe, wonder, meaning and perspective – non-religious people get them from other places like art, nature, human relationships and the narratives we give our lives in other ways', according to Andrew Copson, chief executive of the British Humanist Society (Booth 2012). Faith versus reason aside, what does Copson mean by 'narratives we [non-religious people] give our lives in other ways'? Bound up in this statement is the suggestion that non-religious people tell different stories or tell stories in different ways in order to make sense of their lives or give meaning to their lives. For this very reason it was important for a project interested in religious and secular practices to include interviews with people who did not identify with being religious in order to explore how they make sense of and how they have marked important stages in their lives. Non-believers and secular ceremonies were always part of the project, but in light of our experiences interviewing, it is clear we need to listen carefully given that the religious discourse has tended to dominate such discussions.

The discourses that people draw on to compose their life stories are not random. Within any culture a range of possible identities will exist for interviewees to use when they compose their life stories or try to make sense of the past. An ideal or desirable identity may reinforce the dominant cultural discourse, just as an alternative identity may contest or subvert it. Of interest to the oral historian is how the interviewee draws on these social discourses to construct a narrative they are comfortable with telling. Of concern in this chapter is 'the relationship between the narrative produced by the respondent and the culture that informs it' (Abrams 2010, 66). The discourse of secularisation is a familiar one for the oral history interviewees from all three countries, religious or not. The participants in this project have lived through a series of generational changes in discourses on religion and the secular. Narrators draw on shared meanings and understandings in order to compose their stories. In Abrams's words, 'we can only tell and make sense of an experience if we do so in a way that makes sense to others, and therefore we use common or agreed frameworks and discourses to give shape and meaning to our stories' (Abrams 2010, 66). Narrators tell stories in specific ways in particular contexts. An important consideration when trying to understand stories of the past is that 'The discourses of times remembered may be very different from the time within which the memory is being recalled and testified' (Brown 2001, 115).

In this chapter I begin by locating the RASC project within the current debates on secularisation in the UK. I move on to discuss the challenges of interviewing about religious practice in the context of secularisation and its impact on memories, arguing that the salience of secularisation in the UK presents a framework for interviewees to make sense of their religious past and non-religious present by exploring the testimony of one UK male and one UK female who attended religious services as children but stopped in later life. I then take as my focus the personal testimony of five interviewees (two UK females, one Bulgarian male and two Romanian men). Of interest to me was how each of these interviewees told different stories than those that were commonly told in each country about religious practice. I explore how these stories surface during each interview, drawing on the idea of the religious ceremony as spectacle, theories of composure and the place of individual memory within national contexts. I argue that these stories are 'individual countermemories' (Abrams 2010, 97) that contrast with the dominant narrative commonly ascribed to each country and era in public discourse.

Secularisation and Memory

Having agreed to include non-believers in the interview sample, one of our central research questions was to explore the emergence of secular alternatives to religious ceremonies and how older people experienced and recalled these, if at all. We also wanted to question to what extent religious ritual has any attraction for those in later life who have no explicit religious belief or practice. We were concerned with the secular and those who have no explicit religious belief because in contrast to Bulgaria and Romania religious practice has been cited as being in decline in the UK. Debates around secularisation and atheism are a condition in which British interviewees currently compose their life stories. According to the annual British Social Attitudes Survey, between 1983 and 2008 the number of those who profess no religion rose from 31 to 43 per cent. In 2009, this was found to have further risen to 51 per cent. Those self-described as members of the Church of England consisted of 20 per cent of the population in 2009 compared with 40 per cent in 1983 when the survey was first conducted. In 2008, it was found that 49 per cent of this group never attended services, while only 8 per cent of people who identified with the Church of England attended weekly services (Voas and Ling 2010). It should be noted here that being religious tends to be generalised as the Christian religion in UK surveys. Of course it is also true that many of those who are most committed religionists in the UK are not Christian.

Some of the early interviews from all three countries challenged our understanding and conceptualisation of what is meant by religious practice and highlighted the challenge of asking about practices that are often not spoken about. As oral historian Williams argues:

it is all too easy to go into an interview and to ask questions or to raise topics in a way which suggests that the interviewer merely wishes to hear what the interviewee thought about formal church services and how frequently they attended them. It is another matter altogether to allow the subject of religion to emerge (or not emerge as the case may be) within a structure dictated by the interviewee's own life history and as part of a wide range of topics. (Williams 1966, 29)

For example, one RASC interviewee, John Cruikshank, who was born in 1926 in the East End of London and identified himself as not religious, framed his narrative around the impact of social institutions on his life as opposed to the influence of his family. After being caught by the police for causing damage to factory roofs with his friends, John was sent to a boarding school for young offenders for five years, where he had to attend church every Sunday. At the start of the Second World War and with the imminent threat of bombing in London, 800,000 child evacuees left London to live in the country with host families. John was one of these evacuees to the country, where he sang in the local church choir and attended church regularly every week. Yet despite the circumstances he found himself in, John's participation reflected a common pattern of working-class families' connection to church. Attendance was expected in childhood and throughout the teenage years, enjoyed during courtship, culminating in marriage in church, yet after the first child was christened, it often dwindled (McLeod 1996). Now in later life John does not go to church and says he is not religious but still believes it is important to hold a religious ceremony at key moments in life. John's narrative is an example from the study that fits Bădică's (Chapter 3) 'belonging without believing' thesis.

Historian Brown rejects the long tradition of British historiography that understands a decline in religiousness to have slowly permeated British society since the late nineteenth and early twentieth centuries. For Brown, 'the evangelical narrative structure and the discourses within it had a powerful continuity between the late eighteenth and the mid-twentieth century [in Britain], but both structure and discourses then radically changed in the 1950s and 1960s'. Brown argues that the decline in religiosity in the UK set in after 1945 but did not speed up until the 1960s. This had implications for oral histories of religion gathered after 1960 as 'The liberalisation of religious values and "loss of religious life" … became radically re-remembered' (Brown 2001, 116). Brown's re-analysis of several large UK oral history collections conducted in the 1980s and 1990s highlighted that interviewees composed stories that allowed them to express discontent with their religious upbringing.

This was the case with Polly Rutherford (London interviewee), who was born in 1931 and grew up in Manchester. She identified herself as a humanist before the interview. During the interview, memories of being confirmed in the Church of England at the age of 12 were 'radically remembered'. Polly recalled that her parents were not religious and did not attend church: 'There was no sense of occasions or happenings in my youth which were attached in any way to religion, which seemed to be quite different from quite a number of other children'. Yet when asked if she had ever questioned her parents about why they did not go to church, her memory was jogged and she recalled the 'radical memory' (Brown 2001, 116) of being confirmed:

> When I was about twelve I think it was, people were getting, some people were getting confirmed and I didn't understand what this was and what it was about so I insisted upon going to a class and I was [laughing] I was in fact confirmed. I remember my mother coming to the ceremony and she wore a hat which was very unusual for her [laughing]. But I mean I was confirmed and received into the Church of England. I didn't go [laughing]. I didn't attend.

According to Brown, the radical memory 'becomes evident in oral testimony in the form of laughter, self-derision, grief or even bitterness at recollections of the religious regimes they had followed without question as youngsters' (Brown 2001, 116). Polly's memory was radical because she had not actively remembered being confirmed for many years until the occasion of the interview. She visibly sat up in her seat and between bouts of laughter she closed her eyes to remember the ceremony and her sense of feelings more clearly. Confirmation is a Christian ritual in the Church of England and in the Roman Catholic Church when people strengthen their relationship with God, and can be viewed as a transition point between childhood and adulthood. Confirmation is a rite of passage. For a young girl whose family was not religious and did not belong to any church, witnessing her friends talking about it, confirmation appealed to Polly as something she might want to join in with. Yet after attending the instructional classes and the ceremony, Polly struggled with what it meant:

> It [confirmation] had a sort of mainstream feel to it because of course it was the Church of England and we were English and so on and so forth. But I found great difficulty in believing in God. I couldn't, I couldn't bring myself, and I thought "Well now I'd better wait a bit and see if the great light shines or something" [laughing] And nothing did so I didn't pursue it in any way at all.

For Polly this was a transition point in her life in which she remembers feeling 'rather disappointed', and although she attended the local church a number of times by herself after the confirmation ceremony, her life was changing in other ways as well. Polly's narrative fits that of the scholarship girl given the opportunities that her parents perhaps were unable to provide (Steedman 1997). She passed the 11-plus exam[1] and won a scholarship to the grammar school where

---

[1]   The 11-plus exam was set locally but taken by all children at the age of 10 or 11. Called the Tripartite System, it was designed to divide children according to results by ability. A minority went to grammar schools, preparing them for university or tertiary-level education. Depending on local availability, a second group might go to a technical school,

she studied science, was 'learning new things' and 'reading literature': 'That was filling my mind I think more than – I thought "Well, God can wait" [laughing] but he's still waiting'. She uses wit to deflect and understand these 'radical' (Brown 2001) memories.

Brown's argument that religiosity in the UK only started to decline after 1945 justifies the RASC project's approach to interviewing a group whose memories extend further back than 1945. As Polly's interview highlighted, asking questions about her early childhood and going even further back to ask questions of her parents' generation and views on religion opened up memories that she had long since forgotten. Polly 'radically remembered' taking part in the confirmation ceremony; potentially she might get upset by this memory if it did not fit with her present sense of self. Yet this was not the case as she used wit to make sense of the memory. I would argue that the greater salience of individualism and humanism in the UK may now provide a structure for non-religious interviewees to make sense of their past and compose narratives about their religious upbringing that are less 'radically re-remembered' than those interviewees Brown cites in the 1980s and 1990s.

Spectacle of Ritual in the UK or Belonging without Believing

During her interview Jennifer Renwick (London) composed a life history about her non-religious self within a wider community of religious practice and spectacle. In doing so, she elucidates an understanding of what celebrations and rituals meant within a non-religious working-class East End of London family on the periphery of the church. Here I recount in detail Jennifer's life story. The challenge to the reader is to understand the variety of rituals she recalls witnessing during the 1930s, 1940s and 1950s.

Jennifer is typical of her generation. Born in 1924 she was christened in the Church of England, but like so many it 'was a cultural thing rather than a religious thing' (Polly, London). Like John and Polly and the majority of children in the early twentieth century, Jennifer participated in church activities despite her parents not attending. She recalled that:

> The only time I was religious [laughing] it was a laugh, was when I used to get sent to Sunday School and they used to give you a card and they'd stamp your card and if you had a full card – it's like lottery – if you had a full card you got to go on the outing, which was in the summer.

---

in preparation for work in industry and commerce; there were, however, very few of these schools. The third group, as many as three-quarters, went to what were known as secondary modern schools, where they were taught basic educational skills and given what might now be described as vocational training. Versions of this exam and similar types of provision still persist in some parts of the UK today.

The social aspect of the church was important in working-class areas at a time when there was no welfare state for support. The numbers of families with no regular parental churchgoing emerges from Hugh McLeod's review of UK oral testimony as quite high at 50–60 per cent (McLeod 1996). As a result, the discourse of religious and educational institutions framed Jennifer's experiences from a young age. Having passed an entrance exam that her family were keen for her to take, Jennifer won a scholarship to a Catholic secondary school in 1938. Prior to being accepted, she had to attend an entrance interview with her mother. She recalled the conversation with the nun who was interviewing her:

> And she said to my mother "Of course you're not Catholic". "No". So she said "And what's the child?", who was me. "What does she think about that?" So she looked at me so I said, you know, "That was alright". "Do you go to church?" I said "I go to see the weddings". I'll always remember that and this didn't go down a bundle. So she said "Do you believe?" So I thought well, "Yeah I suppose, you know, something". So she said to my mother "I will accept her", she said. "But I don't often take people who are not religious some way or the other".

Remembering this encounter Jennifer recalls the disjuncture between the official discourse of religiosity that the nun represented and her younger uncertain self. Rejecting belief in the early twentieth century may have had serious social implications. Brown cites an occasion when a 'girl who proclaimed her unbelief in the school playground recalled being taunted and called "a heathen" by her classmates' (Brown 2001, 174). Admitting as much to a representative of the church when your education depended on it must have been difficult. However, Jennifer remembers negotiating this situation deftly and drew on her sense of belonging to the local community in which she vicariously witnessed religious practice to satisfy the nun. Despite the memory of the caustic reaction from the nun when she discovered that the young Jennifer was not religious, Jennifer felt comfortable composing and re-telling the story in later life. She reveals her younger self trying to make sense of what she had been witnessing on the streets and in the churches of her local area. The spectacle of the occasion was the attraction: 'I go to see the weddings'. This helps us to understand how Jennifer composed the rest of her testimony in which she recounts various 'rituals' or ceremonies witnessed throughout her life, not as a member of a church but as someone who had negotiated what it meant not to believe in God in mid-twentieth-century Britain.

Growing up around the busy London docks in Poplar in the 1920s and 1930s, Jennifer experienced a multicultural environment and had the opportunity to witness a variety of different religious denominations' services and practices. Talking about Good Friday and what happened in the local neighbourhood, she recalled:

[On Good Friday] you would get, there was a Baptist church near us and they would, they would have a lot, there would be a lot of people who would go to church on that day. I didn't. I didn't, there were some Catholic children near me who did. And, you know, they would meet up with their mates, and I feel sure that they used to, most Catholic people, would have kept it more than the ordinary. We had a high clientele of Jewish people near me as well.

She used to 'creep into the chapel every now and then' for the Friday afternoon Catholic service for children, and 'every Monday night' she 'used to go to the local Baptist church where they used to show a cinema show with a magic lantern'. Owing to the multicultural area she grew up in and the relative freedom that children had at the time from parental supervision, Jennifer experienced and witnessed a 'broad church' of religious ceremonies. Her natural storytelling manner produces detailed vignettes of dress, emotions and community belonging. She recalls the Catholic processions in the dockland areas:

There were processions in all different parts of the East End. And the churches used to bring out their regalia and their statues of Mary with Jesus or Jesus on the cross. I mean that would – and you would get men who were part of the church with their green braids across and hats too – they would play quite solemn music. The kids would all be dressed, white, boys used to wear black short trousers and a white shirt, white socks, black shoes. The girls used to wear a white dress like a confirmation dress. They would have blue ribbons round their hair. And this procession could be anything up to about half a mile long and it'd trail through the streets.

After capturing the interviewer's attention with the statement 'So this was the ritual', she goes into meticulous detail describing the process by which her father bought paint and prepared the family's backyard to be whitewashed, because on 'Good Friday he [her father] always, I can remember this was something that was tablets of stone I should think, he said "We're going to do the whitewashing of the back yard"'. While this is not a traditional religious ritual or ceremony it clearly had significance for Jennifer, in order for her to recall the practice in later life, and to her father, who as she remembered, 'as a child had been sent, like a lot of kids were when I was little, round to church. And I think you know, sometimes you soak it up.' The rituals and ceremonies that Jennifer recalled were within the context of other national ceremonies, festivals, seasonal change and celebrations of the time, such as Empire Day, Whitsun and the funeral of King George V:

And I can remember when King George the fifth died every blind in the house was pulled down, every house who had blinds. You took part in this, especially if it was a king, a royal funeral. … And if you were sort of able you would go up and you would watch the procession of the coffin being carried through. … But I can remember my dad going up. And there was always a lying in state and that was in Westminster Hall. And Westminster Hall is very difficult to get into. They'll only open it certain times and it's usually if they have a royal burial – it's a burial – and they put the coffin and then you're allowed to march through, pay your respects. I did it for the Queen Mother.[2]

Mourning in public, as a community, was common practice until the 1970s (Wouters 2002, 1). To pay her respects to the Queen Mother when she died in 2002 made sense to Jennifer given the place of public mourning in her younger life, both for the royal family and in her own community.

Jennifer's wider narrative reinforces previous patterns of working-class families' connection to church. After leaving school aged 15 in 1939 she had very little contact with other religious denominations or institutional religion. Owing to the devastation of the East End and dockland areas during the Blitz in 1940, Jennifer and her family were forced to leave their community, friends and family networks in search of accommodation elsewhere, in her case in north London. The period after 1945 was clearly a difficult time in her life, and her testimony reflects this, with gaps in the narrative. She married 'young' sometime in the 1940s and 1950s and had two children, revealing only that she did not 'feel any pressure' to christen either of her daughters. The 1950s are understood to represent the height of an evangelical discourse after the Second World War, when the slightest deviation away from the traditional discourse of religiosity may have been viewed badly (Brown 2001). Jennifer's narrative focus on the 1930s and 1940s may reflect the difficulty she still has in her late eighties in understanding what she experienced in the 1950s. Yet how do we make sense of Jennifer's memories of such a diverse range of rituals?

The answer may lie in Jennifer's memory of the biggest evangelical spectacle (Wong 2004) that came to London, in 1954. When Billy Graham, an American Christian Evangelist, came to preach in London in a brief religious crusade, the atmosphere in the Harringay Arena was 'electric'. Jennifer and four friends thought, 'We ought to go see what this is like' (Jennifer, London). According to Brown, 'nothing like it had been seen before in British Protestantism, and nothing like it has been seen again' (Brown 2001, 6). Brown argues that the high participation rates of women at Graham's crusades would not have happened 'if the discursive power of the evangelical narrative had been seriously diminished' (Brown 2001, 174). Yet Jennifer presented an alternative experience. As a non-believer the significance of the Billy Graham crusade was the spectacle: 'It was fantastic. If you could, stand aside and just go and be what you are without believing anything.'

Jennifer's memories of King Georges V's funeral procession, the Catholic street processions, the whitewashing of the backyard on Good Friday and Billy

---

2   The Queen Mother died on 30 March 2002. Her coffin was moved to Westminster Hall in central London, so the public could pay their respects in a move not seen since the death of Sir Winston Churchill in 1965.

Graham's crusade were memories of public events or spectacles through which she could belong to the local community without believing. Other non-religious interviewees from the UK cited experiencing funerals of friends and families when younger or as an adult that lacked a personal eulogy as a motivation to rethink their relationship with the church and the importance of holding religious ceremonies at key points in life. In contrast, Jennifer recalled a more personalised shared community experience and understanding of funeral rituals that were carried out at home, in the community and extended to the cemetery:

> Well the East Enders had a different way of doing those things. It was much more personal. And you didn't care too much whether it was posh or not. It was just, you know, somewhere where the remains were and you could go over there, you could put your bunch of flowers on it and you could probably put 'em in a jam jar on it.

Accustomed to the personalisation of East End cemeteries and aware of the new individuality presented in funerals today, Jennifer revealed:

> I wanted to go to a dog's – well, to an animal cemetery. I said "Can you be buried in an animal cemetery?" This posed a question. "Don't know". So I spoke to the vet. He said "There are ways of doing it".

Since the 1980s the quest for new personalised rituals to mark death has grown. Wouters suggests that 'the new rituals are not only more varied and informal, they are also more individualised and personal. It seems likely, therefore, that these public expressions signal a rising need to find more public recognition of personal mourning and that, via these rituals, participants are seeking to assert membership of a larger symbolic or 'imagined' community' (Wouters 2002, 2). As opposed to the 'radical memory' that Brown talks about, Jennifer's series of memories of religious and secular ceremonies challenge the collective memory of religiousness of the period. The stories she tells are individual countermemories that challenge the dominant interpretations of the past. The development of individualised ceremonies in the later twentieth century presented a framework for Jennifer to talk about her past experiences of observing religious spectacles as well as to freely admit her aspirations for a very unique resting place at the end of her life.

I will now move on to explore the impact of individual and collective memories on post-communist secular narratives.

Re-composing Post-Communist Secular Identities

The extent and personal experience of enforced socialist secularisation varied in Bulgaria and Romania. The Bulgarian Communist Party followed 'militant atheism' with the introduction of state-sanctioned civil rituals such as guidance on speeches, ceremonies, music, secular tombstones and special buildings to mark life passages (see Koleva, Chapter 6). Yet memories of these secular ceremonies and rituals were scant and they were often not remembered as proper ceremonies by interviewees from Bulgaria and Romania (see Bădică, Chapter 3). With the resurgence of religious practice in both of these former communist countries, some interviewees explained how they had come face to face in later life with yet another change in the religious–secular discourse. In some cases these changes had been experienced within their own familial religious practices.

Oral history research has begun to focus on the construction of subjective identities, individually and collectively, as well as historically and within the interview. Of interest here is the relationship between the narrative produced by the respondent and the culture that informs it. Thomson's early work on Australian men's memories of the First World War, and specifically the Anzac experience, highlighted how Anzacs' own memories of their wartime activities were altered by public discourses in Australia and New Zealand at the time of recollection (Thomson 1994). What this suggests is that we can only tell and make sense of an experience if we do so in a way that makes sense to others. Therefore we use common or agreed frameworks and discourse to give a shape and meaning to our stories. Yet Green warns oral historians against moving away from theoretical understandings of the individuality of memory towards describing the impact of cultural contexts, including public narratives on the shaping of individual memory (Green 2004). Green is concerned that 'Historians are increasingly focusing upon the ways in which individual recollections fit (often unconscious) cultural scripts or templates' (Green 2004, 36). This led Smith to explore the challenges of an apparent simple choice, concluding that memory 'is also the result of social processes that are experiential.' (Smith 2007, 78).

Composing life histories that they felt comfortable telling in the post-communist period was an exercise some of the Bulgarian and Romanian interviewees were still negotiating at the time of interview. Dawson's work on 'popular memory' suggests that we 'compose' our memories to make sense of the past and also of the present. In one sense we 'compose' memories using the public language and meanings of our culture, while in another sense we 'compose' memories to attain 'composure', allowing us to feel comfortable with the stories we tell of ourselves (Dawson 1994, 22–3). Dore, working in a Cuban context, flags Passerini's observation that 'memory seems to have a flattening effect on the concept of totalitarianism' (quoted in Dore 2012, 35). By this she is referring to the remarkable similarity of stories from former communist countries with different experiences being recalled in such a way as to 'have diminished our understanding of life under communism' to stories about 'fear' and 'brutality' (Dore 2012, 35). Dore cites Liljestrom who 'argues that there was a mass cleansing of collective memory in post-Soviet societies where only stories of suffering, repression and dissidence under communist rule were regarded as authentic' (Dore 2012, 35). Mark also argues that 'Oral historians interested in the memory of communism need to pay attention to the ways in which former communist subjects were socialized to think about the very function of *telling their life stories*' (Mark 2010, xxv, italics in original).

Mark explains that 'Before 1989, individuals had been required to write down their own family pasts into official communist histories in public autobiographical writings necessary for job applications or to gain entry to tertiary education.' Those born in the interwar period 'faced immense pressure to reshape their life stories to fit the historical templates of the class and anti-Fascist struggles from communist states which saw these autobiographical procedures as essential to the absorption of individuals' own identities into their own ideological orbits, and to the creation of the ideal socialist citizen' (Mark 2010, xxv). Yet post-1989 previously unacceptable 'truthful' narratives did not suddenly emerge. Instead there was 'a new set of political and cultural values determining what could and could not be said'. Mark advocates that 'the oral method can be used to explore what had to remain hidden, or was newly suppressed, assessing which experiences from their communist pasts individuals thought it worth making public, which they should keep private and which should be reshaped into newly acceptable narratives' (Mark 2010, xxvii).

Social progress in Bulgaria and Romania, as well as in other socialist countries, relied to some extent on an ability to compose an autobiography for oneself that emphasised working-class genealogy, loyalty to the regime and anti-Fascist activities. 'Communist regimes became intensely biographical' (Mark 2010, 129). The practice of 'writing the right autobiography in an age of Communist mass-mobilisation in the 1940s and 1950s in central-eastern Europe was experienced as an intensely political and meaningful act, through which supporters of the regime interwove their personal experiences with official narratives to produce life stories that confirmed them as true believers in the transformatory potential of the socialist project' (Mark 2010, 127). Composing a life story with an appropriate political identity and familial lineage was a skill that could help secure social ascent via employment or higher education, or could be employed simply to avoid discrimination and punishment (Mark 2010, 130).

Given the age ranges of the Bulgarian and Romanian interviewees in this project, the majority will most likely have experienced the necessity of making a 'good biography' in their early adult life. With recourse to oral history interviews conducted in the 1990s, Koleva has revealed some of the most widely employed strategies for making a 'good biography' in socialist Bulgaria, which involved using 'rubrics' based on education, career and political genealogy and ordering them in a formal structure that appropriated the stylistic conventions of official forms that citizens would have had to complete many times (Koleva 2001).

The focus of the life history interviews here was religion and our specific concern was how, if at all, older people remember ceremonies and religious practices throughout the course of their lifetime. Religious practice or belief would not feature in a 'good biography' pre-1989. The act of 'making a clean biography' involved 'an awareness of one's biographical assets and liabilities and arranging one's life at certain points so as to fit a model autobiography' (Koleva 2001). With this in mind it is likely that some of the oral history interviewees would have re-composed their life narratives during the communist period, omitting any religious affiliation, in order to get by. Mark has explored how former communist party members and victims have re-negotiated their 'communist autobiographies' post-1989. Yet religious practice or belief does not feature strongly in either Koleva's or Mark's analysis of post-1989 narratives. In a project such as RASC that probes the place of religious practice in people's life histories, it is reasonable to assume that those interviewees who identified themselves as having a communist background would have had to compose an appropriate narrative about religious or non-religious ceremonies that they were comfortable with telling within the post-1989 discourse. This is not an unrealistic hypothesis. New work in Russia and former communist countries, including Dore's research in Cuba, is 'discovering that some people have been reassessing their past, unearthing memories that were submerged in the fervour of post-communism' (Dore 2012, 36). The following analysis of one Bulgarian man's personal testimony will highlight this.

Diman Vasilev was born in 1935 in the southwestern area of Bulgaria. The manner in which he begins his life history is striking. Composed in 2011 some 22 years after 1989, Diman's narrative begins with a version of what Koleva terms the 'curriculum vitae rubric' (Koleva 2001) in Bulgarian socialist autobiography:

> I will start with the fact that I was born twice. The first time – as a human being. The second one – as an engineering-geologist. The first time I was born here – in Bulgaria. The second time – in Moscow [he laughs]. Yes. Besides, I have at least four weddings. The first one, of course, was with my wife with whom I've been living together for a little more than half a century … What date is today? Yes [he looks at his cell phone], for half a century and five days we've been living together [he laughs]. The other three weddings, it could be said, are professional. I married in 1961, so to say. I was sent to one of the biggest uranium locations. Practically, I made it such at that time – Eleshnitsa. This is 1961, the beginning of February, my wife and me departed for this place. The year 1968 was the time when I married to Mongolia. We went there again with a geology expedition and I worked for almost five years. Finally, my fourth marriage has been to Cuba – we went there in 1984 and 1989 we came back. And now I am actively enjoying my retirement in Sofia, Bulgaria.

By marriage he is referring firstly to his secular marriage to his wife and then uses the term as a euphemism for his professional career as a geologist working within a communist department. He then builds on the CV rubric by outlining his family's communist past, giving details of his father and mother's working-class backgrounds and recounting his father's achievements. Yet he mediates his father's communist autobiography for the purpose of composing his own story post-1989.

He recalls that his father was a railway engine driver, 'member of the party' and 'one of the leaders of the railroaders' opposition in the Dupnitsa region. He was in prison in 1935, when Diman was born, for taking part in an illegal conference of the Railway Workers a year earlier. He recalled that his father was 'an active fighter against fascism. He was recognized as such'. Diman actively re-composes his father's communist autobiography to 'make it good' in the act of remembering in order to understand his own life story. He recalls that 'after I married, after 1961, I could benefit from such priorities and get an apartment too as a son of a fighter against fascism'. He makes sense of this in the act of remembering, explaining 'I don't have a guilty conscience' because he and his wife raised two children and seven grandchildren in the apartment, thus 'we paid back for our priority'. Similarly, he recounts the story when, towards the end of his life in the early 1980s, his father refused to pay the party membership fees when he discovered that the party secretary had not been paying his fees. He goes on to explain that his father: 'Came from the rural areas but never broke that connection. This is the most essential, the most important – never to forget where you come from. From a villager he then became a working class man. All this made him the person he was.' As we can see, Diman is actively trying to re-negotiate and make sense of his past communist autobiography in the act of the interview. He does not fully renounce or purge (Mark 2010, 152) his or his father's communist autobiography because he believes that he is 'a product of such an epoch and I perceive it as nothing else than a necessary fight against this … let's say, obscurantism. It is a fight for a somewhat more just world.' However, his pre-1989 self is challenged by the current discourse of criminalisation and he admits that the post-communist world impacts on his views of the past: 'It's true though, now I see lots of things, now I can estimate from my current situation' (Diman, Sofia).

Religion and religious ceremonies comprise one of those 'things' that presents a challenge to Diman's composure of his narrative in 2011. Early on in the interview he retells a story when his father was invited to be a best man at a friend's wedding:

> back then marrying in church was normal. And he said: "I will be your best man but while you are inside, I will be waiting outside the church. Only when you go out then I will congratulate you". I remember this because it was precisely 9th of September when we were in Dupnitsa and soon after he got invited. A colleague of his invited him. We haven't spoken about religion at all. Neither bad nor good.

Following his father's and his own party credentials as 'a young Septemvriiche',[3] Diman allows the interviewer and reader to presume that he is not and has never been religious. This would have fitted with a pre-1989 communist self. He potentially closes the topic of conversation by concluding 'For me he [his father] was fair and virtuous … in the humane way that is, not the religious'. Yet it is clear that in his re-composed post-1989 narrative he has to negotiate his

---

[3]   A Youth Pioneer Movement established in September 1944. Its members were children aged 9–14.

past communist non-religious identity within a more religious Bulgarian society. Nowhere is this identity challenged more so than in his own family. His daughter's beliefs challenge his post-communist autobiography: 'My mother, she used to be a housewife and as my father, she wasn't religious. In that sense, my daughter [Nusha who is religious] puzzles me a bit. Actually, a lot!'

Nusha's religious practice challenges the communist and non-religious lineage he is proud of in his family:

> Look, I don't want Pharisees, "But daddy!" she would reply, I tell her her again: "No, it's unacceptable!" I understand, yes, I am not so Orthodox or against priests either, and so on. But when there's hypocrisy I cannot accept it. Or else what? I don't enter into church, I am not afraid that I would violate some principles, no.

He continues to try to make sense of Nusha's religiousness: 'What is important is that she tries to do good. This is for me the justification for her, how shall I put it, let's say digression or attitude.'

When asked which holidays he celebrated the most formally he recounted that on birthdays and name days uncles, aunties, cousins and grandparents would gather at their family home and the 'men would play cards on the one end while women would knit and gossip on the other. And with the cousins we would think of some fairy tales.' He made sense of painting Easter eggs and celebrating Christmas by halting his narrative and asking, 'What does a religious holiday mean? Good Lord, to us this is a custom. This is a tradition. No one can say it's his or her own. Neither pagans, nor priests.' Until now he has maintained a sense of his self, but at this point his wife enters the conversation and challenges his sense of composure.

She enters the room periodically throughout and by the end of the interview she and Diman are showing the interviewer photographs from their civil wedding ceremony. When talking about generational differences Diman's wife reveals 'we are baptised, we are Christians'. Until this point Diman has chosen not to recall that his mother and father were married in a church in 1941 nor that he was baptised in order to satisfy the educational authorities and be able to attend school. However, when this information is revealed he quickly defends the situation by clarifying that 'Without such certificate I couldn't attend school. It was absolutely necessary. And they didn't have a choice. I don't know whether they had civil marriage. I'm not sure how it was back then but such a document was necessary.' Such a document was necessary within real life, it was a process that facilitiated real life to function, but within a 'good biography' there was no place for such experiences.

The prominence of religious practice in Bulgarian life today is a condition that Diman and his wife are having to actively negotiate. Their daughter has suggested that, to mark '50 years together', they hold the religious wedding ceremony they never had in 1961. They present a reasoned response as Diman's wife asserts, 'We have been living for 50 years only with one, we can manage with it until the end (the respondent nods in agreement)'. Diman makes sense of generational differences by mediation as he explains, 'I try to keep everyone true to their beliefs'.

We have seen how Diman has had to renegotiate his secular narrative in response to a growing public discourse in Bulgaria of religiosity presented within his very own family. In this next section I would like to explore how some interviewees actively negotiated their memories of religious and non-religious practices during the interview situation in response to the interviewer.

Intersubjectivities: Individual and Collective Memory

Some oral historians draw on the emerging perspective of engaging with the mutual reflexivity of subjectivities between interviewees and interviewers (Patai 1987; Summerfield 2000; Young 2007). Both the interviewee and the interviewer are drawing on their pasts within an interview situation and it is the meeting of these during the interview that is referred to as intersubjectivity. The ways in which interviewees may perceive their interviewer and vice versa are not controllable. Often this perception manifests itself through the way the interviewee frames their stories and perhaps in the way the interviewer frames questions. As Abrams notes, 'even before the interview encounter has taken place the researcher has likely displayed traits of his or her subjective self to the potential respondent that will contribute to how that respondent perceives the interviewer and how he or she constructs and performs their story' (Abrams 2010, 60). Although the subjectivity of the interviewers was not an acknowledged part of the RASC research agenda, subsequent analysis of the reflexivity of some of these relationships reveals how some interviewees negotiated the telling of their memories in response to the interviewer. As Koleva has explored (Chapter 6), some interviewees assumed a shared cultural knowledge of at least the dominant religion of the country of residence, meaning that shared knowledge of religious practices were left unspoken about in interviews. On the other hand, some interviewees identified the interviewer with a change in religious or secular discourse.

In the following exchange I introduced a change of discourse and practice to the interviewee. When at the end of a long interview in which Rita Gardner had composed a well-rounded narrative about her changing religious practices in the Church of England, I asked her if she thought it was important to hold a religious service for births, marriage or death as part of the European Values Study questionnaire, she replied:

> I think it's a very difficult question because I think it's extremely important to
> have something formal, something to mark occasions, but while it's important
> for a religious one for me I don't know that it would, *I mean it's not important
> for you* is it but it's going to be just as much meaningful as mine is to me.
> So I would like to cross out religious service, I would like to put, I think it's
> important to hold a ceremony. [My emphasis]

In the knowledge that I was organising my own humanist wedding ceremony the following month, my personal subjectivity (that I do not believe religious ceremonies are required to mark key points in life) challenged the interviewee's composure of her narrative and she re-adjusted her understanding of the importance of performing a ritual to mark important occasions. Yet for some of the Romanian oral history interviewees the ability to compose a suitable life history that made sense of their past religious self and present non-religious self in light of current discourses of religious practice appeared less straightforward.

Ion Cotescu, born in 1924 in Romania, recalls that his mother and father were religious, but 'dad especially', who was Christian Orthodox, 'would frequently go to church' as he was a member of the 'parochial committee of the church'. When asked if his parents gave him a religious education Ion suggests that the curriculum at school where 'religion was a study object' and his musical ability to conduct 'religious choirs in many churches' comprised the extent of his religious participation and education as a young boy. He recalls that, as a young adult, 'I only went to church on purpose while I was directing church choirs' for a period of about 10 years around 1955. His own church wedding in 1952 and that of a friend in which he participated as the '*the hand brother*' (frate de mana, emphasis in original) aside, he does not recall attending many weddings, religious or civil. Aware of the need to makes sense of his narrative he draws on the discourse he identifies with the interviewer:

> I couldn't describe them ... Weddings ... the usual ones, with some customs, but not this kind of customs that I sometimes see ... Especially you, if you don't mind, you work at the Peasant Museum and you must have plenty there ... No, they weren't like that, glamorous or ... Regular weddings.

Unable to describe the differences between religious and civil wedding ceremonies in the past the interviewee references shared narratives endorsed by the Romanian Peasant Museum, where the interviewer worked. The professional endorsement of an employee from the Museum conducting this research presents one way for this interviewee to view the significance of religious practice today. Again, perhaps because he is aware of a change in attitude that the interviewer represents as a Museum professional, he highlights an awareness of a changing discourse of religiousness in the country: 'I don't know how things happen nowadays, although I have the impression that many things have returned towards the church, in my opinion. This is how it seems to me.' With this statement the interviewee appears to be trying to satisfy the interviewer by acknowledging the religious discourse today.

James Mark argues that 'Nationalist, anti-Communist respondents saw their role as the protectors of pre-Communist traditions within the home' (Mark 2010, 181). From the testimony gathered here it would appear that keeping religious traditions at home and within community networks during the communist period was important to many (see Bădică, Chapter 3). The preservation of national tradition within families and generational cohorts was one way, as Ion explains, in which his family continued to perform religious ceremonies during the period of the 1950s and 1960s when religious ceremonies were suppressed:

> Well, the important days … Of course, we also celebrated, our wedding day, isn't it? But not like a real holiday …

You did celebrate it?

> We celebrated it, why should I say we didn't? Within the family. (Ion, Bucharest).

Ion makes sense of practising religious ceremonies such as baptism and weddings 'within the family' in the past as part of 'family tradition' despite not being religious in later life. He presents a disjointed narrative about religious ceremonies held to mark key points in his life during the communist period. Yet he does not actively recall any memories of secular ceremonies. This could be for a number of reasons. The first explanation is that he did not participate in any. Second, he may have forgotten them (he does suggest that he is losing his memory). Or finally, memories of participating in secular ceremonies do not fit with the narrative he is trying to present of the time being remembered and his present identity. Ion attempts to construct a narrative in which he draws on the discourses of religiosity and enforced secularisation across the period under consideration to deflect attention from his current non-religious self. Aware of the growing religious experience in post-communist Romania, yet unable to identify with this, Ion composes a narrative in which he presents himself as someone who maintained a national identity under oppression by maintaining and performing religious practices covertly. He reinforces his sense of self in later life by explaining, 'I am religious in my own way, because I listen to Trinitas [a contemporary Christian radio station based in Bucharest].'

In contrast when asked about his marriage ceremony in 1952, Viorel, who was born in 1928 in a Moldavian village and became a university professor in economics in Bucharest, recalls the secular ceremony:

> the wedding part was more difficult. We did not have a wedding. We just went to a restaurant with some of my friends and my in-laws. Plain and simple. Yes, my in-laws were there, or only my father in law, yes, only him. There were hard times, think about, we're talking about '52, it was still during my University years.

Conscious that some religious ceremonies at the time in communist countries were conducted in secret or were suppressed, the interviewer prompts him further by asking:

And did you have a religious ceremony?

Sure, the religious ceremony was first and then ...

So how do we explain Viorel's first answer that they 'just went to a restaurant' when, after prompting by the interviewer, he recalls that they had the religious ceremony first? If the interviewer had not persisted, we would have been left thinking he had held only a civil service in a restaurant. The restaurant narrative was the story that it seems Viorel was comfortable telling, one that fitted with a widely received understanding that religious ceremonies had been suppressed, a story that fitted the past communist meta-narrative of the 1950s. However, until the interviewer acknowledged that she was aware that some people practised religious ceremonies in the 1950s he did not feel comfortable admitting to being married in a religious service. Viorel, who no longer goes to church, also cited the importance of maintaining the familial tradition throughout the communist period:

What were the most important holidays in your family?

The major holidays ... Christmas, Easter ... those were the most important. They were important for the atmosphere ... sometimes you get the feeling ... and the moments with your family. We visit them, they visit us, and there is an atmosphere, as such.

These revelations (albeit within a supportive and affirming interviewing atmosphere) of his religious wedding ceremony and that his family celebrated major Christian holidays support Dore's argument that people from former communist countries are beginning to unearth previously submerged memories and feel comfortable telling them (Dore 2012). A narrator may compose different identities for her/himself in an interview depending on what period in their life they are talking about. Who they are telling the story to may also have an impact on the identity constructed. The act of remembering was difficult for the interviewee here and the interviewer noted in the transcript that the interviewee cried during the interview. The emotion and difficult retelling of the story may signal that the interviewee was coming to terms with his past experiences during the act of remembering as he began to reveal previously suppressed memories and struggled to make sense of them. This is not surprising as his individual memories were coming into direct contact with the wider collective memory of the nation and were perhaps being told for the first time. The oral historian Portelli neatly explains the relationship between individual and collective memory:

If all memory were collective, one witness could serve for an entire culture – but we know that it is not so. Each individual ... derives memories from a variety of groups, and organizes them in idiosyncratic fashion. Like all human activities, memory is *social* and may be *shared* ... however ... it only materializes in individual recollections and speech acts. It becomes *collective* memory only when it is abstracted and detached from the individual. (Portelli 1997, 157)

From Ion and Viorel's contrasting accounts it is clear that each interviewee is drawing on their own social experiences in order to express and negotiate their individual memories, thus beginning to challenge the wider framework of a national collective memory.

Conclusions

This chapter has built on Chapter 3 by exploring the significance of changing discourses of religion and secularisation on a selection of cross-cultural interviews with a generational cohort of people over 75 who identified as not being religious. Drawing on the idea of 'composure' (Dawson 1994; Thomson 1994), I have argued that each interviewee constructed a sense of their past self and religious or secular practice that they were comfortable with telling in response to changing discourses surrounding the secular and the religious at the time of interview in each country. In regard to the interviewees, Polly and Jennifer (UK), Diman (Bulgaria) and Ion and Viorel (Romania), I suggest that each actively negotiated their past during the interview in order to make sense of it in the present act of remembering.

Non-religious people's narratives suggest that religious practices can hold alternative meanings and significance. Community, belonging and tradition were ways of making sense of religious practice in the past. The clash of individual memory with a public discourse, such as the growth in individualised ceremonies and the significance of a new generation's religious belief, was a trigger for these interviewees to re-remember their own experiences. Stories surfaced across the geographical spread of non-religious interviewees that we did not expect to hear. First was the story of a young schoolgirl admitting that she was not religious to a nun in the early 1930s. Next we learned that a former Bulgarian Communist Party member had had a religious wedding ceremony. Lastly, to hear how people negotiated stories in the present of their challenges to religious and secular discourse in the past was in itself a revealing process.

Finding ways to talk to non-religious people about their experiences of religious ceremonies involved listening against the grain of the dominant narrative. As these narratives show, collective memory is not fixed. Dominant interpretations of the past shift and alter as formerly marginalised voices are heard and incorporated into the overall narrative. It was the range of stories, different voices and conflicting narratives that made the RASC project so challenging, but it is also these same stories, voices and narratives that will add texture to our understanding of non-religious and secular experiences.

References

Abrams, Lynn. 2010. *Oral History Theory*. London: Routledge.

Booth, Richard. 2012. 'Alain de Botton Reveals Plans for "Temple to Atheism" in Heart of London'. *Guardian*, 26 January. Available at: http://www.guardian.co.uk/books/2012/jan/26/alain-de-botton-temple-atheism?INTCMP=SRCH (accessed 27 January 2012).

Brown, Callum. 2001. *The Death of Christian Britain*. London: Routledge.

Dawson, Graham. 1994. *Soldier Heroes: British Adventure, Empire and the Imagining of Masculinities*. London: Routledge.

Dore, Elizabeth. 2012. 'Cubans' Life Stories: The Pains and Pleasures of Living in a Communist Society'. *Oral History* 40(1): 35–46.

Green, Anna. 2004. 'Individual Remembering and "Collective Memory": Theoretical Presuppositions and Contemporary Debates'. *Oral History* 32(2): 35–44.

Koleva, Daniela. 2001. 'Between Testimony and Power: Autobiographies in Socialist Bulgaria'. Paper presented at 'Texts of Testimony: Autobiography, Life-Story Narratives and the Public Sphere' Conference, Liverpool, 23–25 August.

Mark, James. 2010. *The Unfinished Revolution: Making Sense of the Communist Past in Central-Eastern Europe*. New Haven, CT: Yale University Press.

McLeod, Hugh. 1996. 'New Perspectives on Victorian Class Religion: The Oral Evidence'. *Oral History* 14(1): 31–49.

Patai, Daphne. 1987. 'Ethical Problems of Personal Narratives, or Who Should Eat the Last Piece of Cake?' *International Journal of Oral History* 8(1): 5–27.

Portelli, Alessandro. 1997. *The Battle of Valle Giulia: Oral History and the Art of Dialogue*. Madison, WI: University of Wisconsin Press.

Smith, Graham. 2007. 'Beyond Individual/Collective Memory: Women's Transactive Memories of Food, Family and Conflict'. *Oral History* 35(2): 77–90.

Steedman, Carolyn. 1997. 'Writing the Self: the End of the Scholarship Girl'. In *Cultural Methodologies*, edited by Jim McGuigan, 106–25. London: Sage.

Summerfield, Penny. 2000. 'Dis/composing the Subject: Intersubjectivities in Oral History'. In *Feminism and Autobiography*, edited by Tess Cosslett, Celia Lury and Penny Summerfield. London: Routledge, 91–106.

Thomson, Alistair. 1994. *Anzac Memories: Living with the Legend*. Melbourne: Oxford University Press.

Williams, Sarah C. 1966. 'The Problem of Belief: The Place of Oral History in the Study of Popular Religion'. *Oral History* 24(2): 27–34.

Voas, David and Rodney Ling. 2010. 'Religion in Britain and the United States'. In *British Social Attitudes: The 26th Report*, edited by Alison Park, John Curtice, Katarina Thomson, Miranda Phillips, Elizabeth Clery and Sarah Butt. London: Sage.

Wong, Joanna S. 2004. 'Celebrate 50th Anniversary of "Billy Graham Crusade" in London: A Crusade that Reshaped International Evangelism'. *Christian Today*, 26 May. Available at: http://www.christiantoday.com/article/celebrate.50th. anniversary.of.billy.graham.crusade.in.london/895.htm (accessed 25 January 2012).

Wouters, Cas. 2002. 'The Quest for New Rituals in Dying and Mourning: Changes in the We–I Balance'. *Body and Society* 8(1): 1–27.

Young, Hilary. 2007. 'Hard Man, New Man: Re/composing Masculinities in Glasgow c.1950–2000'. *Oral History* 35(1): 71–81.

Chapter 5

Ineffable Silence and the Sacred: Crucial Moments in Life Histories

Sidonia Grama

The dialogical experience of conducting these interviews, which aim to represent human subjectivity as well as lived history, has elicited several personal narratives of inexhaustible richness. What the narrators identified as key moments in their life histories were actually the most difficult periods they had had to face in their lifetime. These turning points articulated the backbones of the life narratives, providing them with meaning and structure (Bertaux 1997, 32). Some of them were sheer epiphanies of highly transformative and consequential import. With hindsight, they appear to have profoundly influenced the narrators' lives and sense of self-identity. Their confessions led them to express the deepest existential creeds and beliefs.

This chapter[1] focuses on such crucial moments in life histories, seen in their intimate relation to religious beliefs (or disbeliefs) and practices, and envisaged as dimensions of religious identities and (un)certainties. It also attempts to capture the elusiveness of discourses on religious ceremonies, by interrogating certain forms of silences which thoughtfully punctuate life narratives. The presence of silence is an organic part of self-referential discourse. The relevance of life narratives unfolds both through what is stated and through what is kept silent, what is remembered as well as meaningfully forgotten.

This transcultural approach sheds light on criss-crossing life narratives, set against the background of European cultural features, Eastern or Western secularisms and the adversities of recent history.

---

[1] I wish to thank Daniela Koleva for the invitation to participate in this challenging research project and to be part of a valuable team. My effective participation would not have been possible if Ileana Benga had not accompanied me from the very beginning to the end. My special thanks go to Ileana for our (g)old friendship. I have the greatest respect for her substantial field experience in the study of ceremony. Carmen Borbély, the proficient translator of all the interviews from Cluj, has exhibited once again her empathy in conveying the meanings and emotions expressed in Romanian into English. I am grateful to my family for their kindness and support. I also thank all the interviewees for entrusting us their existential meanings; I cherish these Romanian, Bulgarian and British life stories as a treasure.

Silencing Ceremony: A Western (Ir)Religious Mood

Many of the life stories elicited and analysed by the researchers throughout this volume expose hybrid genres of non/(ir)religiosity and describe ambiguous and paradoxical religious identities. British scholars, analysts and mass media representatives have recently diagnosed the state-of-the-art condition of their national religiosity as best featured by the idiom 'neither religious, nor atheistic'.[2] Traces of this ambivalence have also been found, in peculiar and idiosyncratic ways, in some of the UK life narratives. Both Harold Stevenson's and Lewis Farrow's life histories offered fascinating accounts of their transitional thinking from formerly religiously informed persons to late-life atheists. A closer look at these life narratives revealed a meaningfully recurrent oblivion.[3] Although elusive, the amnesia on their own children's christening proved to be a milestone on their way to apostasy and the embracing of a God-free persuasion in later life:

> And we had a christening for our eldest son but not for our second son or for our daughter. Don't know why but we didn't. We didn't, Simon was never christened was he Anne?
>
> [Wife] Yes he was, they all three of them were christened.
>
> [Harold] Oh gosh, I don't remember that. (…) [while listening to his wife recount their children's baptism, he had to repeat] Oh I'd forgotten that; Oh well, memory failure.

Either as episodic memory failures, when the moment of the christening is totally erased from a life review (as in Harold's case), or as semantic memory failures, when the religious content of those ceremonies has been lost (as in Lewis's life story), such oblivions might be considered as symptoms of a broader cultural pattern. In his seminal book on *Memory, History, Oblivion*, Paul Ricoeur has exposed similar forms of active forgetting. They are very close to 'the will not to remember' that lies at the core of different types of social amnesias (Ricoeur, 2001,

---

539–40). If one attempts to scour the depths of the current mood of British (ir) religiousness, epitomised by the 'neither–nor' ambivalence, one might find such cultural oblivion and silencing of the religious meanings and practices that used to fill the lifecycle rites of passage. In the Western disenchanted world oblivion and secularisation seem intricately linked.

The Schism of Ritual: (Post)Communist Duality

In the Eastern part of the continent, some of the interviews conducted by the research teams from Romania and Bulgaria have expressively described peculiar post-communist religious profiles. An 'Orthodox pagan', as Diman Vasilev from Sofia ironically defines himself, or an 'atheist Orthodox', such as Florina Câmpeanu from Bucharest, are rather oxymoronic genres of religious identities. Paradoxical types of 'both-religious-and-non-religious' persons, as those in the East, and 'neither-religious-nor-irreligious' ones, as those in the West, coexist. They seem to be complementary categories of ambivalence which populate the spectrum of postmodern European secularisms.

In this context of ambiguity, a narrative of post-communist life, such as that of Aleko Radev from Bulgaria, is quite revealing. An 82-year-old former member of the Bulgarian nomenclature, Aleko had an important career: under the communist regime, he activated as a prosecutor, an investigating officer, a judge, a member of the Supreme Court and a lawyer. His social biography is a sample of the successful life story of a communist. His professional evolution started from humble, 'healthy' origins, as they were prescribed in the Communist Party membership files from the Soviet Union's satellite countries. A poor orphan, he learned assiduously and came up in the world. His entire life story is structured along this idea. Yet, at a certain point, the logic of his narrative is suddenly interrupted by a different story, left in abeyance at one moment and then resumed in passing. What he evasively calls 'the priest story' refers to his refusal, as a child, to attend the school for becoming a priest. From a narrative point of view, he introduces this story within a story only as a parenthesis, which finally proves to have been a fateful story, the seal of his destiny:

> Oh, [he recalls something], what happened to that priest story! After a lot of insistence on behalf of the peasants, I was sent to a three-month course in Pleven – to become a priest. Just before leaving, however, I stopped in the middle of the yard and I started crying. It dawned on me that priests perform services for dead people. I was a small child and I got embarrassed with this. [...] Unfortunately, later on I worked as an investigating officer for eight years. Throughout this time I didn't perform funeral services for people but I collected parts of dead human bodies. Had I become a priest, everything would have been put together in a coffin, with flowers and a glass of rakia – much better ... *So that's destiny – I couldn't run away from dead bodies.* [My emphasis]

This final revelation concerning the hidden connection between the dead bodies and his own destiny is an epiphanic moment in his life narrative (Denzin 1989, 70–71). Having rejected a religious education when he was a child, he opted instead for a secular, atheistic career, which propelled him to important social (and, inevitably, political) positions. Therefore he defined himself as an atheist in trenchant, categorical terms, although a cognitive dissonance becomes apparent:

And you can't imagine after-life?

No, not at all. It's all nonsense. These things make me laugh. I still haven't lost my mind so I don't believe … Now that my wife is dead we do what's necessary. On the 5th March we'll have the six-month commemoration. *But these are different things.*

The dichotomy between rituals and their religious significance is one of the strongest marks of secularisation: 'We never attached a religious meaning to it [the Easter Resurrection celebration]. It was a ritual', Florina from Bucharest also claims. Moreover, the duality between form and content, thought and speech, beliefs and behaviour represents an unmistakable feature of communism. Despite defining himself as an atheist, Aleko was close to the institution of the church throughout his lifetime. In addition, at a deeper level, his entire autobiography is organised according to the temporal guidelines of religious holidays in the Orthodox Christian calendar. His professional evolution and ideological indoctrination have not managed to erase his peasant origins, which have kept him organically tied to a religious folk tradition, mixed with pagan layers and magic. Beyond the certainty of his instrumental self-definition as an atheist, Aleko's religious identity is a rather strange hybrid of paganism–Orthodoxism–atheism. His life story has a somewhat paradigmatic dimension. It contains the kind of incongruities and dualities that ultimately reveal those taken-for-granted meanings of (post-)communist life. At the end of the day, all of these types of ambiguity might be commonplace strategies of adjustment either to (post-)communism in the East or to (post-)consumerism in the West. They circumscribe a comfort zone of ambivalence that allows most people to be always on the safe side.

Being a Christian in Communist Times

On the other hand, whenever religiosity became profound and authentic, and people took Christianity and its discipline and religious practices seriously, the repressive vigilance of communist state suddenly awoke from its numbness. Christianity's transformative vocation, with its ultimate consequence of irreducible inner freedom, represented a formidable adversary against any totalitarian form of authority. In such circumstances, political power, in its Foucauldian, capillary distribution, reactivated its functions to 'discipline and punish', becoming infiltrated at all levels of society and aiming to marginalise and socially ostracise such persons.

This is the case of Eleonora Moldovan, from Cluj.[4] She is a 75-year-old lady, who is a former professor of foreign languages, mastering a vast number of Romance languages (Latin, Italian, French, Spanish and Portuguese), but also English and German. Right before this dialogue took place, she offered us a highly concentrated version of her life story, in which she simply defined herself as a person whose existential scaffolding consisted of religious faith. On the death of her parents, the most significant others in her life, she experienced an epiphanic moment and made the major existential decision that has marked her entire life:

> Mother died, it was on July 28, a Friday, uh ... on Monday was the funeral, [...] and then I set my mind ... I'd been telling myself, I felt that: If I still want to be in spiritual communion, of mind, with my parents, all I had to do was to start my day with the Holy Liturgy. And since then, since 1 August '72 until today, I've started my day by ... going to church, to the cathedral.

Like any genuine existential choice, the decision to remain faithful to this covenant every day for almost 40 years has cost her dearly. The first consequence was her removal from lecturing. Quite often, in spite of her commitment to her professional activity, she was accused in public political meetings and had to defend herself. Every time, she openly confessed her Christian faith without hesitation, often with candid courage, at the very height of atheism. Eleonora reminisces about the political ritual of such an accusatory meeting, presided over by a well-known professor of Constitutional Law:

> [President of the commission]: "Comrade Moldovan, we are informed that you nourish religious beliefs and we would like to know if you might find it difficult to disavow them". – As if you could change some beliefs you have held for a lifetime like some glove or some dress [Eleonora reckoned] and I say, "It is not hard for me, it is impossible!"

Soon after such a declaration of faith, her academic career ended abruptly. Yet Eleonora has serenely assumed all of the adverse effects on her professional life and the possibilities of gaining a livelihood which have, since then, remained extremely poor. From this perspective, Eleonora's life story is spiritually related to that of our oldest interlocutor, Aurelian Ghelasie, and his wife, Teodora, from Cluj.

---

[4] See also Chapter 8 for this case.

Talking to God

Aurelian's self-presentation is marked by his strong and vibrant Orthodox Christian faith. A 97-year-old Romanian, of priestly descent, he was an economist and a member of the Legionnaires' Movement, a fateful choice for which he was persecuted by different political regimes throughout most of his life. He has nonetheless remained highly loyal to his beliefs: 'Faith in God and love of the country'. Aurelian's existential values were inherited form his father, an Orthodox priest and a patriot, the head of a family with 10 children, a patriarchal figure of authority in their family and community. His father was the founder of Rohia Monastery, 'the first stone church ever made from Lăpușna country' in Transylvania, during the Austro-Hungarian rule, when affirming and preserving the Romanian national identity was extremely difficult. In a legendary way, which echoes a famous Romanian myth, the monastery was founded on the death of Anuța, Aurelian's 10-year old sister. This seems to have been the alpha and omega of his life history, the prologue and the epilogue of his rich autobiography:

> many times I think that God has a plan for each and every man [speaking softly as if to himself] … My sister, Anuța, she was very religious! Very, very religious! If my sister Anuța had lived, she would have become a priestess, that's what she would have become! But, since she died and God took her … […] Now a monastery was built, as you can see … […] And as regards the future, man cannot know his future, 'cause if he could … [inaudible].

Silences and epiphanies consistently punctuate Aurelian's life discourse.[5] There are genuine religious epiphanies whenever he detects the signs of God's presence in his life. With hindsight, those were moments when 'evil happened for the greater good', as he recurrently says. Moreover, silences give a particular rhythm and depth to his life narrative: these are not only silences that reflect his effort of anamnesis but also silences as a way of meaning (Le Breton 2001, 149). The legendary aura shapes his life narrative into a kind of mythic biography (Passerini 1990, 49–60) or an almost exemplary life story. The narrative is very structured, in spite of its multiple stories within stories and embedded temporalities. Although it recounts the tragically intense experiences he has been through and several critical moments when he literally faced death, his life history seems ultimately self-coherent and devoid of contradictions. This is probably why, within his storyline, Aurelian's fateful political choice from his early adulthood – irreducibly controversial and consequential throughout his entire life – is thoughtfully recounted with so much serenity.

5　　Aurelian told his story at a slow pace, with long breaks; he sometimes put his forehead between his hands and closed his eyes, in an effort to reminisce and relive those events. Several times he spoke so softly, almost inaudibly, as if to himself, whenever the testimony reached the most sensitive area and intimate creed.

Against the background of the political upheavals of the 1930s, Aurelian's sense of nationalism as well as religiousness led him to join the Legionnaire Movement. The notorious attractiveness of that extreme-right Romanian movement was a phenomenon that cannot easily be ascertained from a historiographical perspective. Most of its definitions have been ideologically charged, as fighting terms on a political battlefield (Heinen 2006: 13). Within that fateful trinomial combination of nationalism, religion and politics, God was equated with the country, and politics with religion.[6] It seems that this temptation at the heart of the Legionnaire creed ultimately triggered its irreducible antinomies.[7] Twentieth-century history tragically revealed how any combination between those entities – politics, religion and nationalism – was potentially lethal, leading to different forms of totalitarianisms, either fascisms or communisms. From today's privileged standpoint on last century's grand narratives, this is a lesson of History which remains an unforgettable warning.

Aurelian's life narrative organically integrates such a controversial past and reveals the lifelong consequences of ceaseless political surveillance and persecution under various political regimes in Romania. 'Suffering for the whole life long' and the threat of death accompanied him constantly. Flash-bulb memories of the anguishing imminence of death are the milestones of his life history, while silences, ellipses and whispers are the most expressive narrative markers of those unspeakable experiences. He remembers being thrown into a dungeon, in complete darkness, overhearing that he was going to be shot: 'Then I fell onto my knees ... and it passed ... [silence] ... if my faith hadn't been strong ...'. A few times he was about to be shot. Several times he could have died; because of frostbite one winter in Stalingrad during the war or by starvation during the extermination period at the Aiud Penitentiary, one of the most fearful spaces of detention, surveillance and re-education in the frightening geography of Romania's communist political prisons (Comisia prezidenţială pentru analiza dictaturii comuniste din România 2006, 240) . Yet, each time he found himself providentially saved. He recounted that with tender humour and a witty sense of complicity with God's will. Being in the proximity of death, he fasted and prayed. At the end of his seven years of

---

6   There are some attempts to capture the essence of the Legionnaire movement by placing it among the great families of the 'political religions' that have haunted the recent world history: 'the mystique of ultra-nationalism' (Veiga 1995) or the 'Hierophany of the Romanian-ism' (Bănică 2007, 250).

7   The equation between politics and religion is implicit in the Legionnaire political creed as formulated by its founder, Corneliu Zelea Codreanu, in his programmatic writing, *Cărticica şefului de cuib* (*The Nest Chief's Book*): 'If for a politician, politics means business, for a legionnaire politics means religion' (Codreanu 1987/1933, 75). See also http://www.codreanu.ro/carticica.htm. In a recent oral history book of interviews with survivors of the Legionnaire Movement, edited by the Romanian Society of Radiobroadcasting, the idolatry of the country is always referred to in the background: 'Moreover, we considered God – the Country' (Conovici, Iliescu and Silvestru 2008, 69).

political imprisonment at Aiud, when a fellow prisoner asked him 'What is your faith like?', he simply answered, 'Well, I say, it's what's keeping me alive!'

Far from being a victimisation story, his life narrative proves that the laborious work of memory and meaning have reached that much longed-for happy memory, *la mémoire hereuse* (Ricoeur 2000, 643), or exemplary memory (Todorov 1999).

What has definitely guided the hierarchy of his existential values is the supremacy of God and of the Christian faith his entire life history attests to. The story of the 1959 trial and of his last political imprisonment is fascinating for the manner in which this dramatic episode was lived and told in narrative symbiosis with his wife's life narrative. His story and her story are, thus, intertwined with the great History. In Aurelian's trial, the last count of indictment that remained standing after all the other charges were dropped was this: '"Listen, before going to work, do you go to church?" 'Cause they knew ...'.

Aurelian remembered how, ever since he was a student in Cluj, he had gone to churches of different Christian confessions, whether they be Apostolic, Orthodox, Catholic or Greek-Catholic, in the multicultural area of Cluj: 'I went and stayed and prayed'. It was in such a moment of prayer on the steps of the Orthodox Cathedral in Cluj, after his release in 1954, when he had an epiphany that would lead to the providential encounter of his wife:

> Now, here is a more praiseworthy story, if I may say so. [...] – I passed by the Cathedral. The Cathedral ... I sat on its steps, I said my prayer and I prayed that God might bring someone into my life, someone I could build a life together with ... [...].

Shortly after this event, he was to find the love of his life. That is the emblematic moment that inaugurated the third largest chapter of his life history. By the time of our interview, Aurelian and Teodora had already been married for 58 years, their spiritual and political unity being based on enduring loyalty. Coming from a family of priests on her maternal line, and having experienced the condition of political prisoners on her paternal line, Teodora is a religious, sensitive person, without any political involvement, seemingly fragile and vulnerable. However, in the critical moments she has gone through together with her husband, she has mobilised tremendous strength, endurance, toughness, relational intelligence and devotion. She has played the most important role, having been really brave and supported him during and after his 1959 political trial. From this point on, their life stories became symbiotically and complementarily entwined, being articulated at the same key moments they both remember and invest with the same meanings, with various personalised gradients. His masculine, rigorous and rich story is carefully organised by a highly complex chronological linearity, while her feminine story is circular, hesitant, wordy and emotional. They actually mirror each other and are illuminated by special epiphanic moments in which they see, beyond the possibility of denial, the signs of God's presence at watershed moments in their lives.[8]

His(her)story versus History

From the very beginning, the memories of their encounter and hasty, almost meteoric marriage are cast in a fond light. They met in the house of one of Aurelian's cousins, who introduced them to one another. 'When I saw her she was in mourning, 'cause her mother had died. What could I tell you? When I saw her, I liked her. She was exactly as I had wished her to be: slender, thin, dark haired – now what was important was if I also corresponded (laughs)'. Nonetheless, in Teodora's memory, Aurelian does not seem to have matched any of her expectations. In her feminine storytelling, the moment of their encounter is long delayed, mentioned and abandoned several times, after wide loops in the narrative. Aurelian came into Teodora's life when she had a profession that offered her 'the daily bread': she recounted with pride that she worked for 33 years as head nurse in the operating theatre at the Clinic of Urology. While flirting with the thought of becoming a nun, she had suitors who were waiting at her door, as also happened on the memorable day when 'Ghelasie came along':

> That's it! And then came … [she turns towards her husband, who is sitting in
> a nearby armchair, listening to her, and caresses his nape] Prince Charming …
> [she smiles with tender irony].

Her Prince Charming was then almost 40 years old, had already been through a war, on several fronts, had been arrested several times and spent seven years in the political penitentiary of Aiud. She affectionately remembered him dressed in rags, weak and hungry, gaunt and without a penny in his pocket. 'This one, poor thing, my husband, he was right after prison, thin and … woe! (…) He was so meek; now he's not so meek any more [she laughs]. And… the rest was fate!'

---

[8]   My encounter with the Ghelasie family took place at the end of 2010 around Christmas, when we met several times. During the first part of the interview with Aurelian, Teodora sat in an armchair nearby, listening to the well-known life narrative of her husband. During the latter half, when I returned on a different day, the wife was not feeling well and was lying in bed in the next room. At the end of the interview, I asked Aurelian to persuade his wife to grant me an interview when she felt better. It seemed to me that the lady was willing to do so, having discretely awaited the invitation to tell her own life story. During the interview with Teodora, her husband sat in the nearby armchair, rising at times to relax his numb feet, leaning against a metallic framework. As they were growing older and had no children, they were used to listening to each other's story many times, especially with Aurelian being the storyteller *par excellence*.

To the surprise of her close relatives, she suddenly decided to marry this poor old man. In a minor female complicity that arose during the interview, she justified her choice: 'But I got attached to him … [she whispers to me, smiling, without her husband who was sitting nearby, hearing her] – pi-ty, I felt pity – [then, in a loud voice] I got very attached … ['She felt pity for me' says Mr. Ghelasie in a loud voice laughing copiously.] 'And then I came to my sister and told her. I say, "You know what? I'm marrying Aurelian!" "And where are you going to live?" "Under the blue sky!"' Again, a common episode is reflected in a mirror in their life stories. On the very day they had set for their marriage, Aurelian was sacked because politically he did not correspond to his job description. Before the civil ceremony, they met in front of the City Hall:

> A very important thing: [as Aurelian pointed out the relevance of this common autobiographical episode] […] I waited for her and she came; we met and she saw I was rather down. She says, "Why are you sad?" […]

> [Teodora remembered] When I see him by the edge of the sidewalk – I can see him even now standing there – upset … Now I tell him, "This man is sorry about getting married!" I say, "Wait a minute, there's nothing to worry about, we're going back to work, aren't we?" Then he says, "You should know – are you still getting married to me – that I have no job? The company has got dismantled!"

> What's the problem? We'll live on my salary! [Aurelian recalled her saying]

> Then, I say [Teodora remembering her own words]: "This is your trouble now!? We're getting married and we're going to carry … the cross we're going to carry it! Let's get married!" Fine.

'Carrying the cross together' has quintessentially been the definition of their marriage throughout his and her life stories in the face of History. Even the ceremonial nature of their wedding, on which they commented laconically, exhibited these minimalist, albeit essential marks in terms of their religious significance. The austere civil ceremony was celebrated on the same day, followed by the religious ceremony officiated by a priest, in the presence of their spiritual godparents and observing the Orthodox Christian prenuptial ritual of confession and holy communion. Aurelian's arrest was the big milestone of their life together, just as his release was the second one, and their common struggle for survival has unfolded in between these autobiographical landmarks:

> *Tell me, what do you remember, which would be a key moment after you got married?*

His getting arrested! And my being surveyed! I was under surveillance for so long and … God forbid! And beaten up, later and when … […] we've both been through a lot. My oh my, the troubles we've been through!

The night of his arrest is a poignant memory for both of them:

> [Aurelian] What is important to say – I got arrested in '59. 'Cause in '59 they arrested all the former political detainees and had them tried all over again. My wife was the most innocent in this matter. She'd never even been interested in politics, she didn't want to join the [communist] party and she also didn't do any other kind of politics! One night, we had someone knocking at our door at about twelve o'clock. "Who's there?" "The police!" They came, asked for my identification details and they took me, just one, in the car, drove me to the Security and three more stayed with my wife, they searched the house the whole night long.

From then on, in Teodora's life began a period of political terror she endured with courage, tenacity and intelligence. The enormous psychological and physical costs of this period left indelible marks on her life. Fighting to hire a lawyer for her husband, she worked hard to save money, reaching such a degree of starvation, exhaustion and terror that she remembers:

> Every morning I went to church, from church I went to the Security, from the Security to the Military Tribunal – 'cause those people knew me, they didn't stop me and then I said, in the evening, I got home at seven: to a cold, dirty house, famished; there were days when I didn't even have money – my husband has told you how I found 25 lei in the church. I was so upset and sick and tired and … I said, "Lord, if I were to find, Lord, 25 lei, I would pay 10 lei … 20 – to … liturgies for Aurelian and also have something left to buy half a kilo of sugar and a piece, whatever they would give me … of bread; half a loaf of bread". I was hungry!

'The importance of a prayer to the righteous God, that was one outcome of her prayers!', Aurelian concludes, while his face lit up on recounting this epiphanic moment in his wife's life, which is organically integrated in his life story too. Their narratives are thus interspersed, from one end to the other, with genuine religious epiphanies, some anecdotal, others decisive, foundational, all decoded by them as the discreet yet indubitable signs of God's presence in their daily trials. One of the most memorable episodes of their common history, which both interlocutors have relived with intensity, is that of the military tribunal trial. The night before the trial, Teodora visited all the witnesses for the prosecution, former work colleagues of her husband's and, like her mother many years ago, she asked them to tell 'only the naked truth'. For a few seconds before entering the courtroom, his and her eyes met. Aurelian, who had lost weight to the point of no longer being recognisable, smiled at her, while Teodora, exhausted, did not recognise him; then her sister told her:

> "There's Aurelian!" Then I saw him when I entered there. I *made the sign of the cross* when I entered that room and I say, "May God help me, give me strength to go through this, not fall down on the floor, lest he should get scared!" And God saved me from that!

In Aurelian's life story, the same moment meant a lot for his state of mind back then:

> Do you know who entered the first? My wife! And when she entered *she made three big signs of the cross*. And then she spurred me … *I knew God would take care of me.*

The ritual gesture they both remember has symbolic efficacy (Levi Strauss 1978). The sign of the cross is here a living religious symbol (Chevalier and Gheerbrant 1995), in which the transcendental signified and the signifier, expressed through an authentic ritual gesture, are unified, congruent. It triggers the special kind of knowledge that is faith. This is what gave them hope that, eventually, the force lines of the historical and political contingency in which their lives were trapped would enter the orbit of divine justice.

Indeed, the moment was auspicious because most of the witnesses withdrew their allegations:

> A female colleague had said that … – she had to say something – she said I had told her to teach her children how to say their prayers in the evening, before going to bed. And the other said I had rejoiced with Hungary, 'cause there had been the Revolution in Hungary and …

> *Did you rejoice?*

> Yes, I rejoiced, 'cause that was the truth [smiles].

Eventually he could not be convicted on that. Only the accusation that he went to church before going to work remained standing. Aurelian accurately remembered the end of the trial debate, and the words of the judge and the prosecutor resound clearly in his memory even now:

> And they asked the last witness: "But how is he behaving at work?" And that one says: "The first to come to work and the last to leave!" And then the president flung the brief to the prosecutor and said: "This is no man to be convicted!" And you know what the prosecutor said? "We shall carry on with our investigations!"

The echo of this last statement still retains a threatening halo in Teodora's memory. In the prosecutor's technical jargon, this meant that, even after his release, her husband would have to remain in custody at the Security headquarters, being subjected to further investigations meant to coerce him to collaborate. Aurelian had to bear the consequences of his categorical refusal to become an informer for the Security: for a long time, he was unable to find work, except for menial jobs in very difficult conditions. In the common memory of the two spouses, Aurelian's release from his last political detention had an acutely dramatic significance. His wife perceived it as the happiest moment in her life story. The memories of that momentous event were a mixture of joy, surprise, vexation and fear of death, and are reflected in her story and his story, at the crossroads in the history of various periods of communist repression in Romania.

Costs and Rewards of Religious Beliefs

How much did faithfulness to their convictions cost them? For Teodora, her unswerving loyalty to her husband throughout his political surveillance had another price, which she hardly managed to confess, except towards the end of our interview. Perhaps she would never have mentioned the sensitive topic of her failed motherhood, had it not been for the same feminine complicity and reciprocity spontaneously established between the narrator and the researcher, who was then on maternity leave. The life of Aurelian's young wife was marked by repeated miscarriages, caused by poor and harsh living conditions, and the inability to afford a period of rest or appropriate medical treatment during the period of her husband's arrest. Bitter ironical memories of her dead foetuses buried in the garden are particularly touching in her story.

However, the fact that they have been together for so many years and that they still enjoy each other's presence compensates for all these losses. 'We, you know, how? We took joy in one another, it was as if there was a wedding in our house! ... how should I tell you ...?', Teodora confessed, just like Aurelian considered the longevity of their relationship as 'a great gift'. They recalled the beauty of the holy days spent together:

> [Teodora] during holidays we took joy in one another. We both sang carols, on Easter night we went and took Easter bread and we went and took it and came home and sang "Christ is risen!"

> [Aurelian] We always had a Christmas tree! I always ... brought a small branch, something ... and we carolled a lot ... we both carolled. [...] My wife had a voice ...!! My wife used to sing "Your birth, Christ" and ... we carolled at night.

For these eminently religious people, the central axis of their religiosity is prayer, 'man's connection with the Absolute', as Aurelian sententiously defines it. The identity of religion and prayer in their understanding of their lives is strongly evident. When asked, in their case, the superfluous question in the questionnaire at the end of our discussion – 'Do you consider yourself a religious person?' – both their answers are revealing and resonant:

> [Aurelian] The Samaritan woman asked Christ: "Where is it better to pray?" Anywhere, even when walking in the street. [...] whatever prayer you say, it's important that you should pray anytime, under any circumstances. *This is man's connection to the absolute.*

> [Teodora] We ... day or night, we pray. And God helps us! God, you can't even imagine what we've been through and how much ... and we could see with our own eyes how they *opened the gates ... shall I say ... of Heaven, of joy.*

They also experience, as they admit, great, unparalleled spiritual joy: 'very huge soul satisfactions', as Teodora says, confessing carefully, cautiously, with reverent reserve, about their power to pray for others and to have their prayers answered. Congruent with this transcendent realm, their religiosity is also expressed ceremonially, liturgical practice having been essential throughout their lives. Moreover, when asked about the importance of marking life's rites of passage through religious ceremonies, Teodora gives an answer that is as sincere as it is convincing: 'Very important! Because you see life differently! You live life differently!' A completely new worldview opens up whenever the transcendent dimension is existentially taken into account as the ultimate system of reference.

Beyond the negative political consequences, the religious experience of living with God in a period of official atheism brought our protagonists spiritual joy, which they openly confess: 'Every day was a holiday!', as Emil Tatu, a physician and a Greek Catholic clandestinely practising in Cluj, expresses with contagious enthusiasm. 'Clandestinity is very beautiful! It produces effervescence in spiritual life ... and unity; (...) It wasn't easy, but it was beautiful!' He recalls the time when the Greek-Catholic communities in Cluj, whose Church was banned during the communist period, celebrated the liturgy in private homes every Sunday, despite the surveillance of the Security. When asked 'What does being happy mean to you?', Emil answers: 'Being at peace with God, being at peace with yourself and the ones you are close to'.

Spiritual Friendship

As regards Eleonora's kin narrative, although her life history was, in her opinion, devoid of major events and worldly pleasures, since she defines herself as a 'secular nun', we have elicited a grade of 10 – in the self-assessment test – for the happiness she has experienced throughout her life: 'So, Joy – because it's the joy of faith – I'd give myself a 10 here'. She talks about 'the beauty of spiritual friendships with people so special' who have enriched her life. Such spiritual friendships also helped Aurelian survive the hardship of his political imprisonment in the communist penitentiary of Aiud:

'Cause in Aiud my best friend had been Trifan ... [...], and he was extraordinarily religious ... And when I entered the room ... this one wouldn't talk to anybody, absolutely anybody ... he heard what I'd been discussing with a friend, *"Listen, I say that if here in prison we don't try to form our characters, we're here in vain"* ... And he overheard me ... and then he tried to talk to me [laughs softly] ... and then I befriended Trifan. Trifan was a great man [inaudible speaks softly, as if to himself] ... and then ... he formed the younger generations, which later on became the saints of the prisons.

Most of us learned about the Romanian prison universe only after 1989, when the fall of communism brought to light the rich memories of the survivors of that almost unknown and systematically silenced archipelago of political repression. It was then that we learned about survival through faith in the communist prisons. Nicolae Steinhardt called that survival 'the (mystical) solution of faith', a possible way out of 'a concentrationary universe – which need not be a camp, a dungeon or any other form of incarceration; this theory may be applied to any kind of product of totalitarianism' (Steinhardt 1991, 6).[9]

A niche has thus opened in the literature on political imprisonment. It speaks about the power to withstand systematic assaults against human dignity and integrity and about the inner metamorphosis of the prison universe into a privileged space of spiritual growth.[10] There are unsuspected dimensions that Aurelian's

---

[9]   For Nicolae Steinhardt, the Romanian intellectual of Jewish extraction, besides the mystical solution of faith there are only three other possible ways to existentially escape totalitarianism. They are strictly secular and infallible: Solzhenitsyn's, Zinoviev's, Churchill's and Bukovsky's solutions. He invokes them expressively and memorably at the beginning of *The Happiness Diary*, his literary and political testament. 'The first solution, Solzhenitsyn's, consists ... for anyone stepping over the threshold of an investigation organ, in firmly say to himself: I am truly dying this very moment. ... If the individual thinks that, unflinchingly, he is saved. There is nothing that can be done unto him. ... There's no currency for paying the price of his betrayal'. The second solution, Alexander Zinoviev's, consists in utter lack of adaptation to the system. 'Such a man is also immune: no pressures can be exerted upon him, nothing can be taken away from him, nothing can be offered to him'. The third solution, Winston Churchill's and Vladimir Bukovsky's, may be summarised as follows: 'In the presence of tyranny, ... not only do you not give up, but on the contrary, you pull out the mad urge to live and fight'. 'In March 1939, Churchill told Martha Bibescu (an aristocratic Romanian lady): "There will be war. Rack and ruin will come of the British Empire. Death stalks us all. And I feel like getting twenty years younger"' (Steinhardt, 1991, 6–9; translated by C. Borbely).

[10]   Steinhardt experienced the path of faith himself during his political detention between 1959 and 1964, a period that transformed him from a rather agnostic intellectual

confession also discreetly hints at. His narrative approaches these dimensions with reverent caution, through reflexive whispers and silences, because they pertain to an area of inexpressible human experience. This is the luminous and ineffable side of the conversion of 'limit' experiences of political, physical and psychological terror into spiritual experiences. On the other hand, such prison experiences might reach the limits of the unimaginable and the unspeakable. It was the case of the 'Piteşti phenomenon', the terrible communist re-education and brain-washing experiment, to which Aurelian's testimony refers twice, and to which his biography is indirectly bound. 'What happened there, completely unheeded by the West, deserves a special place in the frightful repertoire of concentration camp horrors of the twentieth century', the historian François Furet (1996) states in the preface to the French edition of Virgil Ierunca's book, who coined the term 'the Piteşti phenomenon'. Inspired by the practices of political re-education of the Stalinist 1930s, the Romanian experiment was a specific method of terror. It involved the systematic use of tortured prisoners to torture other prisoners – even their best friends, as evidence of their inner conversion – so much so that the transformation of victims into executioners became almost unrelenting (Ierunca 2007, 9).

What ties our narrator indirectly to the Piteşti phenomenon was, again, a special friendship with one of the survivors of this political experiment. Under terror, Father C. was compelled to testify against Aurelian, who had to serve an additional year in the prison of Aiud. This was a late, mature, serene, even playful friendship, involving the fault of denunciation made out of fear, yet redeemed through confession and forgiveness:

> This one was a good priest. And he kept pumping secrets out of me and he told me everything and everything … after they brought them all back, when the Canal got shut down and he also came … says, "Listen, if you have been to prison at all, you should know it's also because of me … 'cause I rattled about you … what you had told me." He had been at Piteşti. At Piteşti … *you couldn't even imagine* what terror had been there!

It was in this complex context that our narrator elliptically expresses his reflections about the unimaginable evil of the Piteşti experiment, about the (im)possibility of maintaining one's dignity and human honour. His statements are punctuated by thoughtful silences, pauses and whispers that attempt to circumscribe the universe of inexpressible evil. They grant the discourse extremely dense and ambiguous undertones, which are susceptible of conflicting interpretations (see Chapter 2).

---

into a genuine Christian. First published immediately after the collapse of communism in Romania, his highly influential work *The Happiness Diary* testifies on the foundational event of his christening in prison. After his release, Nicolae Steinhardt became an Orthodox monk at Ana-Rohia Monastery, founded by Aurelian's father. There Aurelian Ghelasie encountered him and this is why Steinhardt's personality is connected through biographical and spiritual threads to the life narrative of our interviewee.

The people who'd been at Piteşti, did they ever recover? Emotionally, spiritually?

There were people who could ... but ... like this Gheorghiţă Viorel ... this one, Viorel, who wrote a book. He was a great writer ... he was strong ... when I was at Timişoara. They were ... [this can't be deciphered, he speaks in a very soft voice, as if to himself] Saints, big characters ... And there was another one ... and that one died too ... but I'm telling you, you may accept being shot, but you can't bear with terror, being subjected to it incessantly, 'cause you're going to lose even your moral sense and lose your wits and lose what ... you're lost! And that's the worst calamity! 'Cause after you come back to your senses, you feel that you should have stayed the first time ... not confess ... I've told you that once ... I was having moral classes, 'cause the Legionnaires were raised like that, in the spirit of honour. Honour, no matter what! No matter what, honour ... and faith! And ... 'cause I never said that that one, or the other one ...

... dishonouring ...

I said that the sense of honour was above ... [silence].

Ultimately, this is one of the major interrogations that the two types of totalitarianism of the twentieth century left in their wake: how can one keep one's human dignity under extreme conditions of political terror? The answers seem to be purely individual, as the shattering testimonies of the Shoah and the Gulag experiences reveal. Concerned about the evil of the previous century, Tzvetan Todorov identifies in such testimonies the sole solution for maintaining one's humanity: 'keeping the freedom to choose one's attitude in an extreme situation, even though apparently there is no way to act against it' (Todorov 1996, 61).

All of these life narratives might be considered as precious testimonies about the existential consequences of taking religion seriously during communism, as the high political price that had to be paid and as the spiritual reward that was to be gained. Nothing in these life narratives, in these 'almost final drafts of their life review' and in their inner attitude betrays any regret about the price their authors had to pay for their consistent convictions.

The Category of the Sacred: Religious Experience and Ceremony

While religious ceremonies are present in the above-mentioned life stories of these people, and while their religiosity is unified and fully expressed at multiple cognitive, emotional, performative, relational and existential levels,[11] the

---

[11]   In a multi-dimensional approach on religious commitment there are at least five areas in which religiosity is manifested (ritual/belief/knowledge/experience/life

description *per se* of the sacred ceremonies is rather absent from the interviews.[12] Apparently, this absence of references to the form and content of such ceremonies seems to be as curious as all the other absences in the interviews reported and insightfully analysed by Daniela Koleva (Chapter 6). Still, in this case, there is a different kind of silence, which is pregnant with meaning. It belongs to a whole new dimension, to another order of reality which, surprisingly, tends to be overlooked in social studies on religion and religiosity.

Irrespective of how difficult it is to circumscribe religiosity given its protean forms, what essentially defines the *homo religiosus* is his personal relationship with a sacred transcendence. The religious and the sacred are consubstantial (Eliade 2006), and the definitions of the two categories are often tautological.[13] The sacredness implicit in the relation between a religious person and the transcendent seems removed, detached, severed from many of the life histories elicited. Moreover, even when this dimension is present as a mark of religiosity, it is lost sight of in analysis and research. Eventually, all these symptomatic omissions, oblivions and forms of silencing of the transcendent reality, coupled with the lost meaning of the sacred and holiness, are embedded in the secularised worldview. In this cultural and historical context, what are all the more important are the positions adopted by some analysts: whether religious or non-religious, they have attempted to explain the neglect of religion in the social sciences (Joanna Bornat, Chapter 2), while pleading for restoring religion to the public space (Woodhead 2012).

If the sacred – as a way of being in the world of *homo religiosus* – belongs to another order of reality, then the existential and cognitive relation to this ontological category requires a different type of knowledge, communication and language. What are, ultimately, religious holidays, in general, and Christian liturgies in particular, when they are experienced genuinely, in full awareness, if not community experiences of the sacred and ceremonial relations with God? The life of a practising Christian adopts the rhythm of this sacred time of liturgical celebrations – that continuous, indestructible present; hence, perhaps, the impression of the changelessness and timelessness of religious holidays that many of the life stories in this volume talk about. For the Christians, religious holidays are more than just a return in time, to that mythical, originary time, in *illo tempore*; they are, in fact, an actualisation, a becoming contemporaneous with that *illud tempus* of the sacred events that marked the historical existence of Jesus Christ (Eliade 2006, 68–87). Although open to all those who wish to know it and share it, the meaning of Christian liturgies remains, ultimately, an initiatory type

---

consequences) and these dimensions relate or could vary semi-independently (Swatos n.d., entry 'Religiosity').

[12]   A notable exception is the interview with Eleonora Moldovan, where we discussed the monastic burial ritual of Archbishop Bartholomew at the Orthodox Cathedral from Cluj, a recent religious and media event at the time of our interview.

[13]   Swatos (1998), entry 'The Sacred'.

of knowledge: 'And I will not tell your enemies your secrets', reads the Byzantine liturgy in preparation for the solemn moment of the Holy Eucharist, which is also a Theophany.[14] Therefore the category of the sacred, of the holy is also consubstantial with mystery, not so much as a secret, but as an ultimately revealed truth that one approaches with reverence and awe. It can hardly be uttered; it is something ineffable that common language fails to express and that lends itself only to ceremonial language, to psalms and silence.

Discourse of Silence: The Ineffable, the Unspeakable, Dialogical Silences

There is an intimate relation between silence and the sacred. Reverent silence might be the sign of a privileged relation to God. In most of the world religions, the spiritual dimension of silence is pervasive (Le Breton 2001, 23–4). At stake are the discipline and technique of silence, the silence of deep prayer as communication with God, the silence of man facing infinity. 'The ineffable corresponds to the infinite. Silence respects this organic relation that places the ineffable face to face with the infinite' (Neher 1970, 15). Being a form of the inexpressible, ineffable silence pertains to the impossibility of naming what is transcendent, sublime, sacred. It is something pregnant with a meaning which exceeds human comprehension. Some life narratives reveal the ineffable, epiphanic dimension of a divine experience, detectable in the storytelling thanks to the presence of reverent silences.

On the other hand, another form of the inexpressible is made visible throughout the interviews: the silence which falls upon incommunicable human experiences either because of their meaninglessness or because they are unconceivable and unimaginable. 'The silence of death versus divine silence, the unutterable versus the ineffable represent two modes of the inexpressibility of mystery' (Jankélévitch 2000, 80).

The proximity of death in life is always speechless: the closer death is, the harsher the silence. Critical moments regarding the imminence of death are articulated in Aurelian's life history and deep silences punctuate his discourse. Dehumanising experiences are also unspeakable. The confessions of the survivors of the Shoah or of the Gulag, in another context, 'are torn between the necessity to speak and the impossibility to find the words to do so' (Le Breton 2001, 23). This impossibility limits the historical representation of some events in the recent past.

Given their inexhaustible richness of meanings, the life stories analysed above organically include these rather opposed categories of the inexpressible. We have seen how situations at the very limits of life in the proximity of death were opened up through prayer to divine experiences and how, sometimes, the most critical moments became genuine epiphanies. Within storytelling, the same tropes of

---

[14]   Camil Peteu has generously shared with us this interpretation of the liturgy and far more, in personal discussions in Cluj over many years.

silence condense both forms of the inexpressible: long, thoughtful pauses, ellipses, hesitations, whispers or ways of speaking in a very soft voice, as if to oneself.

Therefore, communicative silences or silent communicative acts (Tannen and Saville 1985) are no longer seen as the absence of speech, but as signs of a laborious meaning-giving process. They are marked by elusiveness and polysemy and thus their interpretation becomes highly challenging. Our research implies a cultural anthropological gaze as a reading grid for these life narratives from various corners of Europe. Let us add to the challenge of difference and contextual complexity that Joanna Bornat underlines in Chapter 2 the intrinsic polysemy of the meaningful silences articulating these discourses. It becomes clear that any attempt to comprehend the life histories elicited by the researchers and analysed from a transcultural standpoint remains inevitably an unfinished process, open to the widening spiral of understanding.

It is against this horizon of meaning that I would suggest interpreting some of the expressive silences that punctuate our interviewees' life narratives. As regards the scarcity of references to the liturgical ceremonies they have always attended, one might identify a double layer here. At the content level, the ultimate religious significance of such ceremonies belongs to the category of sacred ineffableness. Meanwhile, the lack of reference to the form, structure or manner of celebrating liturgical ceremonies corresponds to a kind of dialogical silence. This genre of silence was part of the interviewing encounter and was triggered by a complicity established between the actors of the dialogue, based on the tacit assumption 'I know that you know'. That was the result of a rather subtle mutual questioning and positioning that always preceded the interview.[15] It fostered a specific discourse of familiarity and a shared horizon of meaning that we became aware of and that shaped our discussion *a priori*. Therefore, despite the difference in age and life experience, the dialogical couple interviewer–interviewed tacitly yet knowingly shared the same reference system and meaningful reverent silence. Ultimately, all the performers of this research – narrators, listeners, analysts and readers alike – have been thoroughly immersed in a transcultural language game of sameness and difference. Hopefully, this tension of interpretations may give vent to a more illuminative grasp, albeit not a definitive one, of the memories and oblivions relating to the celebration of life's crucial moments in recent European history.

----

[15]   Each encounter with these persons had, as a preamble, such subtle mutual positionings. To obtain an interview, Ileana Benga and I met Eleonora Moldovan for the first time in her most familiar place, the Orthodox Cathedral, and both had the feeling we were affectionately tested. I was recommended to the Ghelasie family by a lady from the Orthodox Christian Women's Association in Cluj. I got to talk to Emil Tatu, a Christian, Greek-Catholic doctor, at the recommendation of a Greek-Catholic priest, after a long period of courtship, when I had to playfully reveal my own religious beliefs and cultural preferences. It seems to me that all this protocol resulted in an exchange of impalpable mutual signs of recognition, just like the stylised fish symbol, drawn on sand, had recognition value among the early Christians.

References

Bănică, Mirel. 2007. *Biserica ortodoxă romană, stat şi societate în anii 30*. Iaşi: Polirom.

Bertaux, Daniel. 1997. *Les récits de vie. Perspective ethnosociologique*. Paris: Nathan.

Chevalier, Jean and Alain Gheerbrant. 1995. *Dicţionar de simboluri*. Bucureşti: Artemis.

Codreanu, Corneliu. 1987/1938. *Cărticica sefului de cuib*. Munchen: Colecţia Europa. Available at: http://www.codreanu.ro/carticica.htm.

Comisia prezidenţială pentru analiza dictaturii comuniste din România. 2006. *Raport Final*. Bucureşti. Available at: http://www.presidency.ro/static/ordine/ RAPORT_FINAL_CPADCR.pdf.

Conovici, Mariana, Silvia Iliescu and Octavian Silvestru. 2008. *Ţara, Legiunea, Căpitanul-Mişcarea legionară în documente de istorie orală*. Bucureşti: Humanitas.

Davie, Grace. 1994. *Religion in Britain since 1945: Believing without Belonging*. Oxford: Blackwell.

Davie, Grace. 2006. 'Religion in Europe in the 21st Century: The Factors to Take into Account'. *Archives Européennes de Sociologie/European Journal of Sociology* 47(2): 271–96.

Denzin, Norman K. 1989. *Interpretive Biography*. London: Sage.

Eliade, Mircea. 2000. *Sacrul şi profanul*. Bucureşti: Humanitas.

Furet, François. 1996. 'Prefaţă la ediţia franceză'. In Virgil Ierunca. 2007. *Fenomenul Piteşti*, 11–15. Bucureşti: Humanitas.

Glover, Julian. 2010. 'Not Atheist, not Religious: Typical Briton is a "Fuzzy Believer"'. *The Guardian*, 10 September. Available at: www.guardian.co.uk, accessed in September 2010.

Heinen, Armin. 2006. *Legiunea Arhangelul Mihail*. Bucureşti: Humanitas.

Ierunca, Virgil. 2007. *Fenomenul Piteşti*. Bucureşti: Humanitas.

Jankélévitch, Vladimir. 2000. *Tratat despre moarte*. Timişoara: Amarcord

Le Breton, David. 2001. *Despre tăcere*. Bucureşti: All Educational.

Levy Strauss, Claude. 1978. *Antropologia structurală*. Bucureşti: Editura Politică.

Neher, André. 2002. *Exilul Cuvântului. De la tăcerea biblică la tăcerea de la Auschwitz*. Bucureşti: Hasefer.

Passerini, Luisa. 1990. 'Mythbiography in Oral History'. In *The Myths We Live By*, edited by R. Samuel and P. Thompson. London: Routledge, pp. 49–60.

Ricoeur, Paul. 2001. *Memoria, istoria, uitarea*. Timişoara: Amarcord.

Steinhardt, Nicolae. 1991. *Jurnalul fericirii*. Cluj: Dacia.

Swatos, William H. Jr (ed.) 1998. *Encyclopedia of Religion and Society*. Hartford Institute for Religion Research, Hartford Seminary. Available at: http://hirr. hartsem.edu/ency/.

Tannen, Deborah and Troike M. Saville (eds) 1985. *Perspectives on Silence*. Norwood, NJ: Abex.

Todorov, Tzvetan. 1996. *Confruntarea cu extrema. Victime şi torţionari în secolul XX*. Bucureşti: Humanitas.

Todorov, Tzvetan. 1999. *Abuzurile memoriei*. Timişoara: Amarcord.

Veiga, Francisco. 1995. *Istoria Gărzii de fier, 1919–1941. Misitica ultranaţionalismului*. Bucureşti: Humanitas.

Voas, David and Alasdair Crocket. 2005. 'Religion in Britain: Neither Believing nor Belonging'. *Sociology* 39: 11. Available at: http://soc. Sagepub.com/cgi/content/abstract/39/1/11/.

Woodhead, Linda. 2012. 'Restoring Religion to the Public Square'. *U.K.'s Catholic Weekly*, 28 January, 7.

Chapter 6

Performing Social Normativity: Religious Rituals in Secular Lives

Daniela Koleva

The 2008 European Values Study (EVS) has yielded a paradoxical finding: while the levels of belief are not high in most European countries and church attendance is even lower, the share of respondents who think that religious services are appropriate at life transitions is significant everywhere (Table 6.1). In this chapter I try to explain this paradox by looking into the importance that religious rituals could possibly have for non-religious individuals. I start with two findings of the RASC project that seemed surprising: that participants did not talk much about the rituals they went through or witnessed; and that, according to what they said, rituals had not really changed in the course of their lives. I will discuss these findings first in the context of the interview situation. Then I link them to broader social contexts, paying close attention to how interviewees explained their own motivations to participate in or organise rites of passage. I focus on three cases drawn from the interviews illustrating different ways of relating to religious ritual. From this I go on to suggest a hypothesis about the importance that religious and non-religious self-identifications and symbolic practices might have had for the interviewees.

Table 6.1 Shares of positive replies to the question 'Independently of whether you go to church or not, would you say you are a religious person?' versus positive replies to the question 'Do you personally think it is important to hold a religious service for any of the following events?'

Country	I am religious	Religious service important for:		
		Birth	Marriage	Death
UK	46.5%	57.8%	69.4%	75.7%
Bulgaria	55.2%	58.1%	69.8%	78.1%
Romania	80.3%	96.6%	95.8%	95.6%

Source: http://www.europeanvaluesstudy.eu/ (accessed 7 October 2011).

The Narratives: 'Away from Ritual' or 'Discourse of Familiarity'?

Detailed descriptions of rituals are surprisingly rare in the interviews collected in the course of the RASC project. Given that the question about rituals and their uses that older people remember had been a central one, this scarcity seems puzzling. Have our interviewees been drifting 'away from ritual' (Douglas 2003) throughout their lives? Davie's 'believing without belonging' thesis suggests the prevalence of a more personal relation to the sacred, independent of its public performance and unmediated by institutions and collective acts. A couple of our interviewees indeed were of the opinion that no rituals were needed at life transitions. The majority, as suggested by EVS results, considered some kind of ritual appropriate, usually religious. In most cases, interviewees seemed to take such rituals for granted. They did not dwell on why rituals were needed and did not bother to articulate their meaning. Rather, they most often mentioned specific incidents:

> he cried a lot. And my brother was very annoyed because the vicar said "Oh walk him up and down" which was sensible to stop him crying. Because he was being baptised and another couple, you know, two. And my brother thought that was awful. I said, "Well he was just a damned nuisance", crying all the time. [...] My memories of my particular wedding, it poured all day long you see [laughing]. (Kate Osborne, Southampton)

> You know I have moments, fractions of a second ... Certain things remain with you. This memory about my wedding is the same. It seemed that I was walking but I wasn't able to reach the altar. And that choir, that music was divine. So this is how it was, my wedding. (Ioana Georgescu, Bucharest)

> Our village is a big village, 3 to 4 kilometers long, and the groom lived at one end of the village. The bride was in the middle of the village. So we walked and it was this village dust, first class! Oh, it was beautiful, as an event ... so I recorded it among, let's say, my events. (Ion Cotescu, Bucharest)

> The wedding was in Sofia, it was in the Russian restaurant, near the Russian church – there were 15 to 16 people there. ... Those who came were my friends from university. No parents, only her brother and sister, my two sisters, some others and my friends from university. This best friend of mine Boris Kolkovski from the Geography Faculty and Genchev organised the whole wedding. When I gave the money [to pay the bill] – I didn't have enough money. So they started going around with a hat in hand: "Aleko is short of money. Give something so he can pay". That's how I managed to pay. (Aleko Radev, Sofia)

It is not unusual for memory to work in this way. Psychologists refer to so-called 'flashbulb memories' (Conway 1995) to show the importance of emotions and surprise in explaining how some events may be remembered. Anthropologists

(Rosaldo 1986) and oral historians (Niethammer 1988, 45) have noticed that people tend to consider unusual events and obsolete practices worth telling rather than routines. Typical examples in our case are the stories about secretly held religious ceremonies under the communist regime:

> We went to church and got … to that ceremonial. And we even got in trouble 'cause we had a godfather who was a general and couldn't attend the wedding and come to church. … Well it was dangerous in the church, 'cause we only went to church in the evening to get married. (Eduard Vornic, Cluj)

> they were baptised in church, but in a covert manner … we took Adrian to Ploiesti, and Nusa, yes we went to a little church that was hidden. (Viorel Ionescu, Bucharest)

> Cristina [daughter] was already nine months old when my mother-in-law said this, If we didn't have the girl baptised, she would take her for a walk one day and have her baptised … And they did have her baptised there, at the Reformed Church. (Dorina Badea, Cluj)

> at home – we didn't dare have a wedding ceremony in a church. (Andon Igov, Sofia)

> We were clever and we went to Dryanovo. We have cousins there. We went to have our wedding in the church there. (Malina Marinova, Targovishte)

Interestingly, very few of the Bulgarian and Romanian interviewees seem to remember the secular ceremonies they have attended. While in Romania such ceremonies may not have been well developed,[1] the Bulgarian Communist Party followed the Soviet example and took the course of 'militant atheism'. After the open repressions of the 1950s, religion was no longer considered a bastion of a hostile class ideology, but rather a 'survival' of the old way of life. Therefore its eradication was entrusted to mass organisations auxiliary to the ruling Communist Party.[2] Special efforts were made to develop and implement a system of secular rites of passage and the corresponding infrastructure (Elenkov 2009): the enactment of

---

[1]   See Chapter 3.

[2]   On 27 December 1966, a resolution of the Secretariat of the Central Committee of the Bulgarian Communist Party was adopted, entitled 'For further improvement of the work on the atheistic education of the working people'. Following it, the Council of Ministers issued Regulation no. 14 of 4 April 1969, 'On the implementation of civil rituals'.

regulations;[3] the writing of scenarios, speeches and music for secular rituals;[4] and the design of special buildings (*obredni domove*, ritual houses) and objects to be used in secular rituals, including tombstones without religious symbols. Another important task was the training of *ritualchitsi* (ritual specialists), whose job was to conduct rites of passage.

Judging from the interviews, these efforts do not seem to have been particularly successful. One reason may be that participants married and had their children before the adoption of these measures. It seems that the civil marriage ceremony was prevalent, perhaps because signing the marriage certificate was an integral part of it. However, interviewees seldom refer to it as a ritual. They usually say that they 'just signed' and 'had no wedding', and it is not clear if the latter refers to the ceremony or the party. The name-giving ceremony introduced in the later decades of socialism does not seem to have been widely accepted, while funerals obviously used to be a matter of making gestures of compliance in different directions, that is, negotiating secular elements provided by the authorities and religious ones sought by the relatives of the deceased (cf. Kaneff 2004). Talking about these moments now, the interviewees tend to expand on the organisation of the event rather than on the structure and meaning of the ritual. Still, there are some revealing exceptions, such as the description of Muslim funerals given by Demir Hamidov,[5] a Turk and retired teacher of physics, to a Bulgarian interviewer:

> When they dig the grave – there's a special direction, a holy direction ever since Mohammed's times: this is the direction where the Kaaba is, the Holy Mosque from Abraham's times. ... And the grave has to be a metre wide, two metres long and when it's 40 cm deep, you start digging diagonally at the south side and so inside is formed something like a trapeze opening [he shows with his hands] and the deceased is wrapped in a fabric – calico. To the other side, planks are arranged. The deceased is laid in a sort of triangle and is buried. Suras are read. Women can attend the funeral but they rarely go. You aren't supposed to weep and cry. You mustn't weep and cry. You should accept these things more calmly. If you weep and cry, it should be after this ritual.

With priests' families on both his father's and his mother's side, Demir said that he had 'inherited' his faith, although he did not pray as required. At the same time, driven by his intellectual curiosity, he took pleasure in reading and relating religious dogma to contemporary science (for example *in-vitro* fertilisation). He

---

[3]   The regulation on funerals, 'Pravilnik za pogrebeniata' [Rules on funerals], *Darzhaven vestnik* [State Gazette], no. 102, 25 December 1970, treated them as communal services for the population provided by the state.

[4]   A special collection of scenarios, speeches and poetry for every occasion was published in 1975 (*Sbornik normativni aktove, primerni scenarii i slova za grazhdanskite rituali*, 1975).

[5]   See Chapter 10 for this case.

talked to an interviewer who had not been socialised in the Muslim tradition but shared his intellectual curiosity. The opposite was true for the majority of the other cases: the conversation partners (whether believers or not) had been socialised in the same culture, which often implied the same religious tradition. Therefore interviewees took a shared horizon of meaning for granted. Whenever they felt this was not the case, they offered a more detailed explanation. Thus Harold Stevenson, a British secular humanist, described the funeral of his foster parent:

> I was a bit upset because of the nature of the ceremony because there was nothing whatever, apart from mentioning the actual name of the person who died, it just went through the rigmarole of the prayer book and no mention of what they'd done or what they'd achieved in life and that sort of thing, and I felt very empty coming away afterwards… […] It was, it didn't mean anything.

Rather than focusing on the ceremony itself, Harold shared his dissatisfaction with it because of its de-personalising effect and the lack of meaning for him, a fact that obviously had to do with his later turning to secular humanism. The story of this funeral helped him to argument this decision and to introduce a central topic in the interview: humanist ceremonies.[6]

Harold's and Demir's cases stand out as exceptions to the relatively scarce information and lack of reflection on rituals in most interviews. This, however, does not necessarily mean that rituals are unimportant. Rather, it seems that interviewees take for granted not only rituals *per se* but also the shared knowledge about them. Assuming that the interviewers share their own presuppositions, they tend to omit what they imagine as a 'discourse of familiarity' (Bourdieu 1977, 18), whereby one's experience of one's own familiar world finds expression. Since interviewers knowingly directed the conversation towards religiosity and rituals, an expectation that this is their discourse of familiarity would be only natural. Conversely, Harold's and Demir's cases are examples of outsider-oriented discourse, suggesting that the common silence about rituals in the interviews is an example of the 'dialogical silences' referred to in Chapter 5.

The Agenda: Negotiating Normativity

Oral history interviewing is not only focused on the referential aspect of the story but is also interested in its intersubjective[7] aspects: the negotiation of the agenda and the co-authorship of the final product. Therefore it should be kept in mind that, since the project foregrounded religion, it may appear in some cases more salient in the interviews than in the actual lives that the interviewees are recalling, so for example: 'Oh yes, you're interested in the religious, you must keep taking me back

---

[6] See Chapter 7 for his case.

[7] For more on intersubjectivity, see Chapter 4.

there', remarks Barbara Morris (London). Furthermore, the project's topic has stimulated participants to reflect on their own attitudes and perhaps to realise their complexity and, sometimes, their ambiguity. Setting the agenda of the interview, the researchers define the frame of reference for these reflections.

Another major reference that is my focus here is social norms. In some instances, interviewees expanded on practices which they described as deviating from a norm. Alexandra Koleva (Sofia) explained that she did not go to church anymore because she moved with difficulty. However, going to church became a norm for her only when she married into a Protestant family and her father-in-law, a minister, started to take her to his church. Dorina Badea (Cluj) explained that she would have preferred her daughter to be married in church but the high price of the ceremony in Greece, where the couple lived, made a church marriage unaffordable. At the same time she seemed aware that her daughter and son-in-law 'don't give this matter much importance' and was not sure 'whether in their minds or in their hearts it would mean anything'. Usually, interviewees appeared to feel the need to give explanations in cases when they found the reported behaviour ambiguous from the point of view of some norms, even though the interviewer did not refer to them. Alexandra and Dorina may have been trying to reconcile actual practices with norms from which they felt those practices deviated. They did not, however, consider whether the norms themselves had remained stable or had changed.

These instances testify to the existence of a social normativity that – albeit unarticulated – serves as orientation for the participants. It can be hypothesised that, when they speak of 'unchanging' rituals, the interviewees think of the normative models rather than the actual practices. Rituals can be viewed as a mode of relating to religious entities or to fellow-humans via a recourse to culturally available and recognisable scripts. Hinting at their immutability, interviewees seem to refer to these scripts, while the individual ritual acts are probably much more idiosyncratic, drawing as much (if not less) from the cultural script as from what Sered (1993, 106) has called a 'ritual menu', emphasising the bricolage character of contemporary rituals. No wonder then that most of the cases where awareness of ritual change and innovation is present come from the UK, and from interviewees who have been engaged in ritual performances, whether religious or humanist. By contrast, in Bulgaria and Romania, where post-communist attitudes towards religion are often presented in terms of its 'resurrection', interviewees usually seem to imply a return to traditions restricted by the communist regimes. Hence rituals tend to appear immutable.

The Practices: Personal Meanings and Social Norms

The focus on rituals brings forward aspects of lived religion, shifting away from thinking of religion in terms of beliefs towards thinking of it in terms of practices (cf. Neitz 2004, 399) and the emotions embedded in them. Belief is not necessarily the only (maybe not even the central) aspect of day-to-day religiosity. Focusing on practices makes it possible to consider this commitment as 'habitus', a set of unreflected practical dispositions (Mellor and Shilling 2010). From this point of view, rituals are viewed not as *symbolic* practices, whose meanings have to be decoded, but as symbolic *practices*, behaviours, where the performance itself is important, rather than the meaning. The key question then is what participation in a certain ritual means for the participants. Therefore, if ritual practices are broadly viewed as 'texts' (Geertz 1973), what matters are not the denotative but rather the performative aspects of these texts or, paraphrasing the title of Austin's (1975) seminal book: what are the 'things' people 'do' with rituals.

With the initial question about the attractiveness of religious rituals in mind, I will focus primarily on cases where the interviewees stated that they were non-believers – or were not categorical about their religious attitudes – but nevertheless reported to have participated in and organised religious ceremonies to mark their own or their family members' life transitions. I will tap into their motives to engage in religious ceremonies that obviously have lost for them their original meaning, or have never had such a meaning. My hypothesis is that there is a certain social normativity at play here that takes different forms. Among these, I will first focus on conformity as an unarticulated and unreflected ethos. Then I will discuss a conscious morality expressed in solidarity with the immediate we-group and responsibility for family members, and finally will consider the identification with a larger community as an ideology linking religious experience to a cultural memory canon.

'This is how it's done': Conformity as Value

Interviewees do not generally reflect on the reasons why they perform certain rituals. This is also the case when persons who declare themselves non-believers nevertheless stick to religious rituals. When asked about it, they find it difficult to articulate the reasons. Most often, the answers are of the 'this-is-how-it's-done' type, suggesting lack of reflection on the need for performing a certain symbolic act. It seems to have been done 'by default', as a preselected option for which no alternatives were seen:

> it seemed the natural thing to do. (Viorel Ionescu, Bucharest)

> Even when we went to Easter or services, it was because everybody went, I don't know how to say this. (Florina Campeanu, Bucharest)

> he liked those things, it was a tradition and he was doing it in a non-religious way, but it was something superficial, he wasn't much of a believer. (Margareta Calinescu, Bucharest)

Anyway I think we just carried on. I can't remember. When we got married we had a religious ceremony. And when you wanted to get married you had to belong, you had to join a synagogue. We weren't religious, I wouldn't say we were religious. (Barbara Morris, London)

And it was no great problem walking down the street with two kids and going to church, and going with my mother. (Lewis Farrow, Southampton)

Bulgarian interviewees would typically mention health, if they were giving a reason for their religious practices:

I went there and I said, "I can also light a candle for health". (Milena Chakalova, Sofia)

I teach these people how to prepare "the five loaves", ... And they'd ask, "Auntie, what is this for?" – it is for good health and blessings of your homes, that's why the five loaves are made. (Dimana Dimova, Varna)

A prayer in front of the miraculous icon of St Menas for the good health of the child. Buying out a 40 day liturgy for good health, for conceiving a child. It's also a good idea to have your home sprinkled with holy water for good health. (Tanya Teneva, Sofia)

In the church, I started [to help] just for my good health, for the health of my family. (Valentina Vassileva, Shumen)

Polly Rutherford (London) is the only one among the interviewees from the three countries who is articulate and reflective about this attitude. Polly, a retired school head-teacher, divorced and a non-believer, was born in 1931. She presented herself to the interviewer as a 'grandmother', although she was mainly busy with voluntary social work. She had spent her childhood in Manchester in a family that 'weren't church goers'. Her own belonging to the Church of England was only nominal: she would put CoE on forms 'but it didn't really mean anything'. It was 'a cultural thing rather than a religious thing'. At the age of 12 she was confirmed because she felt that church membership was an essential part of membership in society:[8]

Well yes I did actually, no, you've jogged my memory now. When I was about twelve I think it was, people were getting, some people were getting confirmed and I didn't understand what this was and what it was about so I insisted upon going to a class and I was [laughing] I was in fact confirmed. ... I didn't do anything with it but it was, some people, I seemed to get the idea that if I wasn't

---

[8]   See Chapter 4 for an interpretation of this episode as a 'radical memory'.

confirmed I wouldn't be a fully functioning member of British society. It had that sort of feeling about it, but there we were.

Asked to reflect where that feeling came from, Polly suggested it might have been other adults exerting pressure on her parents to have her confirmed, as well as other children who were engaged in church life and whom she envied for 'going to things and doing things'. She reflects now that 'it had a sort of mainstream feel to it'. Although she did not have a church wedding, she christened her first son, trying to conform to what she felt was expected of her:

> I felt, I felt, I felt a sense of duty. And maybe my mother said something, anyway. But I felt I ought to have my first son christened. [laughing] … I was just going through a sort of a phase of wanting to conform a bit I think, or, I didn't want to disadvantage my child by not doing the right thing.

Unlike most other interviewees, Polly appeared to be sensitive to the aspects of conformity in her life, and to the ways in which life had differed from her own ideas of it. She commented that, before her divorce, she had been influenced by feminist ideas but felt that her own life 'didn't match' them. (Indeed, she only divorced and started a career when her children grew up.) The idea that her child might be disadvantaged by her 'not doing the right thing' shows how strong and deeply rooted this kind of normativity has been. A church funeral for her mother also appears to have been 'the right thing' to do and a 'duty' that she fulfilled. Although she did not consider religious services necessary at life transitions, she had not objected to her children's church weddings:[9]

> three of my kids have been married in church, which since none of them were believers or anything else it has been I think mainly with regard to conformity. They've enjoyed the ceremonies, they like dressing up and being the centre of attention and they've been very nice ceremonies in different ways.

Polly even found the wedding ceremonies 'charming' and 'attractive' with their inclusivity. She liked the music and did not feel offended by the religious content.

It seems that relations with others have been very important throughout Polly's life, both with specific people and in a more general sense with those who might pass judgement and include or exclude her:

---

[9]   This seems to be in line with a tendency observed in the relationship between religion and church in contemporary Europe that Grace Davie has interpreted as a shift to consumption (Davie 2006, 281): what has traditionally been an obligation has become increasingly a matter of choice.

I just want people round me. [laughing] And that's it, you know, people make all the difference. And can make all the difference and you have to put your faith in people. I do anyway.

Polly has not only tried to conform but has also taken genuine pleasure in her social life on many occasions. She took pride in her large family (her 'dynasty'), valued her work and remembered with pleasure her membership in a women's organisation. As she reflected, it appeared that what had been most important for her was the feeling of being included, 'being part of it'.

Certainly, the power of rituals to create a sense of belonging is beyond any doubt, with their major role expressed in the interviews as sites of implied although unarticulated consensus. Thus conformity acquires a positive meaning:

Out of habit. Or because it looks good. (Ioana Georgescu, Bucharest)

Well, I think it's a common law. I mean, if they didn't respect it [church ritual], they would be badly judged, so to speak. (Dinu Bunescu, Bucharest)

Of course, we had to take into consideration the situation, but this attitude to religion is persistent and that's how it should be. (Nayden Uzunov, Varna)

Well we knew that this lot believed in something. Whether we believed in it or not I don't think it really mattered. (Jennifer Renwick, London)

My father was an atheist but he liked the conventional things didn't he? (Harold Stevenson, Southampton)

I don't think they give a damn about the words, they're singing and they're just being part of it. (Lewis Farrow, Southampton)

it's about being decent people. (Barbara Morris, London)

The 'default' – whether it is called 'habit', 'common law', 'the conventional thing', 'the tradition' (no one except Polly uses 'conformity') – becomes associated with 'the right thing' and thus acquires moral connotations. Conformity turns out to be compliance with a moral imperative. This stance is even more salient in other types of attitudes that exhibit the same paradox: an actual *choice* is seen in terms of *obligation*.

'Doing the right thing for ...': Solidarity with Family and Friends

The research confirmed the importance of family for transmitting religious and secular attitudes and practices. Only in rare cases did interviewees admit to having questioned models handed down by their parents and grandparents. Most often, as Sylvia Jones put it, 'you just picked it up through your pores':

> So there was nothing imposed on you in any kind of way. It was just lived. And because of the example that we were given we never saw any other way of living. (Sylvia Jones, Southampton)

> That's where traditions in our family come from … my grandmother was particularly meticulous concerning fasting and religious holidays. (Tanya Teneva, Sofia)

> I was a child educated in the tradition of Christianity. My grandmother would traditionally bring me to church, not fanatically though. I enjoyed going to church with my grandmother. When it came to fasting, I would keep fast with her. (Anna Tosheva, Sofia)

For many interviewees, religious rituals have been and continue to be important and meaningful, but with a certain semantic shift. I will consider in some detail Florina Campeanu's case.[10] Florina was born in 1928 into the non-religious family of a Romanian military officer. Mandatory church attendance during her school years did not change her outlook. She earned a scholarship that allowed her to study at university and worked as a high school teacher and principal in Bucharest. The key points of her story, however, relate to her family:

> So on the professional track, I think my life was satisfactory, maybe more could have been done, this is what I did … And on the family side, the fact that I had a child, two grandchildren were born and they were all accomplished as human beings, this is also seems an accomplishment. […]

> In my profession, I don't know … generally, everything in my professional life went well. I still think it was my family life … The fact that Nadia was born, when I so much wanted a child … […]

> When I think of Vlad [great grandson], everything that I did before him seems unimportant.

Like most professional women in socialist countries, Florina had to combine professional life with family life. While communist emancipation encouraged (actually demanded) women's participation in the labour force, it did not tackle the question of their roles as mothers and homemakers. Although early Soviet theorisations predicted a 'dying out' of the family as a bourgeois institution, the 1930s already saw a revision of this thesis and a withdrawal to family values

---

10   See chapters 3 and 7 for other aspects of this case.

(Figes 2007). After a period of propagating women's emancipation in the postwar years, the regimes in both Bulgaria and Romania developed strong pro-natalist policies where the role of family was paramount (Brunnbauer 2007; Kligman 1998). The results of these efforts were so ambiguous that some authors tend to regard family and private life as a site of resistance to the state's attempts to fully colonise society (Brunnbauer and Kaser 2001). Summarising her observations in the later years of Romanian socialism, Verdery found that retirees had key roles in the daily lives of their families: taking children to and from school; cooking; queuing for products; doing small repairs in the house; maintaining kin networks, etc. These turned out to be so important for the functioning of the households that she concluded that social reproduction was 'geriatrized' (Verdery 1996, 65). Similar processes could be observed in Bulgaria as well (Iliev 2001). One way or another, state policies allowed for a wide stripe of traditional views and practices (including those related to religion) to remain within family life and to be passed down between generations. Florina referred to these when she remembered how her in-laws did not celebrate her civil wedding. For them, it was not the 'real' one. She affirmed the values inherited in the family, presenting herself as tradition-bound, although not a believer: 'And we kept Easter, Christmas, I mean all the traditions in the house. Always, we would cook what we had to, what the tradition was, it was respected.'

The traditions she speaks about are not necessarily associated with the faith community but rather with the continuity of generations in the family. The memorable moments of her childhood also appear to be family celebrations of holidays, but not the church Holy days *per se*:

> Holidays. Easter and Christmas. These were more important. ... A special moment in our family was when my father's brothers came. A great table was prepared then with all his brothers and we children tried to mingle but they wouldn't let us stay too long.

Parents and family remained important in her adult life. Being together, helping aged parents was a duty of grown-up children: 'We went very often to the region they were from, and automatically we became closer. We still met with our parents on holidays, on Christmas, on Easter.' As she has aged, family seems to have become even more important for Florina, presumably as a consequence of her withdrawal from other social roles after retirement:

> Thus, the family is the only satisfaction you can afford. Coming from your kin ... Maybe, when I was younger, I was also making plans, in the long run, because it is normal to make plans when you're young. But, now, I'm afraid I think more about how when I will be no more, that it should not be more difficult for the others to live without me. They should deal with it calmly and not suffer from it.

It is in the context of this family bond that Florina has stuck to religious rituals. When specifically asked, she found it difficult to explain. On the one hand, these were festive occasions, where '[p]eople always look for something to get them out of the ordinary'. On the other hand, there seems to have been something more than sheer festivity, something related to the continuity of the family. This is how she struggled to explain sticking to church ceremonies without believing:

> Well, because we knew that all of the children, in our family, they were baptised also. Never, you know … There are some things, I don't know, that run in your blood, you know? You can't, how could you?

Florina was not an exception in this respect. Other interviewees, including some who declared themselves non-religious, offered similar explanations for their opting for church ceremonies. Like Florina's, these explanations most often do not suggest previous contemplation of the issue:

> I could say this is more a question of family tradition? For if this is how it was in the family and the majority I was connected with, let's say in the same age group, they could not … Maybe out of tradition, especially, or the family tradition they could not forget … this is what I think. (Ion Cotescu, Bucharest)

> And especially their parents insisted on keeping these traditions, arguing that it is the right way … (Mirela Dinescu, Bucharest)

> They [parents] always observed traditions. In the past people always observed traditions. Always. (Valentina, Shumen)

In other cases, the interviewees thought of family members' rites of passage as festive occasions, family get-togethers, and associated them with parties, rather than ceremonies:

> [wedding] All brothers came and they made a beautiful party. My father was doing some delicious pickles in cask. (Miron Popescu, Bucharest)

> Like any wedding – with guests and a restaurant. Many, many guests attended, the restaurant was packed. (Alexandra, Sofia)

> They wanted the photographic opportunity and there it was and we strolled round the grounds afterwards and took photographs. (Lewis, Southampton, about grandson's church wedding)

> The whole family was present. Uncle Boris, uncle Atanas, uncle Vanyo. And auntie Nadka, she's still alive, we saw each other the previous day, and my mother. (Diman Vasilev, Sofia)

In these cases, religious rites seem to have lost any original aura stemming from their authenticity but have retained an aesthetic and festive appeal, as well as having importance as social events for the family.

Finally, sticking to religious rituals at life transitions seems to reflect a sense of duty towards other members of the family. Florina has buried her parents with Orthodox ceremonies, and she has observed the Orthodox commemoration rites for the dead:

> On holidays, I always think about our dead. … if I don't do it, I feel restless. I mean, it is some kind of obligation for my conscience. And at the same time, a duty. A sign of respect, the fact that I did not forget them, something like that.

Other interviewees also seemed to regard their parents' and family members' religious funerals as a kind of duty towards them and they reported having taken pains to organise these ceremonies in ways they found appropriate:

> I knew that, you know, I'd done my duty kind of thing by doing the right thing by her, mmm, yeah. (Polly, London, about her mother's church funeral)

> She [his mother] really wanted three priests at her funeral, but there weren't three priests there. There was only one when she died, may she rest in peace. I saw a priest outside and I tell him – so and so, a funeral service for my mother, would you take part in it too, because she insisted on having three priests at her funeral; she was very religious, you see, so with you there'll be at least two priests. Ok, he says, and he went somewhere, he took a stole, he put it on and he took part in the service. That's how I buried her. My brother died in Varna; he was buried according to the ritual. That's it. (Evlogi Anastasov, Sofia)

> [husband's funeral] And I did everything, how it's done in Orthodoxy. … The cemetery is away, far away. Also my parents and my brother are there, and I said because of that … I could bury him elsewhere, closer, but I said no. My parents and my brother are there, so what's the point doing otherwise. (Mirela, Bucharest)

Religious rites of passage for family members seem to be important in various ways, some of which have less to do with religious belief than with a 'co-experienced sociality' (Spickard 2005, 338). They not only call forth a mutual recognition of one's joys and sorrows, expressing and reinforcing family solidarity, but also contribute to the construction of the family as a moral community. Describing how they have fulfilled their duties at family members' life transitions, interviewees reconfirm a moral integrity inherited from their ancestors as a source of stability in the face of change during their lives. This longing for social continuity is more salient in Romania and Bulgaria, where interviewees belong to the generation that lived though unprecedented urbanisation, modernisation and secularisation with an ensuing impoverishment of ritual. While rural–urban migration implied a loss of tradition, family as a moral community was seen as a site of tradition and stability.

'This is who we are': Cultural Memory and Identity

A number of interviewees seem to relate to their religious rituals not only as family traditions but also as a form of cultural heritage. They present religion as a tradition that is part of their ethnic or national identity. Thus rituals acquire a sense of relating as much (or less) to God as to one's cultural background. This form of identification seems more salient amongst minority ethnic members: Jews from London and Bucharest and Bulgarian Turks refer to their religious rituals – both everyday (prayers, food restrictions) and rites of passage (circumcision, bar mitzvah, weddings, funerals) – as part and parcel of their culture. It is interesting, however, that many Orthodox Bulgarians and Orthodox Romanians, unlike most of the UK interviewees, often mention tradition or custom when they speak about religious rituals:

> I was not a believer. But it was a custom. I mean I cared for respecting these customs. (Florina, Bucharest)

> But wait – what does a religious holiday mean? Good Lord, to us this is a custom. This is a tradition. No one can say it's his or her own. Neither pagans, nor priests. (Diman, Sofia)

Andon Igov is a typical case.[11] He declared himself a 'religious Christian', born into a religious family in 1923. His religiosity was, however, intricately linked with his perspective on tradition, itself a 'red thread' in his self-presentation. He graduated from the Naval School and served as a marine officer during the last months of the Second World War. Dismissed from the army on political grounds immediately after the war, he took odd jobs as an unskilled worker until he met a former schoolmate who had become navigation director of a foreign-trade enterprise. This person helped him to get a job in the merchant fleet. When the enterprise was closed down, he became captain of an ocean fishing ship. The greater part of his story is about his younger years and the sharp turn of his life after the communist takeover in 1944. In this context, his references to religion and tradition throughout the interview acquired a complex and multilayered meaning with political overtones. Traditions were related to what he approvingly called the 'patriarchal values'[12] of his parents' family and the society of that time:

---

[11]   See also Chapter 10.

[12]   In Andon's usage, as in most of common parlance in Bulgaria, 'partiarchal' does not have the connotation implied by contemporary feminism. Rather, it is a synonym of 'traditional' as against 'modern', the latter often associated with state socialism.

At that time patriarchal values were above everything else, this was the most important thing. We'd go to church, fast – not only in the family but also at school. ... We'd always go to receive communion in new shoes, new clothes – the tradition has it.

Andon tried to stick to these values during his life in spite of all changes. He openly prayed to God during a gale and his subaltern did not denounce him. However, he was questioned by the party secretary of the Marine about his son's 'Christian' name and explained that it was a combination of the two grandfathers' names, following the tradition to name a child after a grandparent.[13] Since church attendance was forbidden in Bulgaria, he used to visit churches abroad. Now he is pleased to be able to openly practise, again referring to his religious practice as tradition: 'I go to church every Sunday, I keep going to church on Sunday, I observe this tradition'.

Here, the interviewee appears to be reproducing the position of the later communist establishment, where 'tradition' was used as a euphemism to refer to popular religious or quasi-religious practices, undesired but still tolerated because they were considered to be dying out. Conversely, traditional creative practices that were to be encouraged were branded 'folklore', which was a state-organised and state-sponsored activity (Kaneff 2004). Other moments of Andon's narrative, however, point to his broader notion of tradition as regulating the relations between persons and statuses and constituting the normality of pre-socialist society:

Besides, at that time the rank of the military officer was really respected, it was something prestigious. This was a society that was respected, these people had traditions, they observed these traditions – honour, luxury, conduct.

Religiosity appears as an integral part of this broadly conceived tradition and is therefore constitutive of the interviewee's idea of a pristine 'natural' state of the social world:

So we all feared God because it was part of our upbringing. These were our patriarchal values. At that time we didn't feel, we didn't understand, we didn't criticise – we knew this God, we got up with Him, my grandfather, my mother – the icon lamp was always lit ... this unobtrusive, this natural, natural – in a traditional way – creed and religiosity, it was present all the time. I don't know and I can't remember anybody who was negative about religion, at least in my milieu.

---

[13] The name was Hristiyan, a combination of 'Hristo' (Christo) and 'Yanko'. However, the interviewee claimed that the real reason for picking this name was that the child was born at Christmas.

Thus religion, practised in its 'traditional way', appears to be equated with an order in life and society that was reversed by the communist regime. It is very important for the interviewee to identify with that earlier, 'traditional' order as against the abrupt changes that followed in his life. So tradition (and religion as part of it) seems to be a key narrative resource to achieve the coherence of the life story, and maybe also a psychological resource to cope with radical changes across the life course.

Finally, when Andon talks about his son's marriage, tradition links to a historical world and a national identity. To be able to marry in church, the future bride was baptised first, which was kept secret from her parents, who were communists ('more narrow-minded, they've forgotten our traditions'). Approvingly, Andon cites his son's purported ultimatum to his future wife: 'I won't have a civil marriage only, I won't neglect the traditions of our family and of us as Bulgarians – if you don't get baptised, we won't get married'.

Even if his son may not have been so categorical about his church wedding, what is important here is the direct link between family and nation. Andon sees Christianity as an aspect of a Bulgarian identity. This notion can surely be interpreted as a 'longing to belong' – a quest for collective identities as providers of secure and stable we-feelings to cope with insecurity. What is noteworthy is that the construction of this collective identity implies that life choices are governed by belonging to a national collective defined by its cultural memory. Thus the spiritual community of Christian believers overlaps with the nation.

The cases of 'Orthodox atheists' discussed in Chapter 3 are quite similar in terms of how a person relates to religion. Although Andon's case does not fully correspond to Bădică's 'belonging without believing' model – because he is a believer and a church-goer, at least in his later life, it illustrates a perspective on religion as a source of identification with an earthly 'symbolic community' rather than (or not only) a spiritual one. Of course, this can be attributed to a presumed Orthodox traditionalism (Tomka 2006)[14] or the tendency to comprehend Orthodoxy – owing to historical and political factors – not only as religion but also as national and cultural identity. However, the interviews with members of ethnic and religious minorities in all three countries suggest that the feeling of belonging to a larger collectivity acquired from ethnicity and/or religion and enacted in rituals is important for them also as a way of self-identification vis-à-vis other groups:

> that's the tradition, that's what it's like in Moldova. (Tina Cotrus, Cluj)

> The Orthodox can't stand them! They consider that it's a form of dissidence and that they're holding them back. ... and the entire course of life in Romania would have been different if we had been Catholics, like we were in the beginning. (Emil Tatu, Cluj)

---

[14]   The thesis of the stronger link between Orthodoxy and traditionalism has been criticised on empirical grounds. See Flere (2008).

We might go to the synagogue, which we did, – there's something about going to the synagogue, whether you're religious or not – for me. (Barbara, London)

Circumcision is a surgical operation, that's it, there's no religious, it's traditional, customary, carried on from the Arab tradition, Islam has accepted it. (Sunjay Sarvar, London)

Sylvia Jones, a Catholic in the UK, does not challenge this identity resource, but prioritises the universal aims of different religious traditions:

a religious person is somebody that has some, is following a tradition, whether it's Hinduism or Muslim, you know, to make the world a better place that is a tradition which gives you some feeling of awe and worship and gratitude for, you know, what you're given, and try to bring goodness.

Thus, while the tendency towards 'believing without belonging' – a more critical, individualistic and discursive attitude which renders rituals less important – might be a fact,[15] there are also cases that exemplify another model where collectivist and performative dimensions are central, and consequently rituals seem not to have lost their importance. Furthermore, this case seems to justify approaches that view religion as cultural tradition. As Hervieu-Léger has argued, 'there is no religion without the explicit, semi-explicit, or entirely implicit invocation of *the authority of a tradition*, an invocation that serves as support for the act of believing' (Hervieu-Léger 2008, 256, emphasis in the original).

Conclusion

This chapter addresses questions that have emerged during the research: the relatively infrequent thematisation of rituals, the perception of their immutability and the continuing attraction of religious rituals for individuals who do not consider themselves religious. I have tried to make sense of these findings first in the context of the interview: as lacunae in the discourse of familiarity and as results of the negotiation of the agenda between the interview partners. Next, I have discussed the interplay of social norms, cultural models and personal meanings in the continuing uses of religious rituals in situations of diminishing religiosity. I thus approached rituals from the perspective of the individuals who have performed them. Although the focus on ritual foregrounds social rather than personal aspects, the RASC project was interested primarily in individuals' motivations, interpretations and attitudes related to the performance of religious or secular rituals, especially those that mark life transitions. The question was

---

[15]   See Pollack (2003) for empirical evidence interpreted as a tendency towards individualisation of religious belief in 11 Central and East European countries.

why religious rituals retain their importance even when they have lost their relation to a transcendent Power. Exploring it, I have identified three overlapping types of semantic shifts in ritual activities/attitudes. They roughly point to three forms of social normativity. Conformity exhibits an unarticulated moral ethos ('this is how it's done') and is generally not reflected upon. Solidarity with the immediate we-group and responsibility for its members ('doing the right thing') refers to a conscious moral imperative, while belonging to/identification with a larger community ('this is who we are') reveals an ideology redirecting religious experience to a broader cultural tradition.

The cases come from different countries but can by no means be taken to represent attitudes 'typical' of the respective country. To prevent such interpretation, I have looked for evidence in the interviews of the existence of all forms of normativity in the three countries. While the contrasts between the countries at the level of the social and political roles of religions and churches seem obvious, it appears that, at the micro level, as far as individual attitudes and everyday practices are concerned, differences and similarities lie *across* national borders. There are important commonalities in the ways elders from the three countries relate to challenges of later life, such as deteriorating health, bereavement and solitude.[16] There are also commonalities in the ways social normativity works for them. For this generation, it seems that being useful for others is more important than being true to oneself. To make the picture even more complex, it seems that similar behaviours can be the result of different religious 'economies' – the one, of 'religious market', implying choice, and the other, of 'public utility', implying tradition (Davie 2006, 293).

Sharing the assumption that religious beliefs are based on much more than intellectual convictions, that they are matters as much of the 'heart' as of the 'head' (Coleman et al. 2011, 162), I have focused on the diffuse social normativity that requires participation in rituals. Thus rites of passage have appeared to be social conventions rather than – or in addition to being – purely religious practices. That is, it seems that major life events require ceremonial markers in terms of social and psychological needs, not necessarily in religious terms. Rites of passage then relate not only to a religious framework but also to a fairly structured and predictable life course.[17]

Viewing rites of passage as both a religious and a social convention seems to support Davie's thesis of the vicariousness of religion, at least in one of its aspects. According to it, religious rituals are conducted by a minority of 'specialists' on behalf of the majority whenever necessary. They 'maintain *vicariously* the rituals from which a larger population can draw when the occasion demands it' (Davie 2006, 279) and be available as a choice. The idea of vicarious religion implies

---

[16]   See chapters 8–11.

[17]   Their waning then may be interpreted as evidence of the de-standardisation of the life course in the conditions of 'high modernity' as described by Beck (1986) and Giddens (1991).

a possibility of severing the ritual action from its religious meaning. As was hypothesised above, it is the performance of the ritual that is important in such cases, rather than its content. To put it in phenomenological terms, 'shared time-structures can be independent of shared meaning-structures, and experience is not necessarily limited to the latter' (Spickard 2005, 338–9). If this is the case, then the 'truth value' of rituals is not the important one. As Seligman has suggested, the 'meaning' of rituals emerges in their performance: 'Ritual, therefore, is inherently meaning-producing, but it does not produce a meaning that can be analyzed as a coherent system of beliefs about something else. … The meaning of ritual is the meaning produced through the ritual action itself' (Seligman 2010, 14). Thus it is as legitimate to view ritual in terms of its performative nature as in terms of its denotative meaning. With this change of perspective, the fact that religious rituals are performed without a deep understanding of or adherence to their 'authentic' meaning will not necessarily point to a trivialisation or demise of ritual. According to Seligman, rituals of any kind contribute to the creation of a shared 'subjunctive universe' (Seligman 2010, 10) making interactions possible. Since a subjunctive ('as if') world may be illusory but is not a lie, ritual performances cannot be judged in terms of truth, authenticity and sincerity, as might be tacitly implied by the believing-without-belonging hypothesis. Therefore, accommodating religious rituals in secular lives will not necessarily be either evidence of belief or evidence of deceit.

References

Austin, John. 1975. *How To Do Things With Words*, 2nd edn. Oxford: Oxford University Press

Beck, Ulrich. 1986. *Risikogesellschaft. Auf dem Weg in eine andere Moderne*. Frankfurt am Main: Suhrkamp.

Bourdieu, Pierre. 1977. *Outline of a Theory of Practice*. Cambridge: Cambridge University Press.

Brunnbauer, Ulf. 2007. *'Die sozialistische Lebensweise'. Ideologie, Gesellschaft, Familie und Politik in Bulgarien (1944–1989)*. Wien: Böhlau.

Brunnbauer, Ulf and Karl Kaser (eds) 2001, *Vom Nutzen der Verwandten. Soziale Netzwerke in Bulgarien (19. und 20. Jahrhundert)*. Wien: Böhlau Verlag.

Coleman, Peter et al. 2011. *Belief and Ageing: Spiritual Pathways in Later Life*. Bristol: Policy Press.

Conway, Martin. 1995. *Flashbulb Memories*. Hillsdale NJ: Lawrence Erlbaum.

Davie, Grace, 2006. 'Religion in Europe in the 21st Century: The Factors to Take into Account'. *Archives Européennes de Sociologie/European Journal of Sociology* 47(2): 271–96.

Douglas, Mary. 2003 [1970]. *Natural Symbols*. London: Routledge.

Elenkov, Ivan. 2009. 'Kam vaprosa za vavezhdaneto na traurnia ritual i socialisticheskata praznichno-obredna sistema u nas 1969–1971' ['On the

Question of the Introduction of the Mourning Ritual and the Socialist Festive and Ritual System in this Country 1969–1971']. *Hristianstvo i kultura* 7(42): 88–99.

Figes, Orlando. 2007. *The Whisperers: Private Life in Stalin's Russia*. London: Allen Lane.

Flere, Sergej. 2008. 'Questioning the Need for a Special Methodology for the Study of Eastern Orthodoxy'. *Social Compass* 55(1): 84–100.

Geertz, Clifford. 1973. *The Interpretation of Cultures*. New York: Basic Books.

Giddens, Anthony. 1991. *Modernity and Self-Identity: Self and Society in the Late Modern Age*. Oxford: Polity Press.

Hervieu-Léger, Danièle. 2008. 'Religion as Memory: Reference to Tradition and the Constitution of a Heritage of Belief in Modern Societies'. In *Religion: Beyond a Concept*, edited by Hent de Vries, 245–58. New York: Fordham University Press.

Iliev, Ilia. 2001. 'Familie, Ideologie und Politik: Die Grossmutter in der stadtischen Familie nach 1945'. In *Vom Nutzen der Verwandten. Soziale Netzwerke in Bulgarien (19. und 20. Jahrhundert)*, edited by Ulf Brunnbauer and Karl Kaser, 89–114. Wien: Böhlau Verlag.

Kaneff, Deema. 2004. *Who Owns the Past? The Politics of Time in a 'Model' Bulgarian Village*. New York: Berghahn Books.

Kligman, Gail. 1998. *The Politics of Duplicity: Controlling Reproduction in Ceausescu's Romania*. Berkeley, CA: University of California Press.

Mellor, Philip A. and Chris Shilling. 2010. 'The Religious Habitus: Embodiment, Religion, and Sociological Theory'. In *The New Blackwell Companion to the Sociology of Religion*, edited by Bryan S. Turner, 201–20. Oxford: Wiley-Blackwell.

Neitz, Mary Jo. 2004. 'Gender and Culture: Challenges to the Sociology of Religion'. *Sociology of Religion* 65(4; Special Issue: Culture and Constraint in the Sociology of Religion): 391–402.

Niethammer, Lutz. 1988. 'Annäherung an der Wandel. Auf der Suche nach der volkseigenen Erfahrung in der Industrieprovinz der DDR'. *BIOS. Zeitschrift fuer Biographieforschung und Oral History* 1: 19–66.

Pollack, Detlef. 2003. 'Religiousness Inside and Outside the Church in Selected Post-Communist Countries of Central and Eastern Europe'. *Social Compass* 50(3): 321–34.

Rosaldo, Renato. 1986. 'Ilongot Hunting as Story and Experience'. In *The Anthropology of Experience*, edited by Victor W. Turner and Edward M. Bruner, 97–138. Champaign, IL: University of Illinois Press.

Sbornik normativni aktove, primerni scenarii i slova za grazhdanskite rituali. 1975 [*Handbook of Regulations, Model Scenarios and Speeches for Civil Rituals*]. Sofia.

Seligman, Adam B. 2010. 'Ritual and Sincerity: Certitude and the Other'. *Philosophy and Social Criticism* 36(1): 9–39.

Sered, Susan Starr. 1993. 'Religious Rituals and Secular Rituals: Interpenetrating Models of Childbirth in a Modern, Israeli Context'. *Sociology of Religion* 54: 101–14.

Spickard, James V. 2005. 'Ritual, Symbol, and Experience: Understanding Catholic Worker House Masses'. *Sociology of Religion* 66(4): 337–57.

Tomka, Miklos. 2006. 'Is Conventional Sociology of Religion able to Deal with Differences between Eastern and Western European Developments?' *Social Compass* 53(2): 251–65.

Verdery, Katherine. 1996. *What Was Socialism and What Comes Next?* Princeton, NJ: Princeton University Press.

PART III
Death and Loss

Chapter 7

Personal Ideologies of Death: Shaping the (Post)Self in Rituals

Galina Goncharova

In her recent commentaries on the current agenda of the sociology of religion, Grace Davie makes an argument for the use of 'global terms' in order to engage with the dominant thesis of the interrelatedness of modernisation and secularisation in Europe. 'Global terms' in her view encompasses the development of the 'historical churches' and the economic and cultural policies in different parts of the continent that underline not only the thematic corpora of scholarly discussions but also 'the presence of religion in the modern world' (Davie 2007, 6). Based on Runciman's methodology and on his notions of 'reportage', 'explanation', 'description' and 'evaluation', Davie presents 'an attempt to describe what it is like for the individuals and groups involved in religious or indeed other activities; in other words seeing what is happening through the eyes of the religious actor' (Davie 2007, 8).[1] I will engage with these methodological challenges, focusing on the construction of (non-)religious identities in the experience of death.

The relevance to Davie's scheme is great. First, I provide a cross-cultural comparison of models of bereavement and care for the dead in three countries with processes of secularisation and desecularisation of different intensity. In the UK, for example, the ceremonies of secular humanists – gradually gaining popularity – provided reasons for scholars to talk about the privatisation and emancipation of death from church authority as early as the 1990s (Walter 1994). Yet Davie points to the fact that, not only in the UK but also in other European countries, stable practices of Christian burial continue to exist, suggesting that 'Europeans are not so much less religious than populations in other parts of the world' (Davie 2002, 19). No less contradictory is the picture of religious beliefs related to death in Bulgaria and Romania. With the decay and fall of the communist regime and its propaganda of scientific atheism, both countries are experiencing an upsurge of religiosity and of religious practices, including Christian rites of passage: baptisms, church weddings and funeral ceremonies. However, there are differences. If in Romania 'to die Orthodox' means to reaffirm one's national identity,[2] in Bulgaria religious

---

[1]   In comparison, Runciman (1983, 85) speaks about 'the intentions and beliefs of the agents themselves as they reported themselves'.

[2]   See Chapter 3.

prescriptions have loose interpretations that are being adapted to suit the personal visions of relatives accompanying the deceased to their last resting place.

The second resemblance to Davie's agenda is – to paraphrase her words – in the description of what it is like for individuals and groups to be religious in death. The main tool here is the notion of personal ideologies of death that combine existential meanings of mourning and the social roots of religious ideas about end-of-life and after-life. This bridging mostly implies a dense description of certain macro- and micro-contexts of death, from the grand social change reflected in burial ceremonies (such as, for example, the revitalisation of interest in religion in Eastern Europe after the fall of the communist regime) to the personal, intimate and emotional memory of deceased loved ones.

Last but not least, my research combines oral history with gerontological perspectives. An intersection between the two approaches is Robert Butler's (1963) concept of life review, which shares common features with the life story as a recapitulation of one's life. The maintenance of this double perspective allows the variations of religiosity to link with the rethinking of death in the course of ageing and with circumstances such as family background, status attainment and social mobility.

This chapter aims to show how personal visions of the end of life and the after-life are anchored in a complex, dynamic integrity of cultural practices, social networks and religious or non-religious worldviews. The analysis uncovers the pursuit of self-fulfillment and social recognition hidden behind expressions of (non-)belief as well as influences coming from certain cultural models of mourning.

Stories about the loss of loved ones are discussed in the context of the postmodern quest for the privatisation of death rituals and interest in religious practices in post-socialist countries. Finally, the analysis goes back to individual experience, focusing on the encounter of intimate fears of bodily decay with religious identity expressed in the desire for cremation by interviewees who claim to stick to Orthodox traditions. This shift of attention to the interiorisation of collective norms of dying contributes to a deeper understanding of the (dis)integrative effects of personal ideologies of death on self-knowledge and of the dynamics of secularisation in the private space.

Strong Ideologies of Death: The Cases of Ivanka, Harold and Florina

How do we experience, reflect on and talk about death? What are the basic moments of comprehension within the frameworks of a personal worldview and of collective practice?

Most of the RASC project interviewees articulated their experience of death in similar ways. First, they had to answer some broadly formulated questions that influenced the order of their remembering. Second, they were encouraged to share memories of funerals and commemorations of the dead, how they bore the loss of relatives, how they prepared themselves for the end of life and what ideas they had about the after-life. Some interviewees talked extensively about funerals and graveyards, while others focused on intimate expressions of mourning. Of interest here are cases where the practices of bereavement are quintessential for the reaffirmation or denial of a particular value system and where these practices have an integrative effect on knowledge about oneself and, therefore, on the (re) construction of social identities. The strength of 'personal ideologies of death' is evident also in the structure of the life stories. The interviewees frame their life accounts as meaningful in response to encounters with death. Such are the cases of Ivanka Grozdeva, Harold Stevenson and Florina Campeanu. What is common in their experience is the loss of loved ones, overcome only after their (dis)attachment to religious belief which, in its turn, stimulates the development of new social competences and cognitive paradigms later in life.

Ivanka Grozdeva[3] is a 73-year-old woman from Targovishte (a provincial town in north-east Bulgaria), who is a retired librarian. At the age of 27 Ivanka lost first husband in a work accident. Even though she married again a few years later, she confessed, when speaking of her first husband, that: 'Up till today no one has replaced him'. Well acquainted with the Orthodox rituals, after her husband passed away, she began to commit herself to them with a passion that made her a fervent believer. After her retirement she dedicated herself entirely to caring for the 'souls of the dead' and to the 'salvation' of those among the living who were near death. She wrote many mourning services for them, and visited numerous ill seniors with spiritual support, explaining the basic tenets of the Orthodox faith.

Harold Stevenson is an 85-year-old former mathematics teacher. He defines himself as an atheist and supporter of Darwin's evolutionary theory. He reached these conclusions after a period of intensive search for religious meaning. At the age of two he was informally adopted by two women who belonged to the Church of England. They gave him a full religious education, prayers at night time, regular church attendance, etc. He went to two Catholic schools, then a Quaker school and joined the Student Christian Movement; he also took theology classes at university. In the course of time, Harold withdrew from Christianity and, at the age of 55, he embraced the cause of secular humanism. He explains his withdrawal from religion as being due to the formality of religious funerals. Harold mentioned several times how downhearted he felt after the funeral service for one of his adopted mothers because, 'It just went through the rigmarole of the prayer book and no mention of what they'd done or what they'd achieved in life and that sort of thing'. He experienced the same negative emotions about his brother's Catholic funeral when the priest turned down his nephew's request to say some words in memory of his father. Harold is currently very active as a secular humanist and he regularly leads secular ceremonies, including the naming of children, weddings and funerals.

Florina Campeanu is an 82-year-old retired teacher of chemistry and a former headteacher of a technical high school in Bucharest. Her parents respected

---

[3]   For this case see also Chapter 8.

Orthodox traditions but were not regular church-goers. Similarly, Florina observed religious holidays and rites of passage throughout her life as something self-evident 'that runs in your blood'. The deaths of her brother, father and husband occupy an important place in her memories. Despite the fact that she did not remember details of those funerals, she clearly articulated the traumatic experience of such ceremonies. From her husband's funeral Florina remembered the carrying of the body to the chapel and how 'the priests asked me if he had been read the books, as if I knew what they meant. It was the loss of her partner, which happened at her retirement, that Florina mentioned as the most difficult moment in her life. Afterwards she began to pray and to reflect on the question of God's existence.

The Construction of Social Identity and Cognitive Paradigms in Terms of Belief and Non-belief

Contrary to the widespread idea of bereavement as a negative state or period that disconnects individuals from their routine and attacks their mental balance, some contemporary social-constructivist theories of mourning make sense of the period as an opportunity for the reformulation of important existential meanings that ultimately has a positive impact on the re-socialisation of the individual. According to Niemeyer, 'the central process of grieving is the attempt to reaffirm or reconstruct a world of meaning that has been challenged by loss' (Neimeyer 1998, 110), while Attig (1996) talks about 'relearning the world'.

The cases of Ivanka and Harold illustrate how the loss of a spouse or authoritative parent triggers important transformations in a personal belief system and consequently brings new social roles for the individual. For Ivanka, mourning strengthened her religious identity. Even though she claimed to be strictly Orthodox all of her life, her life history shows that the experience of bereavement was a turning point in the strong interiorisation of Orthodox values. She spoke about having a 'mustard grain of faith' since childhood, but her regular visits to churches appeared to start after her husband's death. Further, her memories about her life before the accident lacked any religious meaning; these were stories about first love, university admission, etc. Once her husband passed away everything changed. Most of her days were occupied with religious activities such as regularly visiting monasteries, leading memorial services, conducting requiems, lighting candles in the nearest church and performing her present role of advisor and organiser of commemorations for the dead and their preparation for a peaceful after-life.

In terms of religiosity, Harold's example is contrariwise. In his adult life he renounced the religious identity prescribed for him in early childhood. Unlike Ivanka, he reflected more on the changes that affected his religious attachment and was also conscious of the particularly traumatic impact of the funerals of his stepmothers. In the course of the interview he evoked these events more than once, each time emphasising his enormous disappointment with the ritual. Obviously a rationalist – and a mathematician by profession – Harold experimented with different educational systems in order to make sense of Christian dogmas. In a similar way he entered deeper and deeper into secular humanism. He had been trained and had taken non-religious ceremonies for the BHA (British Humanist Association).[4] Even though Ivanka and Harold adopted different approaches to religion, their accounts intersect when it comes to the new social identity that both have acquired late in their lives, namely 'expert in dying'. Both have gained respect as experts in funeral practices in wide social networks and both receive strong satisfaction as well as recognition for the care they invest in the dead. Here Ivanka describes her charity activities:

> Not only did it help me in the past but also it helps me now, my faith. Daughters, grandchildren. This one gets ill, the other one ... – I constantly pay for holy liturgies, holy 40-days memorial service, as soon as I hear that someone has died. I know they'd never think of it themselves. But I go there and I pay for holy 40-days memorial service for the dead. Because it is the dead who are in greatest need of us, the living – to mention them in our prayers.

> I'm happy because I love a lot of people and a lot of people love me too. My love for other people is happiness for me. I'm happy that I was born and I was probably from such a family that I strongly believe in God. It's God who supports me.

Harold also talked with great enthusiasm about joining the secular humanists and shared details of his ceremonial work. No less than Ivanka he was attentive to the funeral topic:

> I've been taking non-religious ceremonies for the BHA. I was trained by them. And not only funerals but weddings and baby namings as well. And there we try to make a funeral a celebration of a life and we allow people to pay tributes from the family and friends and music, whatever they want. There's a structure to it and it's dignified and many people afterwards, including religious people, come over afterwards and say "Well that was a very fitting ceremony" for the person who died.

As is evident from the quotes, Ivanka and Harold explained their deep involvement in ritual activities through the existential choice that they had made between belief and non-belief. Neither of them seemed aware of the pursuit of social recognition embedded in their ideologies of death. As far as Ivanka is concerned, charity became a natural expression of her convictions. In the interview, however, she narrated the traumatic experience of being downgraded in her professional

---

[4]   In the interview he explained that in 2010 he had resigned from this position in order to make way for his younger colleagues.

position at the County Library of Targovishte as a result of her religious beliefs. The decision was taken by the communist director at the time. She was sent back to the children's department where she had started her career. Engaging in charity, Ivanka regained this forcefully suspended authority in another sphere; either as a librarian or as an expert in bereavement rituals, she could act as a consultant to wider audiences.

As for Harold, one could similarly assume that leading secular humanist ceremonies came, on the one hand, as a natural consequence of his earlier professional work, which also satisfied his spiritual need to experiment over the years with different Christian denominations following his early hesitation between theology and mathematics.

Florina's case is the most difficult to interpret because she was still in the process of mourning the loss of her husband, and her personal ideology of death was not finalised:

> The following thing happened to me. When I went through some phenomena, some processes, you know. One might call them, terrible. I don't know how to call them, maybe important. Yes, important, major events, in general. Like the death of Ion.

When asked about mourning, Florina explained the presence of Orthodox feasts and rituals in her life with common – communal, family or national Romanian – respect for traditions. This respect is what 'everyone shares', as a social convention maintained by family and society but without specific Christian content: 'Always we kept it in our lives. We never attached a religious meaning to it. It was a ritual.'

These firm statements are in stark contrast with her hesitation when she commented on topics of faith, the existence of God and the meaning of rituals beyond any social context:

> But I still think there is a higher power. I am not a believer, let's say one that goes to the church and says the rosary. Sometimes I think that if someone would ask me the reason I pray, I don't even know. I pray in my own way. It's more like I would chat with God. But I still think it proper … I don't know why.

Her hesitations, outbursts and the discontinuity in the dialogue reveal a strong and peculiar versatility in Florina's understanding and imagining of her own religiosity. They also reveal an encounter between two different perspectives of religiosity in general. The first perspective does not differentiate religious from social or cultural–ethnic meanings of regular church attendance and public celebrations of turning points in life. The second perspective attributes the power of consolation to the Orthodox commemoration of the dead and recognises in it a transcendent horizon of individual existence: the idea of a higher power that directs lives. This is how two disparate interpretations come into being, distorting or enriching an analysis of the interview. This may be why Florina's hesitation in discussing spiritual topics leads Simina Bădică to conclude that the Romanian context interweaves 'power and pressure',[5] while someone else could see it as a first step towards finding existential meaning in religion. For example Florina's vocation 'to talk with God', which according to Christian theology coincides with the idea of prayer, should not be ignored. Such an interpretation is reinforced by the fact that her account of the 'most difficult moment in life' coexists with reflections on the healing power of prayer, on 'salvation' through children and grandchildren, and with her recall of her marriage with her deceased husband.

Florina's interview is suggestive of the role of religious belief as a developmental phenomenon in later life (Coleman 2010). It seems that the death of her husband and her retirement – which coincided – were not merely followed by a discovery of a 'high power'l these events were successfully processed through her newly adopted view that a 'divine force leads our lives' and 'we cannot have control'. To a large extent this is also true of Ivanka. After the death of her second husband, she began a legal process to change her family name in order to 'remarry her first husband and so to remain in eternity with him'. Her belief in the after-life not only allowed her to anticipate her own death without fear, but also ultimately to overcome the trauma of her husband's death. Ivanka's case could also serve as a powerful argument in favour of the conclusion that higher levels of religiosity amongst senior citizens provide a coping strategy to deal with such existential problems as death anxiety.

Yet how is Harold's case to be approached? He also demonstrated confidence and tranquility in the face of death, based on the idea that 'this is the only life we have and there's no after-life to follow'. His position could fit with the observation that those who are passionate believers or non-believers fear death less in comparison to those with moderately held beliefs (Downey 1984; Daaleman and Dobbs 2010). This interpretation brings us back to the issue of strong personal ideologies of death exemplified in the three cases discussed here. Ivanka's Orthodoxy, Florina's faith and Harold's humanism are three different value orientations which have the same integrative effect on their self-knowledge and participation in social networks in later life. These ideologies, although playing an important role in their social recognition, contribute to their positive assessment of their current lives. Moreover, the very notion of 'ideologies of death' introduces a way to overcome methodologically binary religious–non-religious beliefs and draws relationships between coherent value systems, the handling of bereavement and preparation for death (Coleman 2010; Downey 1984).

---

[5]   See Chapter 3.

Post-mortem Life Review

The RASC interviews provide the possibility of a comparison between the biographical interview and the life review which old people often practice. What these two types of retrospection have in common is an assessment of personal achievements and hardships. The interviewee and the older person are in one and the same situation, both are remembering and giving meaning to events and people important to them. However, in most of the RASC interviews, this assessment is inseparable from the ritual forms of expression of the value of someone's life. As a result of his disappointment with church ceremonies and as a counterpoint to them, Harold developed the secular humanist concept and practice of funerals without a God. His goal was to emphasise the beauty, depth and meaningfulness of each human life. That is why he encouraged relatives and friends to contribute speeches so that the sadness of death could become a 'celebration of life'. Harold's experience thus exemplifies the idea of post-mortem life review with the assessment of a life as a construction of identity through reminiscence of a dead person triggered and structured in a particular way by ritual practices. It corresponds to Butler's (1963) influential concept of life review as a progressive return to the consciousness of past experience in advanced age, with the basic difference that the evaluation of life history does not precede one's own death, but rather accompanies one's involvement in certain mourning activities. For example, the death of a father leads to reflection on a parent's role, and attending the funeral of someone prominent may lead to comparison with one's own achievements.

In addition, the view from old age (again in agreement with Butler) is an important factor inasmuch as it enables a bereavement memory, in which reactions to death and funerals may be preserved. A major moment in this process is the realisation of the irreversibility, completeness and complexity of another's life and the loss of closeness triggering the demarcation of a life trajectory and the celebration of its ending. This is the reason why Ivanka mentioned that she 'felt liberated and free of worries' when praying for her first husband, regaining his surname in order to 'meet' him in the after-life. Kevin Drake, the 'oldest street pastor' in Southampton (as he described himself) directly addressed the role of mourning and funerals as a source of meaningfulness: 'Well I think that the common denominator they all have is that it provides a turning over point if you like and you can't get on with your life until you've finished with the funeral'.

The post-mortem life review has much in common with what death studies term post-selves or posthumous reputations (Shneidman 1995; Leming and Dickinson 2002; Kamerman 2003), the live images that will be left in the memory of the communities where a person had memberships. Within our sample, the UK interviewees express the greatest interest in posthumous reputations, mostly in the context of the funeral. Many of them considered the tributes, speeches and eulogies as the most significant part of the ceremony, because they created a living picture of the deceased person though their achievements, thus transforming grief and triggering reflection on one's own significance and dignity.[6] Matilda Hastings was particularly eloquent in this respect. She belonged to the Church of England and for many years she used to participate in services, playing the organ. Listening to the eulogies she felt truly involved in the funerals:

> And, as the son, he was the best one to do it. But I think it went on for about half an hour [laughing] and it was so interesting and in places very entertaining as well, you know, and you had a little joke here and there. And I thought, "Well I'll remember that, you know, when …". Cos I knew her very well over a long period of time as well and he'd brought in a few things that I could identify with and I've got a, actually I had a copy now, I've got upstairs a copy of his eulogy because it was just so good in that case. But some people do manage to do very good things. I find that very interesting listening to what other people have done.

She was impressed even by the memorial services of people unknown to her, for example the service of the owner of the Southern Town Football Club:

> *Interviewer: So the biography that was read about him was interesting to hear?*
>
> MH: Yes, yes, well it wasn't so much a biography because it was just really him as a man and the short time he'd been – because it was just a year – been there. And it was for the benefit of all the fans and the people who were, you know, the football team were there and all the dignitaries and the mayor and everything like that. (…)
>
> *Interviewer: It makes you think, yeah. Does it – well you think about your own life and your own …?*
>
> MH: Well yes, yes, yes, and sometimes you think "Oh gosh, fancy that person has done all that", you know. And I haven't done anything.

In the UK interviewees' accounts, the post-mortem life review is very often found not only in the eulogies but also in other elements of the scenography of the funeral with the music and flowers. What remains prevalent is attachment to a particular vision of how the individual has to be presented in or after death. Matilda was in complete agreement with her 'lady priest who used to go out of

---

6   For example, Rita Gardner was much in favour of a tribute to the life of the deceased which would say some pleasing words. She would like this for her own funeral. Kate Osborn was impressed by her grandchildren's speeches at her husband's funeral. Kevin similarly had nothing against the tributes which relatives made and he did his best not to change anything 'because it's what they want'. John Cruikshank was happy with his wife's 'good service' because 'he spoke about different things and I think somebody got up and spoke about Hetty and that, you know'.

her way to make sure people had some piece of music which they could, you know, relate to'. So she played Frank Sinatra's 'My Way' with pleasure at a funeral service. Sarah Hazelwood (Church of England) liked the music at her stepfather's funeral and wanted it played at her own funeral service. Negative emotions could also influence the preparation for a dignified celebration of the end of life. Polly Rutherford, for instance, was repulsed by the anonymity of the religious ritual and by the traditional exposure of the dead body. She wanted a secular ceremony for herself because she could not find meaning in 'the ceremony that they provide, these anonymous clergymen, who talk about this person that they've never met, you know, and all the rest of it'. Polly found the costly coffins and hearses that transported the body to the church unacceptable. She was also not keen on the idea of using the services of undertakers 'living at the corner next door'. All that Polly wanted was for her family to take entire care of her funeral and to cremate her in a recycled coffin.

These last examples show that the post-mortem life review is indispensable to a personal ethos and worldview, and as such is an integrative part of personal ideologies of death. A common trend that could be observed in the UK interviews is the desire to include a flavour of the person, that is, the individualisation of death through personalising the religious ritual with music and eulogies or even through a complete divorce from it, as in the cases of Harold and Polly. Perhaps the most curious example of this tendency is Jennifer Renwick's idea of burial in a pet cemetery.

By contrast, personalisation does not imply neglecting or undermining religious beliefs and prescriptions in the Bulgarian and Romanian cases. On the contrary, there is a strong attachment to Orthodox rituals with no reflection on or narrative of the biography of the deceased. In addition, the Bulgarian and Romanian interviews rarely report any desire for a civil funeral and generally other rituals are emphasised more than the ceremony. As in the cases of Florina and Ivanka, saying prayers, lighting candles and conducting memorial services are interpreted as a duty to the deceased's loved ones and a sign of respect for their post-self. No wonder that 91-year-old Dimana Dimova, who had observed Orthodox traditions since childhood, put funeral candles and incense on the list of things needed for her funeral, along with clothes. These items are the visual expressions of relatives' care for the after-life of the deceased.

What conclusions could be drawn from the absence of a critique of the religious funeral, of an aspiration for humanisation and personalisation of the ritual message in the Romanian and the Bulgarian cases? Are these two radically different experiences of individualisation in death that might eventually correspond to different collective attitudes towards the religious rites of passage?

Grief Systems in Three Contexts of Secularisation

The choice between a religious and secular ceremony, between eulogies and prayers, should also be understood in relation to the norms and meanings of mourning that reflect the impact of historical and cultural changes shaping individual experience. This broad cultural background of personal encounters with death could be defined as a grief system or 'rituals, local cultures and discourses that shape the significance of loss within human communities' (Neiymeyer et al. 2002, 237; see also Walter 1999). Hence, what remains perhaps beyond the interviewees' awareness but demonstrates differences in the rituals aimed at unlocking and preserving memory of the deceased are the specific historical dynamics of grief systems.

In the interviews discussed so far, one significant difference between the Anglican and the Orthodox funerals was specifically noted. The former include 'a personal section, reflecting on the person's life and their role in the Christian church'[7] as well as a poem or a passage from the Bible. The Orthodox funeral, similarly to the Catholic, does not include such a section, which explains why the Romanian and Bulgarian interviewees do not problematise posthumous reputations.

Religious traditions and normativity related to death and dying could also be seen in the light of the processes of secularisation in the three countries. Walter, declares that 'the revival of death' in contemporary Western society accompanied the secularisation or the replacement of 'the old authorities – whether the church, the tradition or duty – by the authority of the individual self' (Walter 1994, 27). The UK case is exemplary in this respect. The media provide plenty of evidence of the secularisation of the national grief system. One widely discussed topic is the so-called Modern British Funeral,[8] which the website 'My last song' represents as: 'a mixture of secular and religious music and readings; greater participation of family and friends in reading tributes, specially written poems, contributing live informal dress code and colourful eco-friendly coffins and caskets'.[9] Secular funerals in the UK as a whole contain the same sections and elements, but they are not organised in a Christian (Jewish, Muslim, etc.) structure and are not charged with religious meanings. They are actively promoted by humanists, who developed a network of trained and accredited celebrants as an alternative to the church authorities and priests as advocates of common human values. The celebrants plan the funeral in full accordance with the ideas and the desires of the family and friends without

---

[7]   See http://www.bbc.co.uk/religion/religions/christianity/ritesrituals/funerals.shtml (accessed 21 January 2012).

[8]   Grace Davie termed it 'a mixed economy funeral', giving the example of Princess Diana's funeral (Davie 2006, 278).

[9]   See http://www.mylastsong.com (accessed 21 January 2012).

any guidance and help from outside. For example, an article in the *Guardian*[10] newspaper tells the story of a funeral of a 'Jewish atheist' woman, organised by her brother with loving concern for the personality of the deceased and a healthy sense of humour. The author's desire for a 'kind of validation' to be given 'to all of us who want to live and die as non-believers' almost directly corresponds to the ceremonies of the humanists.

The tendency to modernise and personalise funerals in the UK is clearly reflected in the interviews, with comments on speeches and music, rejection of the anonymity of the prayer corpus and original and provocative scenographies. The interviews also provide evidence of complex and multiple changes in mourning practices. Confirmation and repudiation of the classical Anglican funeral coexist. On the one hand is the recognition of the modern funeral with the endearing words of the relatives and Frank Sinatra's music (Sarah and Matilda), and on the other the ceremony 'without God' and without undertakers or any interference from outside the family (Harold and Polly).

In post-communist Bulgaria and Romania a radically different revaluation or reinvention of the traditional grief system is emerging. The Romanian and especially Bulgarian communist elites supported the propaganda of Marxist–Leninist 'scientific atheism' and tried to control religious beliefs and rituals, including those related to death and dying. Meanings were revised in accordance with the concept of the individual as a collective being who achieves full meaningfulness only through contributing to socialist construction and the triumph of the proletariat. Where religious practices were preserved, their symbolic content went through specific transformations in line with the dominant ideology. In Bulgaria state-sponsored institutions conducting secular funerals (as well as marriages and the naming of babies) appeared as early as the end of the 1940s (Metodiev 2010; Elenkov 2009). Their structure was similar to the ceremonies of the secular humanists: a trained ritual clerk made a speech and turned the music on and off, etc. The major difference was that personalisation was only superficial since they followed a scenario that the relatives could not compose or change. As Anastasia Pashova noted in a semi-ironic fashion, 'the only thing which differentiated the deceased was the date of birth, the date of death, his status in the labour and social collective and those were all the significant things to be said about him/her' (Pashova 2006, 335).

The secular funeral in Bulgaria went through different phases of popularity and acceptance. In 1970 a report to the Central Committee of the Bulgarian Communist Party claimed that 80–90 per cent of funerals were still religious; however, other estimates suggest that in early 1980s religious and secular funerals comprised around 50 per cent each (Elenkov 2009). The influential folklorist Todor Iv. Zhivkov reported at a national conference in 1981 the alarming adoption of eclectic versions of the funeral ceremony:

---

[10]   From 9 May 2011; see http://www.guardian.co.uk/commentisfree/2011/may/09/ my-sister-wanted-godless-funeral?INTCMP=SRCH (accessed 21 January 2012).

> The most difficult problem is the one with the funeral rites. The present practice shows a variety of versions which would not have been troubling if it wasn't a variety not only in the form but also in the content of the rite. Even the absence of church representatives does not always deprive the rite of religious meaning. Not to mention that the rite is divided – the formal part is secular and the informal part (the transportation of the deceased to the grave, their placing in the grave, etc.) is religious ... Obviously we need a differentiated approach here but in any case we have to do away with the Christian and the Muslim burial in Bulgaria and the funeral itself has to become an entirely secular rite. (Zhivkov 1981, 150)

With the fall of the communist regime, the tendency of rediscovering religious frameworks for life-course and death experiences was reinforced. If, in the 1950s, secular funerals were a novelty or an encroachment on local habits, after 1989 they became a negative symbol of the communist regime. This is another possible explanation as to why Bulgarian interviewees did not discuss music and speeches at the secular funerals they had attended. Only very few among them, such as Tanya Teneva, a professed anti-communist, discussed the ritual promoted by the communist elites:

> Now I'll tell you. The funerals – there was no burial service. There could be one only if you wanted. And then they introduced this ritual funeral, which consisted of ... the speeches of the comrades. My aunt, since she had a communist husband who didn't work at all and my father provided for them and well, afterwards, he became a big guy ... When her husband died I was pregnant with Cyril in 1968, I didn't go to the funeral but when we went to the memorial service a year after my dad came and said out loud to my mum: "No candles, nothing. Those screwed Pharisees at the funeral. Gathered those parasites, the communistars there."

While religious knowledge existed semi-legally under the umbrella of socialist rituals, today religion comes up as an adaptation to (personal or collective) private visions for walking beloved people to their last resting place. Since the 1990s the national dailies and the tabloid newspapers have paid special attention to the funerals of key figures in the Bulgarian shadow economy; these combine Orthodox ceremony with non-Orthodox elements, often contradictory to church tenets.[11] The opening of churches for memorial services received broad and widely positive public acclaim (during communism it was an unwritten rule that memorial services could only be held in the church of the Central Sofia Cemetery). One of the Bulgarian interviewees, Naum Ruskov, expressed his deep satisfaction at this

---

[11]   These funerals comprise crowded processions with crosses and priests and pop-folk songs (the funeral of Ivo Karamanski in 1999) or masonic rituals (the funeral of Ilia Pavlov in 2003), all of them aiming to emphasise the Mafiosi's unique biography on the borderline of legality.

change in the place of the services: 'I think that this practice that was introduced, namely the memorial service to be done in the churches in downtown Sofia, is better than all of us waiting at the cemetery; it's more solemn, nicer, isn't it?' At the same time, some donors required that in the churches sponsored by them 'there shouldn't be mourning rituals but only joyful ones'.[12] The Bulgarian funeral portal informs its clients in an equally comprehensive way on topics varying from price lists to church requirements and folklore (including pagan) practices, and offers an innumerable choice of scenarios for the ceremony.[13] Some of these could be found in the interviews. Dimana, for example, in addition to the candles and incense, insisted that her body be washed in wine and basil before being laid in the coffin. Evlogi Anastasov buried his mother according to her desire 'with three priests' and Tanya had prepared in advance everything needed for her funeral, including photographs to be laid in the coffin at the side of her body.

In this context of re-evaluation and reconstruction of religious knowledge and normativity, it became possible for Ivanka to become 'an expert in dying'. Similar to the way the ceremonies of secular humanists have become popular in the UK for achieving a more authentic and personal expression of grief, the Orthodox memorial service (together with the commemoration services) has become more authoritatively a way to overcome the socialist legacy and return to what is seen as true and right in caring for the dead.

In Romania, similarly to Bulgaria, religious rites of passage were on the periphery of the public sphere of the socialist state; according to our interviewees they were observed privately, often in secrecy. However, there were no systematic efforts to establish a practice of secular funerals. On the contrary, funerals of party activists in accordance with Orthodox ritual gained popularity in the 1970s. Under Ceauşescu, ceremonies of baptism, Christian marriage and burial services were even encouraged (Stan and Turcescu 2000, 1469). Democratic changes capitalised on this prior state of the national grief system 'cleansing' layers of socialist symbolism from it. Thus, according to Bădică, the Orthodox funeral has remained a 'particular symbiosis of religious and national identity with a strong respect for tradition'.[14] It is important, however, to point out that respect for tradition does not necessarily mean a denial of individualisation of the commemoration of the dead and it is not a unilateral argument in favour of the thesis, widespread among scholars of the region, of an 'undeniable religious revival' in Romania (Tomka 2006). According to Gog, 'Death starts to be handled by private for profit companies and sometimes the priests have only a formal role. Both in the terms of death related practices and meanings people attach to dying, we can notice in post-socialist Romania a gradual secularization' (Gog 2011, 28–9). Even though the Romanian interviews do not give evidence for the secularisation of mourning, they do show a formalisation of the religious funeral as, again, in Florina's words,

---

12   See http://www.24chasa.bg/Article.asp?ArticleId=565481 (accessed 12 January 2012).
13   See http://www.pogrebenie.bg/gk/sofia.php (accessed 12 January 2012).
14   See Chapter 3.

'We never attached a religious meaning to it. It was a ritual'. The search for a religious meaning for death is substituted by a concern for the after-life or the memory of the deceased while the observance of specific rituals is accompanied by random and unstable interpretations of religious doctrines.

Is there a 'resurrection' of death in post-communist countries that is related to the rediscovery of religious rituals and that is running counter to the processes of secularisation at a global scale? The examples discussed here clearly reveal the complex dynamics of privatisation and release of religiosity from the grasp of the totalitarian state, resulting in a wider spread of Christian values, their intertwining with national meanings and, ultimately, their reinterpretation and integration in personal value systems. Yet these processes often enter into conflict with Orthodox (and not only in the sense of Eastern Orthodox) religious norms and prescriptions. What emerges is actually a heterogeneous, fragmented and contradictory symbolic space of new non-communist ideologies of death that cannot be comprehended within categories of either contemporary revitalisation or the decline of religiosity. This space relates in dubious ways to the pluralisation of spiritualities observed in Western Europe.

Projections of the Body in the After-life: Grief Systems and Religious Identities

If the individualisation of the funeral paradoxically suggests a compatibility with, or at least a reference to, collectively built and shared grief systems, then what is the most personal of the ideologies of death? Two types of imagery can be clearly differentiated in the interviews: 'reputation' or post-self, which has already been discussed, and 're-membrance' or post-body. While reputations perpetuate and back up virtually – in communal memory – the cultural and social identities of the dead, 're-membrance' and post-bodies are connected to the projections of the body in the after-life and to the intimate experience of the physical presence of the lost loved one. This is 'presence' at the verge of reality when, willingly or not, one enters in communication with the dead. They are called to hear the words of their family members and to help them solve their problems, or they appear unexpectedly in their dreams, or are perceived to be tangibly, palpably, corporeally present. Constructivist–psychological conceptions of mourning regard this attitude as an 'ethical act of "re-membering"', that is, 'to recall or recount; … to reattach the limbs of the body (suggesting that forgetting is a form of violence to the dead, a kind of dismemberment); and … to grant the dead their autonomous membership in the living community' (Becker and Knudson 2003, 694; see also Boszormenyi-Nagyand and Spark 1973).

Re-membering is very much connected and even coincides with what is defined by recent attachment theory as 'continuing bonds with the dead', which in contrast to the Freudian understanding of grief work do not threaten, but foster the emotional health of the mourner (Klass, Silverman and Nickman 1996). They help them to construct a 'durable biography' (Walter 1996) and to integrate in a non-traumatic way past and present experiences of strong relationships.

The universality and importance of communication with the dead is evident in the accounts of interviewees who clearly render cultural models of mourning irrelevant as they experience a unique and entirely private relatedness to the deceased loved one. The Orthodox Bulgarian Tanya was convinced that, on the night she had spent gravely ill in a hospital, her dead husband was on vigil there at her bed. She kept his photograph with her, on the back of which she wrote a message of love. Ion Cotescu, who described himself as non-religious, decided to transfer his wife's grave to his native town, 'For now she lives, if I can say so, in Bragadiru'. A Greek-Catholic Romanian, Ioana Georgescu, reported having regularly heard the steps of her brother when she was alone. Rita Gardner, a Presbyterian from the UK who also attended Church of England services, admitted that she had always wanted to see a ghost, especially after her mother's death:

> I did hope very much that when my mother died I would be able to feel that she was around. I think I did feel that she was for about the first two or three weeks but after that I didn't. And so my views on the after-life and things are very hazy.

In addition to communication with the dead as equal members of the community of the living, interviewees mention objects, usually favourite belongings of the deceased. For instance, Molly Stevens repeated several times that she could not dispose of her deceased husband's shoes because they reminded her of him. She clearly expressed the idea of the continuing bond with the dead, explaining that the lighting of a candle for her lost partner was: 'That I remember him, you know, and perhaps where he is he's remembering us'.[15]

Unlike Molly, whose memory is anchored in items her husband used to wear, John Cruikshank entered into direct contact with the post-body of his wife through kissing the urn containing her ashes, which he kept at home. Smith explained such re-collection of different parts or traits of the dead person as the necessity to overcome the physical reality of death: 'The abandonment of the body to its final transformation leaves a problematic space between the disposal of the corpse and the dead's placement into memory. In this space, there is a jumble of heterogeneous materials. To organize these is to demarcate the decaying of the dead body from the living memory of the dead person' (Smith 2006, 233).

Imagining the dead as alive not only allows the living to reconfirm or re-define their relationship with them, but also articulates the traumatic contents of personal visions of the after-life. Thus the dead not only watch and care for the living but also follow and trouble them. Bulgarian interviewee Nina Ganeva provides a good example of this. She spoke of the fear that possessed her while watching her dying sister's convulsions and when later she 'heard' her sister's steps in the empty room. As a result Nina developed such a strong fear of dead bodies that the

---

[15]   For this case see also Chapter 8.

only request she made to her son regarding her own funeral was that she should be cremated. Naum Ruskov's identical decision came from his troubled memories of the Second World War: 'I would like for example to be cremated. I want this because I have seen many dead people, on the battlefield I have seen bodies without heads, without arms or legs'.

These cases reveal two important aspects in the construction of personal ideologies of death. The first is the impossibility of recovering the decayed body and reconciliation with the physical evidence of death and with the notion of one's own imminent decay. Both Nina and Naum were confronted with the reality of an alienated, decomposing, body and the intimate image of the living person, a dichotomy that they could not resolve inasmuch as their choice of cremation kept the fixation on the physical parameters of death. Rita, on the contrary, came close in her reflection on death to the source of her desire to see ghosts. She begins her comment with the sight of dead bodies, 'How they can be cut up, how they can die at sea, disintegrate and what not ... It's quite obvious that our bodies are mortal and just little atoms'. Immediately after this she recalls the short ghostly existence of her mother only to conclude with a confession about her own 'hazy views' on an after-life.

These 'hazy views' draw attention to the second important aspect of the construction of personal ideologies of death: the encountering of phobias and fears of physical decay with the grief systems and religious identities which, in its turn, undermines the coherence of self. Rita defined herself as a religious person and yet she could not decide for herself whether people fell 'asleep' after death or went to heaven. Nina expressed a sense of guilt that she related to her desire to be cremated (she said she knew that 'this is not right'), because cremation is at variance with the Orthodox understanding of the importance of burial as a step towards the future resurrection of bodies.

The interviews demonstrate how common religious prescriptions are adjusted to the profoundly personal projections of the body in the after-life without reflection on specific religious meanings. Ivanka, who categorically defined herself as a passionate believer, did not see any problem with the fact that, when her husband died, she refused to eat, drink and sleep because 'he doesn't eat, drink, sleep'; any reflection on transcendence, on the separation of body and soul, was absent in her discourse. This corresponds directly to her claim at the end of the interview that death is a biological law rather than, for example, a consequence of original sin. The Bulgarian Turk Audan Berber considered himself a pious Muslim because he obeyed the quasi-religious prescription of personal hygiene and at the same time he claimed that there was no life after death and he did not want to die because the grave 'is very dirty'.

Despite the fact that the dichotomy body-decay versus living image of the dead concentrates itself in the emotional contents of a particular biographical experience, it could equally stabilise or destabilise personal ideologies of death inasmuch as its successful resolution depends on the development of a religious identity and attachment to specific cultural models of mourning. In Naum's case the memorial services that he attended could not displace the disfigured corpses he remembered from the war while Ivanka coped with her depressive state after her husband's death by regular visits to churches and monasteries. In this way the projections of the body into an after-life allow the observation of both personal religiosity and the interiorisation of grief systems.

Conclusions

For secular humanists the meaning of the funeral and the mourning is, Harold puts it, to get the 'flavour of the person'. This formulation articulates a universal human conviction concerning the ownership of death: ownership of the expressions of mourning and of the schemes for encountering the end of one's own life. The examples of personal ideologies of death discussed here question this ownership or at least reveal that what motivates it is a complex compound of a search for social recognition, religious or non-religious beliefs, cultural practices and stereotypes, the impact of historical changes and the interplay of particular biographical situations. Thus in the cases of Harold, Ivanka and Florina, the work of mourning became a turning point in their religiosity that encouraged the development of new social competences and cognitive models. Similarly, preparation for death is inseparable from tributes to and assessment of another's life in speeches and music during the traditional Anglican and Modern British Funeral. Even the profoundly personal anxieties of body decay are realised or resolved in the encounter with grief systems and (non-)religious identities.

Harold's phrase, 'a flavour of the person', draws attention to another important problem related to (post)modern experiences of death. In light of contemporary theories of secularisation, the search for individualisation of funeral rituals (as well as of rituals in general) is not only a proof of emancipation from sacred authorities but also a sign of the loss of trust in religious institutions and their potentially supportive role in borderline existential situations. As Wouters argues:

> Traditional ways of regulating emotions, as via rituals, lost part of their "defence" or "protective" function. As the demands for a more personal identity and individual authenticity rose, they increasingly came to be experienced as "stiff", and their performance as too obvious, as "insincere", even as a "fraud" or as "deceit". In this development, to the extent that the old mourning rituals were attacked and abandoned, the shelter they used to provide by evoking the sense of being connected to traditional "symbolic *communitas*" was demolished. (Wouters 2002, 7)

Even though the cases under consideration partly reveal the instability of religious identifications – the attack on religious beliefs by the idea of the body's decay – this does not abolish the protective function of rituals with their symbolic communitas. This is not least because even the bravest inventions of tradition do not deny the essential role of rituals for the marking of life transitions (including death), which is the reason why humanists acclaim such rituals (Wilson 1991). Moreover, even if rituals are conceived as formal and superficial, and are followed only because 'We kept it all our lives' (Florina), they open spaces for expressing solidarity with the deceased through a post-mortem life review or through projections of the body in the after-life. This gives reasons for thinking about what is hidden behind the flavour of the person, communal respect to the tradition and the prospect of life without the shield of religious prescriptions and authorities, yet not without an aspiration for membership in a community of the dead and the living.

References

Attig, Thomas. 1996. *How We Grieve: Relearning the World*. New York: Oxford University Press.

Becker, Scott and Roger Knudson. 2003. 'Visions of the Dead: Imagination and Mourning'. *Death Studies* 27: 691–716.

Boszormenyi-Nagy, Ivan and Geraldine Spark. 1973. *Invisible loyalities*. Hagerstown, MD: Harper & Row.

Butler, Robert. 1963. 'The Life Review: An Interpretation of Reminiscence in the Aged'. *Psychiatry* 26: 65–75.

Coleman, Peter. 2010. 'Religion and Age'. In *Sage Handbook of Social Gerontology*, edited by Dale Dannefer and Chris Phillipson, 337–61. London: Sage.

Daaleman, Timothy and Debra Dobbs. 2010. 'Religiosity, Spirituality and Death Attitudes in Chronically Ill Older Adults'. *Research on Ageing* 32: 224–43.

Davie, Grace. 2002. *Europe: The Exceptional Case*. London: Darton, Longman and Todd.

Davie, Grace. 2006. 'Religion in Europe in the 21st Century: The Factors to Take into Account'. *Archives Européennes de Sociologie/European Journal of Sociology* 47: 271–96.

Davie, Grace. 2007. *The Sociology of Religion*. Los Angeles, CA: Sage.

Downey, Ann Marie. 1984. 'Relationship of Religiosity to Death Anxiety in Middle Age Males'. *Psychological Reports* 54: 811–22.

Elenkov, Ivan. 2009. 'Kam vaprosa za vavezhdaneto na traurnia ritual i socialisticheskata praznichno-obredna sistema u nas 1969–1971' ['On the Question of the Introduction of the Mourning Ritual and the Socialist Festive and Ritual System in this Country 1969–1971']. *Hristianstvo i kultura* 7(42): 88–99.

Gog, Sorin. 2011. 'Secular and Religious Identities in Post-Socialist Romania', PhD thesis summary. Available at: http://doctorat.ubbcluj.ro/sustinerea_pub lica/rezumate/2011/sociologie/gog_sorin_mihaita_en.pdf (accessed 10 January 2012).

Kamerman, Jack. 2003. 'The Postself in Social Context'. In *Handbook of Death and Dying*, edited by Clifton Braynt, Vol. 1. Thousand Oaks, CA: Sage, 2003.

Klass, Deniz, Silverman Phyllis and Steven Nickman (eds) 1996. *Continuing Bonds: New Understanding of Grief.* Washington, DC: Taylor & Francis.

Leming, Michael and George Dickinson. 2002. *Understanding Death, Dying, and Bereavement*. New York: Harcourt College.

Metodiev, Momchil. 2010. 'Mezhdu viarata I kompromisa. Pravoslavnata carkva I komunisticheskiat rezhim v Balgaria' ['Between the Faith and Compromise. The Orthodox Church and the Communist Regime in Bulgaria'.] Sofia: Siela.

Neimeyer, Robert. 1998. *Lessons of Loss: A Guide to Coping*. New York: McGraw-Hill.

Neimeyer, Robert, Holly G. Prigerson and Betty Davies. 2002. 'Mourning and Meaning'. *American Behavioral Scientist* 46: 235–51.

Pashova, Anastassia. 2006. 'Dnes ostana prazno edno rabotno miasto (Nova ideologia za smartta i pogrebalnata obrednost na darzhavnia socializam v Bulgaria ot 50-te – 70-te godini na 20 vek)' ['A Workplace Remained Unoccupied Today (The New Ideology of Death and Funerary Rituals of the State Socialism in Bulgaria in the 1950s–1970s)']. *Balkanistichen Forum* 1–3: 319–40.

Runciman, Walter. 1983. *A Treatise on Social Theory*. Cambridge: Cambridge University Press.

Shneidman, Edwin. 1995. 'The Postself'. In *Death: Current Perspectives*, edited by John Williamson and Edwin Shneidman. Mountain View, CA: Mayfield.

Smith, Warren. 2006, 'Organizing Death: Remembrance and Re-collection'. *Organization* 225: 225–44.

Stan, Lavinia and Lucian Turcescu. 2000. 'The Romanian Orthodox Church and Post-Communist democratization'. *Europe–Asia Studies* 52: 1467–88.

Tomka, Miklos. 2006. 'Is Conventional Sociology of Religious able to Deal with Differences between Eastern and Weastern European Developments'. *Social Compass* 53: 251–6.

Walter, Tony. 1994. *The Revival of Death*. London: Routledge.

Walter, Tony. 1996. 'A New Model of Grief: Bereavement and Biography'. *Mortality: Promoting the Interdisciplinary Study of Death and Dying* 1: 7–25.

Walter, Tony. 1999. *On Bereavement: The Culture of Grief.* Buckingham: Open University Press.

Wilson, Jane. 1991. *Funerals Without God: A Practical Guide to Non-religious Funerals*. London: Prometheus Books.

Wouters, Cas. 2002. 'The Quest for New Rituals in Dying and Mourning: Changes in the We–I Balance'. *Body and Society* 8: 1–27.

Zhivkov, Iv. Todor. 1981. 'Socialisticheski obredi i socialisticheska kultura' ['Socialist Rites and Socialist Culture']. In *Miastoto na izkustvata v savremennite praznici i obredi* [*The Role of the Arts in the Contemporary Feasts and Rites*]. Plovdiv.

Chapter 8

Belief in the Context of Bereavement: The Potential Therapeutic Properties Associated with Religious Belief and Ritual

John H. Spreadbury

Introduction

The role played by religion in the context of coping and adjusting to significant bereavement has continued to be a relatively neglected area of research in both psychology and psychogerontology. This is perhaps unusual considering the wealth of mainly American research that has repeatedly identified the positive effects of religion on physical health and psychological well-being in samples of varying ages, including older adults (see Koenig, McCullough and Larson 2001). It is also unusual considering that religion tends to be of more importance to older adults compared with younger age groups (Coleman 2011; Coleman, Mills and Spreadbury 2011), and that significant bereavements from one's peers, siblings and spouse tend to occur more frequently in later life (Spreadbury and Coleman 2011). It could also be considered unusual as the search for cost-effective coping resources for increasingly ageing populations has become a focus of government policies and social scientific research throughout Europe.

Despite being an under-researched area, however, recent years have witnessed a growing interest in the area of religious coping and significant bereavement. The recent reviews of the empirical literature by Becker et al. (2007) and Wortmann and Park (2008) have provided useful overviews of the religion and bereavement research and highlight a number of important observations about the research in this area. According to these reviews the majority of the studies conducted appear to report that religion can have a positive influence on adjustment to bereavement. However, the reviews also highlight a number of significant limitations: very few of the studies have been based solely on older adults, very few have been conducted outside of a mainly North American Protestant context and there has been relatively little qualitative research conducted. This latter limitation in particular has had noticeable theoretical consequences. Theoretical explanations for how religion influences coping and adjustment to bereavement have tended to lack detail about the theological or philosophical content of people's religious belief and practice, and how belief and practice are drawn upon, used or applied in circumstances of bereavement and grief. Moreover, the findings involving religion have usually not been discussed in the context of existing theories of bereavement and grief.

Recent British research by Spreadbury and Coleman (2011) has attempted to address some of the above limitations. Spreadbury and Coleman (2011) interviewed 26 older adults of Church of England and Catholic denominations about their religious belief and practice and their experience of spousal bereavement. The aim was first to identify the Christian beliefs and practices most important in coping and adjustment, and second to examine whether these religious coping strategies fitted with the predictions of bereavement and grief theories. Interview transcripts were analysed using Interpretative Phenomenological Analysis, and four themes were identified that represented how religion was used by this sample in coping and adjusting to spousal bereavement. The four themes were labelled: *benevolent religious cognition*, *biblical assurances*, *religious ritual* and *spiritual capital*.

Benevolent religious cognition referred to positive and optimistic beliefs about the nature of God, and related to belief in a life after death, that in different ways were used in the grief processes of sense0making and benefit0finding, processes central to reconstructing meaning in bereavement (Gillies and Neimeyer 2006). *Biblical assurances* referred to how participants for whom reading the Bible was a part of their religious practice were able to use Biblical scripture to support benevolent interpretations about their loss. The theme of *religious ritual* referred to how, through engagement in the behaviours and activities involved in the practice of one's faith, participants were able to regulate grief and encourage a sense of closeness with their deceased spouse. Performing religious rituals in this case provided mechanisms for continuing bonds (Klass, Silverman and Nickman 1996) with deceased loved ones. Finally, the theme of *spiritual capital* represented how, through engagement in regular roles and jobs related to the running of one's church, participants were able to find new sources of meaning and purpose in life, and develop a new post-bereavement identity.

The findings by Spreadbury and Coleman (2011) resonated some significance because they emphasised and supported not only that religion was a multi-dimensional construct, something that has been widely theorised in the psychology of religion (see Paloutzian and Park 2005), but also importantly that religion's influence in the context of bereavement and grief was multi-dimensional at the level of the believer. Different dimensions of religion such as belief or church attendance could be drawn upon in coping and adjustment but religion was also experienced by individual believers at more than one level, for example at the level of thought, emotion, behaviour and social interaction. This observation provided explanation for potential variations in how religion is experienced or found beneficial during bereavement and grief. For one person belief in a life after death is most important; for another the sense of emotional closeness to deceased loved ones experienced through lighting a candle in church or through prayer, for another identifying with Biblical characters of suffering or finding motivation to cope in Biblical scripture, and for yet another finding new sources of meaning in life through performing jobs or activities on behalf of one's local church.

In addition, from a methodological perspective, what was also important was that many of the beliefs and activities observed by Spreadbury and Coleman (2011), for example belief in a life after death reunion with deceased loved ones and engagement in religious rituals and spiritual capital, have no dedicated psychometric instruments and are thus not being measured in the present body of mainly quantitative research. With these findings in mind, it is now of interest to investigate how older adults in other European countries belonging to the other major branches of Christianity articulate using their belief and practice in circumstances of coping and adjusting to significant bereavement.

The present study draws on cases from the RASC project to investigate how older adults describe the role of their religious belief and practice in coping and adjusting to significant bereavement. From participant descriptions potential therapeutic properties associated with belief and practice will be discerned and discussed.

The cross-cultural analysis of cases is presented in two parts. First, an overview is given of the bereavement and religious ritual characteristics based on all 60 cases. Second, two case studies from each country are presented that provide examples of the different ways in which religion is used in coping and adjustment. It should perhaps be noted at this point that all the cases presented are women. This was not in an attempt to specifically sample for women,[1] but it happened to be the case that these participants provided rich examples of religious coping and bereavement. However, it could be hypothesised that, owing to differences in traditional gender roles and gender mortality rates, it was females who were arguably more likely to experience significant bereavements in these countries in the pre- and post war years, and that it is older females today who are perhaps more willing to talk at length about the importance of their personal beliefs.

For the purposes of the present chapter, *religious ritual* will refer to the specific behaviours and activities involved in how one practises or expresses one's faith. This conceptualisation attempts to represent religious ritual at a more specific level of analysis than general religious practice. As such it can be considered that, when one practises one's faith, one does so using religious rituals. Religious rituals in this sense guide, facilitate and make possible religious practice.

Cross-cultural Analysis

Bereavement and Religious Ritual Characteristics

The overall sample described a range of significant bereavements that included bereavements related to parents, grandparents, spouses, siblings, friends and one's children. Memories for bereavements and funerals related to one's parents and grandparents appeared to be the most frequently described across the sample,

---

[1]   See Chapter 10 for a focus on women specifically.

while memories for bereavements related to one's own children were the least frequently described, and only in the Bulgarian sample.

With regard to bereavements related to one's spouse, more than half of the participants from the Bulgarian and Romanian sample, and only three participants from the English sample, reported experiencing this type of significant bereavement. One interesting observation was that, for participants who were asked what their most difficult experience in life was, both the Bulgarian and Romanian samples were far more likely than the English sample to report a significant bereavement. The latter were more likely to report an illness or life regret.

In comparison with the English sample, not only did the Bulgarian and Romanian samples provide more frequent descriptions of bereavement experiences, but they also described more frequent and more richly detailed examples of engaging in religious rituals and ceremonies in coping and adjusting to bereavement and their on-going grief. The English sample provided relatively few such descriptions, although some examples will be illustrated below.

With regard to the use of religious rituals *per se*, again in comparison with the English sample, the Bulgarian and Romanian samples described engaging in a much wider variety of activities: lighting candles, burning incense, receiving communion, confession, using holy water, crossing oneself, bowing and kneeling, venerating icons, fasting, marking Saints' days, giving alms, asking religious ministers to bless one's home, preparing religious foods (e.g. koliva, kozunak, the five loaves, coloured eggs) and making periodic commemorations. Although not all of these were described specifically in the context of bereavement, they were on some occasions a part of the process of longer-term adjustment and acceptance of a significant bereavement. In contrast, the religious ritual activities that seemed most important to the English sample in the context of bereavement included the funeral service, prayer and candle lighting.

We will now explore below in more detail selected cases from across the three countries that demonstrate the different uses of religious belief and practice in the context of coping and adjusting to significant bereavement.

Case Studies

English Sample

Kate Osborne

A particularly good example of a participant whose personal faith in God and life-long religious involvement had been useful in coping and adjusting to a significant bereavement was Kate Osborne. Kate was 85 years old and was a retired medical doctor. She had studied medicine during the Second World War and had married her husband shortly after the war, with whom she had two children.

Kate had attended Sunday school as a child and from childhood had developed a strong sense of God as protecting and caring for her that was still very important to her: 'I have God's protection knowing that I'm His child'. Indeed, some months before being interviewed, Kate had felt that this sense of God's care and protection for her had helped her emotionally by bringing her a feeling of 'peace' during a traumatic experience related to an operation for a broken hip. Kate's sense of a close personal relationship with God was also reflected in the way that she felt that God had guided her at certain times throughout her life.

During her life Kate had belonged to and worshipped within more than one Christian denomination. Although she now belonged to the Church of England, earlier in her life she had worshipped within the Plymouth Brethren and Baptist Church. As such, Kate took the opinion, which she had held since she was a teenager, that the type of denomination was of little importance in belief. What was of greater importance for her was the sincerity of the Christian believer: 'I very strongly felt that denominations were not important. But I suppose if you pushed me I would say [I am] Church of England ... Well churches are manmade aren't they? And to be a Christian is basically one's belief and trust in the Lord Jesus you see and that's where we ... but I think, I mean, the Biblical teaching is that we should get together and worship together.'

With regard to the content of her belief, Kate's reply captured what was arguably typical of many of the highly religious Christian participants in the English sample:

> Well I believe that God is the creator and the sustainer of the universe and that man chose to go his own way rather than follow in God's way. Which I think is described to you right in the beginning of the Bible. That it all began then when man decided he'd prefer to go his own way rather than the way that God chose. And I think I believe that God sent His son, the Lord Jesus Christ, into the world and Jesus lived a life on the earth showing us in a way God and finally gave His life, He was crucified. I believe that He died and I do believe in the resurrection, that He rose and is now living with God in eternity.

Concerning her religious practice, Kate reported that she attended church more than once a week, that she prayed on a daily basis, and that she read Biblical scripture in the form of a study guide every morning: 'I do spend about an hour's time, it is usually about an hour, reading the scriptures and thinking and contemplating and just spending time with God'. Interestingly, Kate also reported that she talked to God regularly and this reflected the sense of a close personal relationship that she felt with God: 'And then of course I'm always talking to the Lord as I do my daily routine and go places and things.'

With regard to her bereavement experience, Kate had lost her husband in 2002 to cancer, just two years after moving to Southampton. She described the experience of coping with her bereavement shortly after moving to a new city where she knew very few people:

> How did I cope? Well it wasn't all that easy because I was a newcomer to Southampton and I hadn't really made, or at least we had very little opportunity to make friends, cos my husband was not well and we didn't get out and about much. So I found it quite difficult but I realised that I'd been very fortunate in the marriage that I'd had and I knew that my husband was with his Lord and I decided that what God wanted of me was to try to sit still and just take things very quietly. So whereas most people find things to do as quickly as possible, I felt God was saying to me "I want you just to learn to just be quiet on your own and be with me" and I did that for, I think, a good two years. And then I started feeling that it was right for me to get more involved with the church and that's it really.

Kate continued by describing how she became more involved in activities related to her local church following her bereavement. Kate's description is similar to that reported by other religious British older adults who have also lost a spouse and find a new post-bereavement identity through becoming more involved in church activities in the months and years following spousal bereavement (Spreadbury and Coleman 2011). Kate described her experience as follows:

> Well I started first of all going to a prayer meeting on a Friday evening when there was just a few of us and we used to pray for the church and members who were abroad and any issues, you know, which arose. And then I went to a, I joined a home group, and I also went to a Thursday morning group which is held at the church hall. I can't remember times – I eventually found that it was really in the prayer line that I was most involved and so I became part of what is called the prayer ministry. So if people at church had needs someone will pray with them. We always prayed in twos. Then I joined in that.

For Kate, although religious rituals seemed to form an important part of her daily and weekly activities in the form of daily prayer, daily reading of the scriptures and regular church attendance, it was arguably her strong personal faith in God that she had had since childhood that was experienced as most helpful in coping with her bereavement. Kate articulated a belief in the resurrection, a belief in a life after death and a belief that her husband was with God, and these religious cognitions appeared to be important factors that helped her accept and understand her bereavement, as Kate commented: 'I quite honestly felt that it was my trust in God and resting in Him that gave me the peace'. From this position of cognitive and emotional acceptance, the religious rituals that make up her religious practice and her involvement in church activities were then able to facilitate her longer-term adjustment to a new way of living.

Molly Stevens
Molly Stevens described using her belief and practice related to the loss of her husband in a different way to Kate Osborne. Molly was born in London in 1926,

had left school in her early teens and had spent the majority of her adult life living in London as a housewife and mother. Molly had been brought up as Catholic, had a practising Catholic mother and had attended a Catholic school and Sunday school. Starting from a very early age, Molly had experienced several significant bereavements in her life. Her father had died prior to the Second World War when she was a child and her mother had died in 1939 when Molly was only 13 years old. Molly described this latter loss as devastating and it occurred while she was separated from her mother as a war evacuee. Molly was only informed of her mother's death in a letter many weeks later in an insensitive and traumatic way. In addition, Molly was the youngest of five children and during her life had lost two sisters and a brother. She had also lost her husband, whom she had married in 1945 and with whom she had two children.

Molly appeared to have a straightforward, yet private religious belief, and remarked that generally she did not like to talk about it with other people. Yet she appeared to be deeply committed to her religious practice. Indeed, Molly reported that she had been a church-going Catholic throughout her life and had felt it important to raise her children as Catholics. She reported preferring the traditional Latin Mass, and attended Mass every Sunday, often with one of her grown-up sons, and reported praying every night before going to sleep.

Although Molly provided few details about her bereavement experiences or how she had coped and adjusted, she did feel it important to describe how she used religious rituals and ceremonies that are meaningful to her to remember and commemorate her husband on both an annual and a weekly basis: 'I always have a Mass said for him in here when it's his anniversary and birthdays and that, you know.' She also described lighting candles in church for her husband on a more regular weekly basis:

> I light candles, yeah. I go in nearly every – well, two or three times a week and
> I light candles in there, you know. Just to say I remember him, you know, cos
> he was good. He was a good dad and he was a good husband. You can't ask for
> more can you?

Interestingly, when Molly was asked what she thought candle lighting meant to her, she replied in a way that reflected her belief in a life after death: 'That I remember him, you know, and perhaps where he is he's remembering us.'

Perhaps one of the most striking things about Molly was that, despite experiencing several significant bereavements early in her life, at the age of 84 years there appeared to be no feeling of bitterness or regret; indeed, she repeated that she had a sense of being happy, content and thankful for life. Moreover, the ritual practices she engaged in for her husband, although appearing simple or straightforward, seemed to be satisfying enough for her and provided ways for her to continue to commemorate her husband with a sense that he may be aware of her behaviours.

Romanian Sample

Ioana Georgescu[2]

Ioana Georgescu was born in 1924 and was living with her daughter in a house in Bucharest where she had lived the majority of her adult life. Ioana had worked as a pharmacist and in personnel, but had retired from full time work at the age of 44 years owing to poor health. Reflecting on her life, Ioana said 'I had a hard life', which was marked by perceived sacrifices and loss. In particular Ioana highlighted the early loss of her parents, the loss of her older brother, and the separation from her husband, with whom she had two children, as amongst the most difficult experiences in her life. Indeed, when asked what was the most difficult moment in her life Ioana replied:

> My dear, that was when my mother died, when my mom wasn't with me anymore, when my dad died [I] was too young, I wasn't able to understand, but when mom, that I felt it, I felt that … After that my brother, he was all that I had left in the world, there wasn't anybody else that I could go to after that. I was left by myself, I had to fight for my children, I had to give up on certain things but that seemed normal to me.

Ioana's formative years had been unsettled and had included significant bereavements, moving between different schools and homes, and a period as a war refugee fleeing the advancing Soviet Army in 1944. Following the death of her mother when Ioana was 12 years old, her eldest brother became her guardian and she would describe their relationship by saying that he was both mother and father to her. Yet her brother was unable to look after her immediately following their mother's death as he had to complete his military service. Thus, although Orthodox herself, Ioana was sent away to a Catholic boarding school. However, it appeared that some stability in her early life was provided by her childhood religious education and experience. Ioana remembered her time at the school and her daily religious practice with positive memories. She also remembered the 'need' she felt to attend church following the death of her mother.

> After my mother died and I had to go to boarding school, there was a morning service there … there was such a beautiful chapel, a big chapel, with an organ, it was very beautiful and they had a service in the morning. There was a priest, he came from town, it was the sisters' choir who answered, it was sublime you know. I was in [a] bad state, you know. I felt the need to go to church. And I went, but I didn't know, I didn't know, it was new to me and I didn't know the rituals. The Catholic rituals are very different than ours. And almost every morning I was going to church, to the religious service.

---

[2]   For this case see also Chapter 11.

Indeed, Ioana's experience of the Catholic boarding school appeared to have had a significant influence on her and seemed to have provided the foundations to how she would think and behave as a Christian throughout her life. In describing the religious education she received at the boarding school she highlighted the strict emphasis placed on fasting, communion, confession, prayer and self-reflection, following religious morals, being honest and having a clear conscience. All of this seemed to shape and structure what she called her 'Christian learning'.

Ioana had a strong faith but was no longer able to attend church regularly because of poor health. She reported a strong belief in a life after death and a belief in the importance of Christian love and forgiveness, and remembered the words her mother would repeat, that 'God is everywhere'. With regard to her religious practice, Ioana reported the importance of candle lighting and having her home blessed by a priest specifically for protection, and as with many of the highly religious Orthodox participants, the importance of fasting (despite being on medication).

However, what is particularly interesting about Ioana is that during her life she had become something of an expert with regard to the ritual and ceremonial uses of food related to commemorating significant life events, especially those related to bereavements and funerals. In addition, Ioana also placed great importance on the giving of alms. Both practices were described in the context of 'honouring the dead' and Ioana possessed a detailed knowledge of how these activities should be prepared and conducted. Interestingly, Ioana spoke about preparing koliva (a sweet dish made from boiled wheat kernels and decorated with a cross) for the dead or the giving of alms with a sense of mysticism and related to dream premonitions. She recalled how she prepared koliva related to arguably the most traumatic bereavement of her adult life. When she was in her mid-twenties and pregnant with her son, Ioana's eldest brother, who had been her childhood guardian and with whom she had lived when she left boarding school, died suddenly at the age of 39 years in a motorbike accident. Remembering the event Ioana recalled:

> I could not cry during the funeral … I had to live with my sister-in-law, she was afraid to be alone, and I stayed with her until his 40 days commemoration service. It was quite interesting that before The Transfiguration, I made for my sister-in-law, koliva. My sister-in-law from Pitești was doing this for her husband, it was a pledge, preparing koliva for her husband's health, on August 6th which was The Transfiguration. I don't know why, but I had this on my mind for a long time now, that I had to prepare koliva! And indeed, now I was preparing it for my brother. My brother however, died on a Sunday.

Ioana also described in detail how it was important for her to give alms related to significant bereavements. She had vivid childhood memories of her mother giving alms when her father died and this had no doubt shaped how she had continued this tradition throughout her life.

Interestingly, related to Ioana's belief in a life after death, she also described feeling an enduring relationship or attachment with the deceased loved ones who had been most emotionally significant in her life. Ioana described how she could feel in close proximity to them, and importantly that she felt they had the ability to help her in times of difficulty.

> I do believe there is life after death. I don't know what else. I mean, I think that, besides God who helps us … we have next to us, I'm thinking many times of my mother or my brother, my dad not so much, I ask for their help me. When I go through hard times, I felt my brother next to me.

Indeed, speaking specifically of the enduring attachment with her eldest brother who had been her childhood guardian, Ioana said:

> Traian is here, next to me, not there [in the cemetery]. There you just have a bag of bones. He's dead for 60 years now, God rest his soul! No! I have him here. And when I go through hard times, I think of them to be next to me.

For Ioana, her belief and the practices she engaged in for honouring the dead seemed to be helpful to her in multiple ways. These practices formed part of a larger tradition that stretched beyond herself, linking back to positive memories of her mother and her childhood, and extending to her daughter, with perhaps the hope that her daughter would continue them. Furthermore, these practices seemed to provide Ioana with a strong social role and a sense of purpose and, importantly, with a proactive response to death and significant bereavement. They practices also provided physical mechanisms and vehicles to help her maintain an intimate cognitive and emotional link with her significant deceased loved ones.

Eleonora Moldovan

Another Romanian participant who, similarly to Ioana, described feeling a 'need' to attend church following a significant bereavement was Eleonora Moldovan. Eleonora was 75 years old and was living in an apartment with her sister's family in Cluj–Napoca, the city in which she was born. Eleonora had been a university professor of foreign languages and had never married or had children. Although now in retirement, she was still active as a volunteer curator for a library in the university.

From the early 1940s Eleonora's childhood had involved a period living with her religious grandmother in the countryside as a war evacuee from the allied bombings, while by 1944 she had experienced a period seeking refuge from the advancing Soviet Army. Eleonora also had clear memories of the details of the postwar years that included the abolition of the monarchy, the formation of the Romanian Worker's Party and the atheistic educational reforms whereby in her schooling the learning of religion was replaced with the learning of Russian. However it was perhaps the postwar poverty and the example of stoicism and integrity set by her parents in the face of these and other challenges in her childhood that left a particularly powerful impression on her character.

Perhaps one of the things that made Eleonora a particularly striking case was the conviction and certainty with which she held, and spoke about, her religious belief and the importance of her strong faith in her life, particularly during times of difficulty. An Orthodox Christian, Eleonora emphasised a strong personal faith in God and His power. Eleonora described her belief and practice as not only a priority in her early life: 'I went to church every Sunday, this – our religious education was a priority, so we went', but it was also a priority in her adult life: 'I think that is the priority in my life and it really helped me; and belief in the supernatural and in the power of prayer. I think it ranks first in my life and after it come all others.' Furthermore, Eleonora highlighted the supportive nature of her faith: 'faith is the scaffolding on which I built my whole life and faith and with the power of prayer I came through situations in which others might have surrendered'.

Interestingly, Eleonora was able to identify the moment in her childhood where she first felt the power of God in her life, to the backdrop of the allied bombings:

> In '42 – it seems to me it was in '42 – the Anglo-American bombings began! Brasov was badly bombed and, to make matters worse, it was right at Easter time that year. So, I know that it was '42, I think. I know for we had just got out of church, from the Resurrection service, I do not know what, and I had gone out with my sister for a walk; we were young, 'cause in '42 we were how old? About seven ... and the alarm, the siren ... Brasov was badly bombed. My father and mother had remained in Brasov, because they were tied to their jobs ... Well, and here I felt for the first time, let's say, and I realised what God's power meant – and I should note in parenthesis that my very religious grandmother constantly reinforced our religious beliefs and educated us ... And I remember that one day I said to her, "Grandmother", I say, "Grandma ... we must believe in God so much, that if there were a storm as strong, with lightning and thunder" – for that was for us, children, so to say, the ultimate criterion of fear, "so – we must say: "We believe in one Lord", and then we won't have to fear anything". And indeed, in life, this is what has happened to me, more or less. Well! ... For indeed, faith in God helped me get over everything. And, as I say, it was here that I felt, that I even realised a little, when I was a small girl, the power of God.

In thinking about her religious upbringing and education, Eleonora also remembered her parents' influence on her engagement in religious acts of worship and on her moral development. Perhaps unsurprisingly, related to her strong conviction in her faith was the fact that she also described experiencing intense religious emotions often during or following her religious practice, from crying and sadness to feelings of joy and love.

> Happiness for me comes from the fact that … happiness is given by faith! Faith in God and this is my only happiness and yes, this is how I pull through everything! … My happiness is, first of all, in my clear conscience and the fact that through faith I can pull through everything.

Eleonora emphasised throughout her interview how her belief had been important to her during the most difficult moments of her life, which centred on her demotion from her job during the height of the atheistic Socialist period for attending church, moments of financial austerity, the near loss of her home and the deaths of her parents:

> My conviction and I say it out loud – I never felt how powerful God is except when I was in the most difficult of circumstances. In order to really feel the power of God, you need these limit situations, hard tests, and then the power of prayer and faith in God – these simply make wonders! […] only for this you have to be steadfast in prayer and also try your best in Christian behaviour, so and … yes, never forget that God is above you and that He helps in all […] I always have a certain attitude to people, to life and go through life with my convictions even in difficult times, God won't abandon you!

During the most difficult moments in her life Eleonora also described being able to draw on Biblical scripture to make meaning out of difficulties and to reinforce and support her strong faith. She described one episode of drawing on the Bible in a moment of difficulty that captured some of the complexity of her cognitive search for meaning and understanding:

> I read, and at night, Psalm 90, which ends: "He shall cry unto Me, and I will hearken unto him. I am with him in affliction, and I will rescue him and glorify him. With length of days will I satisfy him, and I will show him My salvation." And so … then I read it … "I will rescue him and …". How can it be?! God does lie! What He promises here "no evils shall come nigh thee, and no scourge shall draw nigh unto thy dwelling …". I know that by heart … and I say: "This can't be! God does lie! God does lie." And this idea and with faith in God and … I say: "How? Does God not see that I thank Him wholeheartedly and sincerely feel this spontaneous need to thank Him and through religious service and He sees me going through hardships and could He turn His back on me?" No! That was my conviction, which I've had all the time. Yes.

Eleonora highlighted that the bereavement of her parents was one of the most difficult experiences in her life, but was also a key turning point, especially with regard to the strengthening of her religious belief and practice. Eleonora's grandmother and father had both died in close succession in May 1967 while her mother at that time was recovering from surgery for cancer. Four years later her mother's cancer returned and she eventually died in July 1972. She described being very 'attached' to her parents, particularly to her mother, who at the time had been ill in bed for more than a year and Eleonora had been caring for her on a daily basis. Eleonora seemed to have clear memories of her mother's death and also of her religious response to it:

> Mother died, it was on July 28, a Friday, uh ... on Monday was the funeral, the next day, Tuesday, it was 1st August and then I set my mind ... I'd been telling myself, I felt that: If I still want to be in spiritual communion, of mind, with my parents, all I had to do was to start my day with the Holy Liturgy. And since then, since 1st August '72 until today, I've started my day by ... going to church, to the cathedral.

Eleonora continued on the subject of her religious response to her mother's death and the 'need' she felt to attend church every day:

> I started going to church every day after mother's death and there was a time when I couldn't even mention death – the death of my mother: "Mother is gone! She's no longer amongst us!" And after the first ... so it was a new experience for me to feel the need, need that I wanted to come to church every day and then I realised and I ... and something happened inside me because I said to myself: Wait, now I'm coming out from the liturgy – liturgy is communication with God, with heaven and He asks something of us – and then I felt that covenant that I now must supervise my thoughts and language and deeds.

What is particularly interesting about these descriptions is the language Eleonora used to describe her need to continue or maintain a perceived attachment or relationship with her parents. Eleonora described a desire for 'spiritual communion' and identified the religious liturgy as providing a method of communication with God and heaven, and presumably therefore with her deceased parents. Thus, by attending church daily, Eleonora could still feel in daily communion with her parents. Furthermore, Eleonora used the word 'covenant' to describe her new solemn commitment or agreement with God, creating a more intimate relationship with God and producing a new sense of self-identity. Eleonora described the new sense of self-improvement or edification she experienced as part of her covenant: 'I proposed myself not to speak; not only not to speak ill of anyone, but not even to think bad things about anyone and then I felt so, so suddenly, this feeling, of purification and had a positive and optimistic vision of the world.' Moreover, for Eleonora going through such difficult yet significant life events, far from negatively affecting her faith, actually had the opposite effect and she experienced a strengthening of her faith: 'I've always felt that my tests have spiritually fortified me and from every trial I came out more robust emotionally and strengthened spiritually.'

Bulgarian Sample

Ivanka Grozdeva[3]

Ivanka Grozdeva was born in 1937 and was living alone in an apartment in the city in which she was born. She had trained as a librarian and had spent her entire career of 33 years working in two different libraries. Ivanka had been married twice and had two daughters from her first marriage.

An Orthodox Christian, Ivanka reported having had a strong religious belief ever since childhood. In reflecting on where she 'inherited this strong faith', Ivanka highlighted the importance of her religious grandparents. She reported receiving very little formal religious education at school, but recalled at the age of 9 years feeling a 'spiritual hunger' and asking her grandfather to obtain for her a Bible to read. She recalled that some of the happiest moments in her life were when her grandfather would read to her from the Bible. For Ivanka, belief in childhood was an essential prerequisite for strong belief in later life. She expressed her thoughts on the role of early exposure to religious belief on belief in later life as follows:

> It's true that upbringing matters. But I'd also say this. If you don't have faith, a grain of faith, if you remember the poem "Spring"[4] – in the days of prosperity, it can't sprout. So it seems to me that in each person there should be such a grain; if he has this grain, there comes a time, even in the last years of his life, when he returns back to God. That's what I think. This grain has always been in me because my grandfather.

Ivanka continued on this theme by alluding to the Gospel of Saint Matthew, Chapter 17, Verse 20: 'I should tell you that upbringing has its influence but I tell you again that if you don't have this mustard grain of faith that can lift mountains, you can't do anything. So this grain should be there.'

The aspects of Ivanka's strong personal faith in God that appeared particularly salient to her was her strong sense of God's care and protection for her and the confidence she had that God would help her should she need it. An example of these strong protective beliefs was in how Ivanka expressed great faith in God with regard to maintaining her health. Ivanka reported that she had experienced three significant strokes in her life, the first in 1987, the second in 1992 and a third minor stroke more recently. However, when the interviewer encouraged Ivanka to

---

[3]   See also Goncharova (Chapter 7) and Karamelska (Chapter 10) for other aspects of Ivanka Grozdeva's case.

[4]   The interviewee refers to another poem, 'Faith', also written by communist poet Nikola Vaptsarov (1909–1942); it does not refer to religious faith but rather to the 'faith' that 'tomorrow/life will be better/life will be wiser'. Both poems have been part of the school curriculum ever since the 1940s and are very popular. Probably this is the reason why Ivanka does not find it problematic to illustrate her views on her religious upbringing with a metaphor from the poem.

take care of herself she replied: 'I don't take care of myself. That's the problem, I don't take care of myself. It seems that God takes care of me. He really does take care of me. He sends me a lot of ordeals, a lot of difficulties but He also gives me strength to overcome them.' In addition, Ivanka also attributed in part her sense of happiness specifically to God: 'I'm happy that I was born and I was probably from such a family that I strongly believe in God. It's God who supports me. It's probably God who gives me happiness in life, too. He protects me. That's what I think.'

Ivanka was very active in her religious practice and reported engaging in daily prayer, reading the Bible, lighting candles for the dead and attending up to three different churches. Indeed, she light-heartedly commented that, from the perspective of her family, 'I hardly ever leave the church'. Moreover, Ivanka appeared to derive a great sense of purpose in life through her religious practice. She described regularly preparing 'the five loaves' for Sunday liturgy and reported that it was important to her to 'contribute her mite' to the churches she attends and through the church to the prosperity of the Bulgarian people. In addition, Ivanka emphasised that since childhood an important aspect of her religious belief has been to be charitable, 'for me God is to do good deeds, to love', and reported her involvement in pro-social activities such as charity work and caring for other older adults, especially those who were sick or close to death.

An experience in Ivanka's life related to her belief that was particularly salient to her was how she defended her right to hold and practise her Orthodox Christian belief during the height of the communist regime. During her working life in state-run libraries, Ivanka described occasions where she witnessed opposition to Orthodoxy and experienced work-related prejudice specifically because she held a religious belief and attended church, which brought her on occasion into conflict with her superiors and colleagues. Although Ivanka was never explicitly told to stop attending church, she was 'warned' to attend church 'inconspicuously', something that was arguably against her religious principles. However, a source of satisfaction for Ivanka was in how she repeatedly refused to become a party member when invited.

With regard to significant bereavements, Ivanka was one year old when her father died and her mother was left at the age of 27 years to raise two young children. Ivanka experienced a very similar bereavement pattern in her own life. Her first husband died in a car accident in 1965 when Ivanka was 28 years old and she was left to raise two young daughters, one three years old and the other five. Ivanka recalled her behaviour in the days following bereavement from her husband that provided a glimpse into her life at the time. She described being at her husband's grave 'day and night'. She recalled getting up at 4 o'clock each morning, leaving to go to the cemetery at 5 o'clock, then going to visit her sick mother in hospital, returning home to prepare her children for kindergarten, then leaving for work herself. Although these events had occurred 45 years earlier, as she spoke the memories triggered observable upset. Ivanka continued by recalling the practices she used to commemorate her religious husband's death during the early stage of her grief that were openly religious but also inclusive of the communist ideology of the period.

> This would happen at 4 in the morning. Then at 5 I'd leave home, I'd go to church to light a candle for him. All these things for 40 days in a row. His collective – 70 people. I'd gather them. They'd all take part in the organisation – lambs, korbans, and things like that. They respected me for my strong faith. There were different people there – party members, all sorts of people. No one ever showed that they disapproved of this, that I shouldn't do this. I keep the cross, I keep the photos [she cries], I have a whole album, there he was at the front with the cross; I also have a photo of them, there were red stars too. But I brought the cross so that he was buried with it. And that's the way I did it. Not only because he was religious. But my faith in God … So the 40 days passed, many more days passed and my only support was God. This was the only thing – I waited for nine days, three days, 20 days, 40 days. I had this from my mother, from my family. I grew up in this way, with all these Christian, these church rites. And I observed everything. And the three months, the six months, the nine months, a year, a monument and so on. My mother-in-law … says, "Thank you, I'm so grateful that you will do everything for my son." Pay attention to this. "But I don't have the belief to believe that he's alive." And I embraced her and I kissed her and I told her, "I feel sorry for you, mother, [she cries] because what helps me now is my faith in God, my faith that he is alive. His spirit is alive."

When Ivanka was asked directly whether her faith had helped her, she replied: 'Not only did it help me in the past but also it helps me now, my faith'. Ivanka highlighted a significant practice that she used to commemorate the dead. As with many regular church-goers, she reported making a financial donation to have a liturgy dedicated to those who have died. Indeed, she carried out this obligation even though she herself was experiencing financial difficulty: 'I constantly pay for holy liturgies, holy 40-days memorial service, as soon as I hear that someone has died. I know they'd never think of it themselves. But I go there and I pay for holy 40 days memorial service for the dead.' However, what is particularly interesting is the logic articulated by Ivanka behind why she does this, specifically her belief that these types of religious rituals can help the dead, with the full extension of this idea being that the actions of the living can help the dead in their life-after-death existence. Thus, this idea adds an interesting dimension to the reasons why some believers engage in religion-related grief rituals and ceremonies. Indeed, this idea of helping the dead also ties in with the belief underlying the importance of marking the first 40 days since death, during which the deceased, or soul of the deceased, is believed to be on a journey from an earthly existence to a life after death.

> Because it is the dead who are in greatest need of us, the living – to mention them in our prayers. Not everybody leaves this world having confessed all their

sins, not everybody fasted and received Holy Communion or was allowed to receive it. So the living have to help the dead and to pray for their sins. That's the way I see it.

Valentina Vassileva

Another Bulgarian participant who, similarly to Ivanka, also highlighted the importance of honouring the first 40 days since the death and periodic commemorations was Valentina Vassileva. Valentina was 71 years old and was living with her daughter. Valentina had been a manual worker in different industries during her working life but had retired from full-time work at the age of 52 years to look after her grandchildren.

Unlike many of the highly religious older adults interviewed from the three countries, Valentina did not come from a particularly religious background. Although her parents, who had been farmers, had observed certain religious festivals and traditions when she was a child, Valentina commented that her parents had not been religious and that as a child she rarely went to church. Valentina reported only becoming religious at the age of 40 years when, on one Holy Thursday, while she was at work, she described feeling a strong desire to attend the divine service, and she began to pray to God. Since that day, Valentina described a feeling of being drawn closer to God: 'Since then, it seems to me, God has drawn me closer to Him, He has drawn me closer. You see, God calls on you.' Indeed, at the time of the interview Valentina had been working as a sexton at her church for the last six years.

Valentina had a strong personal faith in God and attributed to God much of her health and well-being. She had a strong sense of being thankful to God and emphasised that she felt God's help and support in her life: 'God drew me here. Thank you, Lord! He always helps me, He helps me a lot, I count on Him only.' Valentina also expressed her belief that events in life occur in accordance with God's will or power: 'Thank God, He saved me. That's what I say. Everything is through God's help, God's will and God's power.'

Valentina described engaging in a wide variety of religious practices and highlighted the importance to her of receiving communion, of confession and fasting. She also reported preparing the five loaves, lighting candles for deceased loved ones, and dedicating Saturday to the dead. Moreover, Valentina provided a revealing glimpse into her more personal daily religious practice:

> I go to bed with a prayer, I cross myself before bed, I cross myself when I get up. Always. I sometimes make up my mind to go to bed and watch TV and I drowse. So I get up. I say the prayer, I don't know if it's wrong or not, then I cross myself and I go to bed again. We [Valentina and her daughter] sometimes burn incense over our beds, we sprinkle them with holy water. That's what we do, both of us.

Valentina also described her prayer and veneration related to religious icons, be they in her home or in the church:

I have icons here and in the other room, they are from the monastery, they've brought me icons from monasteries. I pray to them. But I mostly pray to the Holy Mother. And of course to Jesus Christ. I even read in the newspaper the other day that when you enter a church, you must first go to Christ's icon to bow and then to bow to Mother Mary's icon. That's what I do.

In addition, although Valentina reported some non-specific health problems that had recently prevented her from attending church as frequently as she would like, she did feel that her physical health problems were relieved when at church:

Whenever I go to the church here, even if I have some aches and pains, the saints relieve them all. They relieve my pains. There are no pains there, all my aches and pains are gone. When I go there, the saints take away all my burdens.

When Valentina was asked directly what was the hardest moment in her life, she replied: 'The hardest moment was when my husband died. I had to cope with male and female work. It's very difficult to be the man and the woman in the family. It's very difficult.' Valentina had lost her husband 21 years ago after a two-year-long illness. Two months after her husband died her father-in-law also died. She recalled some of the grief she experienced following the loss of her husband: 'You can't imagine how much I cried, if you could return a person from death by crying, he would have come back a hundred times.' Valentina described how she commemorated her husband's death in the days following her bereavement:

Forty days after my husband died, I didn't have a single work day. Forty days I kept going to the cemetery. That's how it was in the past. Now people don't observe this. Every day I'd go there on foot. But now I can't walk, I haven't got the legs for this. It's only after that that I started work. His father – I asked my neighbours to go there after the 40th day, to visit him, the man was gone because of the worries. It was really bad to face your child's death. May God protect even my worst foe from this.

Valentina commemorated the death of her husband and father-in-law using a practice that combined Christian ritual with earlier tradition.

Father Dimiter came and performed the service. The service was here. At the cemetery. We couldn't ignore this. There was also a service after the 40 days, we also have it each year. I've always observed the church things the way they should be. For my husband and for my father-in-law. When they both died – three lambs. It was necessary to slaughter either one or three lambs for votive offering. Therefore we bought three lambs for my husband, we bought three lambs for my father-in-law's commemoration too. I've always observed church traditions. For the deceased.

Discussion

In thinking about potential therapeutic properties associated with religious belief and practice, and in particular religious ritual, in the context of significant bereavement, the present case studies provide examples of several ways in which different religious dimensions may exert a positive influence. For the present sample of case studies, certain religious cognitions appeared to be particularly important during their bereavement and grief experience. Perhaps the two beliefs that were most frequently emphasised were belief in a personal relationship with God, and belief in a life after death.

All of the cases reported a strong belief in God and perceived a personal relationship with God in which they could communicate with God, often through religious rituals such as prayer or during the communion service, and perceive the influence of God in their lives. The majority of cases had felt or experienced their personal relationship with God since childhood, often introduced to this way of thinking and feeling by parents or grandparents, or through their religious education. However, this was not always the case, as for example Valentina appeared to have developed her belief and sense of a relationship with God as an adult and her belief seemed to have grown stronger with age and since her bereavement. In the context of bereavement, in different ways this sense of a relationship with God was often felt as God caring for, protecting and supporting the person in their bereavement and grief. In some cases, such as Ivanka, God was perceived as being her only support. Similar to the function provided by human relationships, the perceived relationship with God is likely to have ameliorated some of the feelings of loneliness, vulnerability or abandonment elicited by significant bereavement. Indeed, for most of the cases, faith and belief were often associated with indicators of psychological well-being and meaning in life.

Similarly important was belief in a life after death. Although participant descriptions of this belief lacked detail, it seemed to capture how, although the deceased was no longer physically present, from the perspective of the participants, the deceased still continued to exist in some form, somewhere, in a location that transcended human understanding, be this in heaven or in the presence of God, and importantly that the deceased had the potential to be aware of the living. Related to this, it seemed that a part of this belief meant that deceased loved ones were still in some way accessible, albeit indirectly, or that their presence could be sensed, evoked or communed with, specifically through engagement in religious rituals.

Similar findings have been identified by Spreadbury and Coleman (2011) in religious British older adults who had lost a spouse. However, one significant difference from the present case studies is that, in the British sample used by Spreadbury and Coleman (2011), in addition to believing in a life after death, it was also important for some participants to believe in a life-after-death *reunion* with one's spouse. In the present sample of cases there seemed to be little or no mention of a belief in a reunion with deceased loved ones. One possible explanation for this observation may reside in the different attitude to death influenced by the branch of Christianity each participant believed in and identified with. Of the case studies presented, four were Eastern Orthodox and it may be that Eastern Orthodoxy, in comparison with other branches of Christianity, perhaps encourages an attitude of a greater or on-going sense of deceased loved ones still being present in one's life and perhaps even a greater sense of responsibility for the dead.

For those who placed importance on certain religious rituals, there were several ways in which these religious activities seemed to be experienced as helpful in the context of bereavement and grief. Perhaps one of the main ways in which religious rituals seemed to be useful was in how they provided proactive ways for responding to death and bereavement and in providing on-going ways of managing and expressing one's grief. These ways of responding may be in the short term and immediately following a significant bereavement, as in engaging in daily prayer for the dead during the first 40 days, preparing food to honour the dead or giving alms, or longer term during the on-going process of grief, as in regular candle lighting, periodic commemorations or dedicating services to deceased loved ones. In this sense, religion through its religious rituals was able to provide both immediate and longer-term continuous ways of behaving, thinking and feeling related to death, bereavement and grief. In addition, for some believers such as Ivanka, performing religious rituals was perceived as a way of helping the dead in their life-after-death existence, and may therefore hold great potential for offering some believers a sense that they are doing something positive or useful. As such, through engagement in religious rituals, it may be possible for some believers to develop a sense of control or certainty during a period that would otherwise be experienced as uncontrollable and uncertain.

Performing religious rituals, as well as having a belief in a life after death, also had the potential to function as continuing bonds processes (Klass et al. 1996) related to significant deceased loved ones. Through engaging in religious rituals such as praying, lighting candles, dedicating services to the dead or attending liturgy, it was possible for some cases to feel a sense of continuing a relationship with deceased loved ones. Indeed, through performing religious rituals and having a belief in a life after death, some cases, such as Ioana, were also able to evoke, when needed, a feeling that significant deceased loved ones were in close proximity and had the ability to help the living.

Indeed, extending the theory of continuing bonds with deceased loved ones, it could be considered that at some level there may be perceived a tacit or latent interactional relationship with the dead. This idea refers to a relationship in which, for some religious believers, deceased loved ones are perceived as being able to help, or at the very least support or accompany, the living, especially in times of trouble, and the living are perceived as being able to help the dead by performing religious rituals to help the dead in their life-after-death existence. Cases such as Ioana and Ivanka lend some support for the existence of a hypothesised perceived interactional relationship that may generalise to other highly religious older adults.

There was also evidence from the cases for powerful psychological and attachment processes at work that perhaps deserve mention. For example, both

Ioana and Eleonora reported feeling a powerful 'need' to regularly attend church liturgy following their respective significant bereavements from their mother, and this seemed to be an attempt to increase their emotional proximity to their mother and to continue their feeling of attachment as a method of on-going coping and adjustment. Thus, their strong attachment needs to feel close to their mother following bereavement seemed to be satisfied or facilitated through their being able to attend church on a daily basis and experience the liturgy. In addition, for Eleonora, the bereavement of her parents seemed to strengthen her belief and practice and was also accompanied by a significant change in her attitude, in that she wanted to think and behave in a more moral way and to perceive the world more positively, while for Kate following the loss of her husband she experienced a period of two years in deep personal reflection until she felt ready to socially interact with others again specifically through activities related to her local church.

In summary, it is arguable that, without such religious beliefs, rituals and resources to engage in, the present sample of case studies perhaps would have felt increasingly disempowered in the face of death and bereavement and would have found their personal experiences of significant bereavement even more difficult or challenging. In addition, for the present sample of older adults, particularly those in Romania and Bulgaria where communist regimes attempted to introduce secular rituals and ceremonies to replace religious ones,[5] religion may have been experienced as more satisfying than secular and atheistic alternatives, specifically because religion provided psychologically helpful ways of continuing bonds and attachments with deceased loved ones.

References

Becker, Gerhild, Carola J. Xander, Hubert E. Blum, et al. 2007. 'Do Religious or Spiritual Beliefs Influence Bereavement? A Systematic Review'. *Palliative Medicine* 21: 207–17.

Coleman, Peter G. 2011. 'The Changing Social Context of Belief in Later Life'. In *Belief and Ageing: Spiritual Pathways in Later Life*, Peter G. Coleman et al., 11–33. Bristol: Policy Press.

Coleman, Peter G., Marie A. Mills and John H. Spreadbury. 2011. 'Ageing and Faith: Trajectories Across the Lifespan'. In *Belief and Ageing: Spiritual Pathways in Later Life*, Peter G. Coleman et al., 59–77. Bristol: Policy Press.

Gillies, James and Robert A. Neimeyer. 2006. 'Loss, Grief, and the Search for Significance: Toward a Model of Meaning Reconstruction in Bereavement'. *Journal of Constructivist Psychology* 19: 31–65.

Klass, Dennis, Phyllis R. Silverman and Steven L. Nickman. 1996. *Continuing Bonds: New Understandings of Grief.* London: Taylor & Francis.

---

[5]   See Bădică (Chapter 3) and Koleva (Chapter 6).

Koenig, Harold G., Michael McCullough and David B. Larson. 2001. *Handbook of Religion and Health*. New York: Oxford University Press.

Paloutzian, Raymond F. and Crystal L. Park. 2005. *Handbook of the Psychology of Religion and Spirituality*. New York: Guilford Press.

Spreadbury, John H. and Peter G. Coleman. 2011. 'Religious Responses in Coping with Spousal Bereavement'. In *Belief and Ageing: Spiritual Pathways in Later Life*, Peter G. Coleman et al., 79–96. Bristol: Policy Press.

Wortmann, Jennifer H. and Crystal L. Park. 2008. 'Religion and Spirituality in Adjustment Following Bereavement: An Integrative Review'. *Death Studies* 32: 703–36.

PART IV
Gendered Ageing and Religion

Chapter 9

Social Change and Well-being: The Place of Religion in Older Bulgarian Men's Lives

Ignat C. Petrov and Peter G. Coleman

This is the first of two chapters examining different perspectives on men and women's ageing and its relationship to religious belief and practice. The present chapter examines in depth the well-being of the older men interviewed in Bulgaria, in relation to the social changes they have experienced over their lives, particularly changes in regard to religion. We begin by reviewing previous studies on the effects of social change on the experience of ageing before presenting our analysis of the older men in our sample in Bulgaria. We purposefully evaluate the well-being and its sources in men both with and without strong religious faith. In the concluding sections we comment on the apparent stability of these men's attitudes to religion with age and draw some comparisons with the older men studied in Romania and the UK.

However we begin by introducing the subject of religion and well-being in later life. Across the life course, religion has been thought to provide a sense of significance, belonging and rootedness to both individuals and societies. These functions may become more salient in the second half of life as the social and psychological processes of ageing encourage greater reflection on the meaning of life and death, to which religion can bring a greater sense of coherence. However the interaction between religion and mental health remains complex. In certain circumstances religion can heighten feelings of guilt and anxiety, but empirical evidence indicates that religious belief and practice have, in general, a positive influence on mental health (Coleman 2010). Religious faith prevents depression by both promoting positive mood and counteracting despair. Religion encourages healthy behaviour, cultivating an attitude of respect to the body and against attitudes of despair. Persons aged 50 and over who engage in religious activity are less likely to commit suicide (Nisbet et al. 2000).

A recent study of ours on samples of rural elderly aged 60 and over in Bulgaria and Romania revealed lower levels of spiritual belief and significantly higher levels of depression in the Bulgarian compared with the Romanian sample (Coleman et al. 2011). Analyses of the data suggest that spiritual belief may both influence and reflect physical and mental illness. The predominantly US literature on religion and mental health suggest reasons for this. Religious faith and practices have a social importance. Church participation and membership of a religious organisation both encourage activity and provide a potential support network. Religious belief can increase resilience and help older persons to cope more effectively with the stresses and losses of later life (Levin, Markides and Ray 1996). The attitudes that are learned from religiously committed peers may benefit one's health through encouragement of healthy behaviours and lifestyles, lowering the risk of disease (Levin and Chatters 1998). The most striking findings relevant to health and ageing come in studies of longevity. An extensive cross-state study in the USA has found a life expectancy difference of more than seven years between those never attending religious services and those attending more than once weekly (Hummer et al. 1999).

The gender aspect of religion has been little studied in relation to ageing, which is surprising since, certainly in Western Christian societies, women tend to be more religiously observant than men, whereas religious ministry has been traditionally confined to the latter (Woodhead 2004). However some theorists have argued that the process of ageing, with its potential for greater androgyny in personality characteristics relating to dependency, aggression and need for control, leads to greater openness to religion in men and greater scepticism in women (Gutmann 1987; Henry 1988; Coleman, Ivani-Chalian and Robinson 2004).

Much better studied are gender differences related to health and longevity. Women live longer, men die earlier, but older men may have more years in subjectively judged good health (Kryspin-Exner, Lampimayr and Felnhofer 2011). The study of inherent behavioural differences between women and men is compromised by societal expectations. The traditional masculine model of behaviour includes more competitiveness and more rationality displayed in the taking of responsibility, decisions and risks. Women on other hand are expected to be caregivers to a much greater extent than men, and to be somewhat more intuitive, sensitive and empathic. Women soften and counterbalance men. Males tend to engage in high-risk activities more frequently than females, and may incur higher levels of stress in some circumstances. However, in more economically advanced societies the roles of men and women have converged to some extent. Thus their characteristics have become less dissimilar than they were in past historical periods. Late middle age and old age is a period of both convergence and loss. Role convergence means that men and women face less differentiated worlds with the transition to retirement, physical decline, illnesses and widowhood.

Social Change and Well-being in Later Life: The Case of Eastern Europe

Relationships between social milieu and well-being, including psychological well-being, are complex. It is assumed that in all historical periods individuals and groups of people have been greatly influenced by times of abrupt political and social changes (Schaie and Elder 2005). These might be wars, revolutions, sharp economic changes or technological changes in common ways of living. Studies conducted in the UK in the 1970s and early 1980s documented the distress experienced by many older people who found the social changes originating in the

1960s too much to bear (Seabrook 1980; Coleman and McCulloch 1990). They commented especially on perceived changes in younger generations' attitudes to social and religious values.

The lives of those persons aged over 75 years interviewed in this study have occupied a period of considerable political and social change. In the earlier part of their lives they witnessed the mass destruction and upheavals caused by the Second World War. Their middle adult years differed greatly between those living in Eastern and Western Europe. Whereas those in the UK observed the birth of the welfare state and increased liberalisation of attitudes towards, for example, norms of sexual behaviour, those in Bulgaria and Romania saw the installation of cruel totalitarian regimes. However, interestingly all three countries, in this period of their life, saw concerted and generally successful attacks on the influence of religious authority within their respective societies. In their later years our participants have experienced further changes, threats to end the postwar welfare consensus in the UK and the dramatic collapse of communist rule and a return to capitalist principles in Eastern Europe. We expected that our informants would provide us with valuable information on their subjective experiences related to these changes.

Of course social change is an almost inevitable aspect of ageing. Even the most traditional and stable societies show some change over a person's lifetime, and some degree of adaptation is required of all people as they grow old. Yet older people in modern societies have often experienced multiple changes in their lives. The individual qualities of resilience, personality outlook and values, as well ties within the close environment could modify the effect of macro-social changes. Family structures and quality of relationships are particularly important for the maintenance of older people's well-being through a period of major social change.

A number of studies have examined the well-being of people in Eastern Europe during and after the fall of the communist regimes, but without distinguishing the particular attitudes of the older part of the population. Thus Muller (2004) studied the social attitudes in East Germany after the unification of the country, and found that, although 45 per cent of the East Germans were more satisfied with life in 2000 in comparison with 1989/1990, 30 per cent were more dissatisfied and 12 per cent found no change.

The first author of this chapter has been one of the few to study the feelings and attitudes of older people towards the changes that occurred in the mode of life during the transition to democracy and capitalism in the early 1990s (Petrov 1996a, b). These revealed a considerable variability of views. In analysing the reported feeling and attitudes to the changes, five categories were established: positive and/optimistic (+); mixed but predominantly positive (+ + −); mixed (+ −); mixed but predominantly negative (+ − −); and negative and pessimistic feelings and expectations (−). Around 70 per cent of the older people studied were polarised at the extremes: 35 per cent (+) and 35 per cent (−). Mixed views were held by much smaller numbers: 19 per cent were classified as (+ −), and only a few cases were (+ + −) and (+ − −).

The most commonly shared positive feelings towards the changes were of relief, inner liberation, joy, enthusiasm, faith, confidence, happiness, hope and optimism. The most common negative feelings were of disappointment, apathy, sadness, incertitude, anxiety and pessimism. The main plusses concerning the period post-1989 involved freedom as a central value; freedom to speak, act, think and listen to radio; freedom for initiative, self-realisation and enterprise; and better prospects for the country. The main minuses defined were: economic difficulties with insufficient income compared with the sharply rising prices; lack of discipline, authority, law and security; mistrust, disunion and aggression among people and especially among politicians; morale and culture decline; criminality; ruination; and concerns about the future of the country (which were heterogeneous – fears of a return of communism as well as concerns about national unity, and fears of war).

To some extent, the older people with negative views were more extreme in their statements. Usually they did not see anything positive in the situation. Many of the elders with positive views had mild criticism, noticing some negative aspects of the time of transition, but they firmly believed the minuses were transient and would dissipate with the advance of the democratic process. Among 34 personality, health and social variables calculated, nine correlated significantly ($p < 0.05$) with positive versus negative views on the changes. Favourable factors were: living with another person; having a surviving spouse; having good relationships within the family, including with children; higher level of education; stable personality characteristics; and higher self ratings on the scales of happiness, health and intelligence from the Self-Evaluation Test.

There are many aspects to the impact on well-being of the communist mode of life as well as of the post-1989 changes in Eastern Europe. During the 1950s and 1960s mortality decreased and life expectancy improved throughout much of Europe. In the late 1960s and 1970s this began to change. The steady improvement in West Europe contrasted sharply with the stagnation and decline in Eastern Europe. By 1989 there was a striking gap in life expectancy between East and West (Bobak and Marmot 1996). The further evolution was uneven in the different Eastern countries; Bulgaria and Romania began to show improvements only in the late 1990s. Most of the East European countries have experienced rising adult mortality since 1970 and in the majority of them the mortality rates continue to be high compared with the European average (Nolte, McKee and Gilmore 2004).

Assessing Well-being in Later Life

From a gerontological point of view it is important to look for the signs of subjective well-being recorded in the interviews, their links with religious and non-religious beliefs, and their evolution in the life course. Did the interviews reveal some evidence of changes with age in attitudes and characteristics of the participants? Were these changes linked to ageing *per se* and/or with the 'external' changes in the person's mode of life? From a psychogeriatric viewpoint it is interesting to see whether the sharp political, social and economic changes endured by the interviewees have had some impact on their mental health and well-being.

An examination of the 60 interviews shows that they vary in the degree of knowledge they give about the personality and psychological well-being of the interviewees through their lives. In some interviews this evidence is more extensive and informative and in others cases it remains scarce. For an appraisal of the psychological well-being we rely on:

- the presence or absence of psychological or mental health problems such as depression, anxiety and feelings of loneliness;
- the global narrative, and in particular, data about positive and stable development of the personality, for example, in family and social life;
- the personal experience of life satisfaction and happiness according to the Self-Evaluation Test data (Petrov 1976) and the rest of the interview.

At the time of the interview the majority of the respondents seem to have been in a good mental state. In only one case (Aydan Berber from Shumen) might it be suspected that the interviewee was in a state of some mental disorder. Five interviewees shared data about one or more depressive episodes in their past life. Almost all of them had overcome these difficulties and at the time of the interview were in a state of positive psychological well-being. A few of the participants demonstrated mild signs of depression or anxiousness at the time of interview.

The Self-Evaluation of Personality and its Social Coherence Test (SET)[1] was developed from procedures in which individual persons were asked to project their perception of personal well-being on a scale of one (or more) vertical lines. The full SET consists of two parts. For many purposes, and also in this study, we used only the first part with five scales of self-evaluation of health, intellect, character (or personal qualities), others' attitudes and happiness. The procedure involves the interviewer drawing, in front of the participants, a vertical line (*c.* 10 cm long) on a blank sheet of paper and at the same time asking them to imagine that the top end stands for the most optimal health and the bottom end for the worst possible health. When the respondent has completed the marks on the five lines, the interviewer restarts the conversation by asking for comments on each in a (partly) reversed

---

[1]　Tamara Dembo, a disciple of Kurt Lewin, studied disabled persons in the USA, asking them to mark their position of happiness along one vertical line. She demonstrated this method during a psychological conference in Moscow and Susanne Rubinstein acquired it. Rubinstein (1970) used four consecutive vertical lines. A similar method was used by Fernand Clement in Paris. The author borrowed the method from Rubinstein in her laboratory at the Moscow Institute of Psychiatry and later developed it for use in Bulgaria (Petrov 1976). Further details on the administration of the SET test are available from the author.

order: happiness, health, intellect, character and others' attitudes. Happiness is the most general category; it is presented last but comes first in the comments.

The projective elements of this test come from the way of presenting the task and the suggested/assisted personal freedom of choosing on a continuity of innumerable positions along the line and the subsequent explanation of their choice. Combining this projective approach with a biographical interview about important life themes proved to be a useful way of obtaining valuable information about the older person's health, personality, values, subjective well-being and quality of life. It appears to harmonise with the inclination of the ageing personality towards life review and, in some older people, also towards an alternative mode of thinking. The SET test has been found to be understood and performed by older people of all levels of education, even by those who are illiterate. It has also proved to be a quick and sensitive instrument in the early assessment of depressive and cognitive disorders of older people.

Older Bulgarian Men with a Religious Identity

The first two examples presented in this category are Bulgarian military officers who displayed stable subjective well-being arising from a family education based on the values of honesty, patriotism and Orthodox religion. Their mature life and military service had taken place in a difficult time when the communist regime was establishing itself and making particular demands of the army. Both had encountered problems in adjustment.

Naum Ruskov was an 84 year old army officer and engineer. He was well-educated, moderately extroverted, physically healthy and moderately religious, with a successful family and professional life, and with high levels of subjective well-being. Naum was a widower and lived in Sofia together with one of his two daughters. He had been born in Karnobat in 1924. His father was also an officer and engineer, his mother a teacher. Naum had grown up in an Orthodox religious family.

> My first religious performance was to hold the train of the bishop's cloak ... I must have been three or four years old ... For us religion is ... not something you can learn. It is something that you naturally acquire; it is an element of your upbringing ...

> You approach something and you start believing in it. Initially it's only a kind of intuition ... The mystery in the church, the sacrament itself, the atmosphere there, the silence, all builds in you a kind of respect, respect to something that is not material. It's something spiritual. It makes you more humble. I am not a religious fanatic; I perceive it as something that exists for me, something existing in me. I believe in it without any doubt ... The feeling inside – this is a faith.

Naum was engaged in the latter part of the war in 1944–1945 against Germany. After 1944 he was on the brink to being discharged from the army. The policy of the new government was to replace the old regime officers with people devoted to the communist ideology. However, owing to his competence as an engineer he succeeded in staying in the army until 1956, although during all of this period he felt himself under suspicion. Being an acting army officer Naum organised his civil marriage in 1947 in the town where he served, but immediately after that there was a church ceremony in his native town onthe opposite side of the country. For a period of several years he ceased to enter a church – '*it was a taboo for an army officer*' – and in that period of Stalinism he prayed at home with an icon-light. Naum was now attending a church on all the great holidays and regularly visited the graves of persons close to him.

> The grave is a sacred place to me.

There were no indications of major physical illness. Naum seemed to be healthy for his age and talkative. The interviewer described him as an energetic man. He was evidently stable and well-balanced. He had been well educated and had had a successful career. After being discharged from the army he had worked in business and travelled much in Europe. Although now a widower, he had had a happy marital life. His religious belief was something natural for him, acquired in the childhood. It gave him calmness, confidence and hope. His subjective well-being seems to have remained stable throughout life. Concerning outward observance of religious ritual, he was wise to conform to not exhibiting his religiosity at the time of Stalinism when he had been an army officer. His innate personality structure, his family education in patriotism and Orthodox faith, a happy family life and a relatively successful professional career appear to have fostered his subjective well-being.

Andon Igov, whose case has already been discussed in some detail in Chapter 6, was another older man with high level of subjective well-being, but not without substantial difficulties in his life. Born in Stara Zagora, he had worked as an officer in the navy. A widower, he was now living in Sofia with his son and daughter-in-law. He presented as a cultured man with a well-balanced and differentiated personality. The interviewer described him as 'energetic, tall and good-looking man. He speaks clearly and confidently'. Andon had grown up in Kazanlak in a patriarchal family with Orthodox religious parents. His grandfather was a priest. All of the family members fasted and received communion regularly and dressed in their best clothes. He developed a strong religiosity during childhood, and still described himself as a 'religious Christian'.

Andon applied for the Navy school and studied there. He was interested to see the sea and to experience romance and travel, especially to exotic places. Moreover the financial situation of his family, with four children, had become difficult. His father was already ill. Early in his life, at the age of eight, he had come to realise that his two elder brothers were really stepbrothers. For him this was a shock to understand that his mother had had a previous marriage. She had reassured him, and in fact he appreciated that her attitude to each of her four children had been equal.

He was satisfied with the years spent in the Military Naval School, which was situated firstly in the small Black Sea town of Sozopol and then in Varna. In the School, just as in his family, he became accustomed to the full range of Orthodox religious rituals. During his first year there his father died. He discovered this only as he approached the family home for Christmas. He was in his uniform and he remembered telling himself: 'I am a soldier and I have to console my mother in this time of grief.'

Andon was promoted to the rank of officer in 1944. The stable moral system he had acquired, his religious faith as well the upbringing in honesty and patriotism, helped him both to resist and to overcome serious difficulties after the *coup d'etat* of 9 September 1944 with the subsequent political repressions. He encountered a series of difficulties with misunderstandings and suspicions from supervising Soviet officers sent to the Bulgarian fleet. As a captain of a ship on the Danube but supervised by a Soviet political officer, Andon had refused the order of the Soviet political officer to remove the Bulgarian flag and replace it with a Soviet flag. He was put under arrest for three days, then liberated and permitted to raise again the Bulgarian flag. After the war Andon was rudely dismissed in spite of the fact that we had been awarded the Medal of Honour.

> They told me to leave Rousse in 24 hours. I had a girlfriend there, we were about to get married ... When she understood I was not an officer any more, she started crying, "I wanted a man with golden buttons ...". We split up and I went to Varna. Soon I had to leave Varna too, because if you don't become a member of the Party, you are no longer wanted in Varna. I took leave for 24 hours and went back to Kazanlak.

Earlier, in May 1944 one of his brothers had been killed by communist partisans. In response his other brother had written an open letter to the partisans and an arrest warrant was issued for him after the 9 September. Andon was arrested for a period as a suspected initiator of that letter. Subsequently he went back to Varna and found work digging canals. However, then he was ordered to leave Varna by State Security and came to Sofia to work. It was in this period that he married and had a child while living with his mother-in-law. Eventually he managed to find work in Black Sea fishing fleet. Captains were needed, but again he encountered problems. It was noted that he had given his son a Christian name (see Chapter 6). Even though he overcame this obstacle, it was not long before he was accused again of religious activity, that when he was abroad he often visited churches and lit candles there.

To the question of which were the hardest moments of his life, Andon referred to a number of events: the discovery that his brothers were actually step-brothers; the loss of his father; the order to leave his ship at the end of the war; a period of personal remorse when he had not told the truth in matters affecting his friends; and dramatic events in his life at sea, saving Russian sailors from their ship which exploded three minutes later, and a subsequent dangerous situation with his ship in the severest of storms in the North Atlantic.

Andon was a remarkable man with many positive features – honest, brave, decisive, tenacious, critical of himself, firmly religious and patriotic, tolerant and a man of culture. His religion went together with an ethical system of honesty and patriotism, both of which were acquired in the family and at school. His religious and moral views had helped him to resist and preserve his subjective well-being as well as his sense of self. His religious faith was stable, with some deepening of mystical feeling in old age (see Chapter 11). His attitude to religious rituals had remained unchanged. They were part of his sense of self as an Orthodox Bulgarian Christian.

Evlogi Anastasov, our third example, was a well-educated man of 84 years of age, and was somewhat less religious. Born in Varna into a middle-class family, his mother had been very religious and had taken him to the Russian Church as a child. He became well acquainted both with the liturgy and the priests. However, after the revolution of 1944 he was sharply acquainted with political terror, and thereafter remained afraid of possible repressions.

Soon after the events of September 1944 he happened to visit the office of one well-known communist[2] in Varna, looking for a seasonal job. She saw the chain with a silver cross that Evlogi always wore around his neck and responded with force:

> "Oh, c'mon, what is this? Are you with a cross, are you religious, do you do these stupid things?" … She even tried to hit me, she tore one of the buttons of my shirt, she grabbed the cross and she threw it in the corner of the room. Of course I was furious, but I couldn't do anything; at the same time I was really scared … the fear that was in the air was another thing – a lot of murders had happened between '44 and '45, loads of people had disappeared without any sentences – this one had disappeared, the other one had disappeared. Everybody knew that these people were either shot or drowned in sea and so on. So this cross played a trick on me. However, I picked up the cross from the ground. She told me, "So what? Are you planning to hang it on yourself again?" "No", I said, and I put it in my pocket.

He spent many years studying part-time in Sofia while working at the (opposition) social-democratic newspaper *Narod*, always concerned about the possibility of repression. He studied medicine and then law, and finally graduated in journalism. He married, but only in a civil ceremony because of his cautiousness. However

---

2   'A sinister woman', she was said to have killed General Christo Christov, the commander of Third Army while he was waiting for a presentation of the officials in front of Marshal Tolbuchin in September 1944.

all of his children were christened (in a 'hidden' way), and his close family were buried with a religious service conducted by a priest.

Evlogi was later divorced and continued to blame himself for this, even though it was his wife who asked for the divorce. He thought they shared the guilt for the failure of their marriage, which he thought had had an unfavourable impact on the development of their two children. He was religious, with a good awareness of Orthodox Christianity, but no longer observed the rituals so strictly. He continued to visit the church, but not every week, and prayed usually only in circumstances of difficulty. He was inclined to believe in an after-life – like his mother. Probably possessing introversion and conscientiousness as his principal personality traits, he may have been helped to some extent by his religion, but appeared to be rather unhappy. Perhaps he felt lonely.

The two last religious examples were both members of the Turkish community living in Targovishte in North East Bulgaria. The political and social changes during the communist regime in Bulgaria, and especially in the 1980s, were especially painful for the Turkish and Bulgarian ethnic Muslim minorities (pomaks) in the country. They probably suffered even more than Orthodox Christian Bulgarians because:

- the majority of Muslims lived in economically less developed and poor regions, such as Targovishte;
- their mode of life was mostly traditional/patriarchal;
- the modernisation of 1944 and later was combined with atheistic– communist propaganda and regulations on marriages and births;
- a forced change of Arabic names to Bulgarian ones was imposed on these specific groups in the population during the 1980s.

Murad Sezgin was 80 years old, poor and living alone in a village near Targovishte. He was religious but also tolerant in his views. He felt sharply the changes in life within his region. He thought that life had been better before 1944:

Then we had less to eat, we used to eat poorer food, but we were merrier. My people, specially, they didn't use to quarrel … Our faith was stronger, we were happier, and we got on better with each other … Here in Targovishte we lived together Turkish and Bulgarian. We had Bulgarian and Turkish teachers … I remember in the past in our village we had a Turkish and a Bulgarian school. Some would finish fourth form (in the Turkish school) and would go to the Bulgarian school … We studied together with Bulgarians … There are people from my "mahala" [neighbourhood] – they studied in the Bulgarian school for a couple of years.

Now, when I look at the young, they don't show respect, because they don't respect our faith either. But it is because communism destroyed our faith; it destroyed the Bulgarians' faith too … [*So elderly people were more respected when you were young?*] Of course, my father couldn't do anything without first asking his father – my grandfather – for permission.

Murad was born in a village near Targovishte. His father and especially his mother were religious. He had a difficult life, studied seven classes and then worked hard on his piece of land. Murad had a family with three children, but his family has disintegrated. Under the influence of her communist sister, his wife had gradually showed a desire to be more independent, to oppose him and not to obey. They had separated. He had quarrelled also with their junior son, who had taken the side of his mother and tried to beat his father. Murad had left his home and escaped to another more remote village. Thereafter he had spent some years in Turkey with his other son, who had emigrated there. Finally he had returned and now lived alone. He was also not pleased with his daughter, who did not care for him – 'she is ill-bred and knows only to ask money from me'. However, he was very fond of his 10-year-old grandson, and kept up with his advances in study and also his religious education.

The forced changing of the names during 1980s was the worst period for Murad.

> I had hard times because I was religious. I even had problems with sleep …
> There was a lot of bullying, especially for the older people. I was about 50–60
> years old at that time … They even changed the cemeteries, "dzhnanam" [my
> dear]. Now there are a lot of Turkish people in Bulgarian cemeteries – you can
> say there are Muslims in Bulgarian cemeteries, yes, yes. [*How did you lament
> over your dead people then?*] How can you lament over them? It's impossible!

Murad remembered the negative social changes, with attempts to eradicate traditions, occurring throughout all the period after 1944. The changing of the names was the climax, the most dramatic moment. As a result the faith of the majority of young Muslims weakened.

> They destroyed the school and made the playground so that our roots disappear
> … they destroyed the old laws and the child doesn't listen to his parents, the wife
> doesn't listen to her husband and so on, and so on. We were used to the old ways
> … So, a lot of bad things happened then.

All his life Murad had been religious. Now he seldom visited the mosque, and preferred to pray at home. He observed all Muslim rituals. He thought that his religious faith helped him. It kept those who believed calmer, so that they lived longer.

> I can see it – faithful people live longer. It's always been like this … They don't
> cheat … My mother, for example. She would stay hungry and thirsty, but she

would keep Ramadan. My mother lived till 90 ... you can say, she prayed all day long – she worked and prayed. Every day, five times a day, even if she was at home.

The interview with Murad was carried out in one of the rooms of Targovishte's mosque. The respondent looked old and ill, and his hair was white. He seemed bent with the age but his blue eyes were bright and sparkling. On the SET test he expressed his feelings clearly:

[*Health?*] I'm not healthy, I have various pains. First I don't have money; second, there's nobody to help me – I have hernia in two places ...

[*Happiness?*] Some people believe in wealth ... But I am happy, because God has given me long life. I always manage to find something to eat, something to drink ... I have no friends, no relatives any more ... If God doesn't help me, if he doesn't give me strength to take care of myself ... If your brain works and your legs move a bit, you manage to get along, you see.

It seemed that the subjective well-being of Murad had been shaken by a chain of unfavourable personal events. The social changes he had experienced had also contributed to his pessimistic views. Murad felt ill and lonely, lacking help from other people. However, at least he felt he could he rely on God. His personal philosophy was rooted in strong religious belief and this helped him.

Demir Hamidov, a 74-year-old physics teacher, came from a background that contrasted strongly with Murad's. He was descended from a local Turkish elite. Both the families of his father and mother had included imams. His grandfather was a 'hogja', which signifies also a teacher of religion to children. His father was a teacher as well. He had obtained a theological education at the Muslim school in Shumen before studying physics in the University of Sofia. He had retired from teaching in Targovishte schools 12 years before. Married, he had two sons, both of whom had graduated in engineering at the University of Varna and now worked successfully in the field of informatics and computers, one in Sofia and the other in the USA.

In his childhood Demir has been brought up in a religious spirit. He said that his father was a man of high culture and morals. In their native village near Targovishte, Turks and Bulgarians had lived harmoniously together; they celebrated together Christian and Muslim holidays and exchanged respective presents (for example, coloured eggs at Easter). The Bulgarians in the village had also spoken Turkish. Demir thought that nowadays the Turkish people in his region are less religious, especially the younger Turks. They have been turned into 'atheists', also the Christians. 'Things have become faded. In our state there is an unbelief now. There is nothing to rely on'. In his narrative Demir mentioned that at some time in the past he had wished to become a member of the Communist Party. He alluded to the fact that Communist Party was somewhat like a religion, but that the power of the Party has weakened along with religious belief. At the same time Demir described himself as a very religious person.

> I believe deeply in the existence of Allah. I believe deeply that God will help me … If a man believes, it is easier for him. Belief provides assurance and calm. Religion can direct and discipline people.

Demir was proud to be Turk, but he was also proud to be a Bulgarian citizen. He considered Bulgarians and Turks to have a very similar mentality. Many other things, including the cuisine, were very similar. Living 500 years together was the cause of this. Demir thought that the commonly used Bulgarian expression 'Turkish yoke' (турско робство) was not the right designation. It was better to say 'Turkish domination' (турско владичество). He indicated that the Turkish domination may have had some positive influence on the Bulgarian people. Demir was now a member of the political party 'Movement of Rights and Liberties', which represented the interests of racial and religious minorities, and thought that it had had a positive influence on society. During the 1980s period of name changing he had agreed to change his name to Bulgarian form. He had entered into a brief and polite discussion with the commission in which he had admitted that he knew only three generations of his ancestors (i.e. previous ancestors may have had Bulgarian names).

Demir had a deep interest and knowledge in history and religion. He said he knew well all three Abrahamic religions, Islam, Christianity and Judaism. In comparing them he found that Muslim ideas of God were the best (they avoided ideas of man's similarity to God). He compared their rituals, especially in regard to funerals. He thought that the funeral ritual was a unifying influence among people and built mutual confidence; this was a stronger feature among Muslims. Demir had on his night bedside table both the Koran and the Bible and when he had trouble sleeping he used to read one of these books. Every morning he read the introduction to the Koran, but he did not observe the five Muslim rituals during the day.

At his first meeting with the interviewer (in the office of the Director of State Archives in Targovishte), Demir arrived well dressed but seemed reserved. One year later, he invited the interviewer to his home, a well-upholstered apartment with many books. It seemed that Demir had been affected by the abrupt political changes and especially by the forced changing of names, but he also had some opportunities to adapt and collaborate with the system, as he had some acquaintances within the local elite in Targovishte. His religious feelings, as well as his culture, his interest in religion and his successful professional and family life seemed to help him in preserving his self-esteem and sense of well-being.

Older Bulgarian Men with a Non-religious Identity

Our sample provided two clear examples of older Bulgarian men with a non-religious identity. Both presented clearly articulated alternative attitudes to life. Diman Vasilev was a well-adjusted man of 75 years who displayed a combination of positive personal qualities, professional and cultural experience, good physical health and good family relationships. It is noteworthy that he had been brought up in an atheistic family. Although not religious, he accepted that there was something spiritual in interpersonal relationships.

Diman's life history has already been referred to in Chapter 2 and more extensively described in Chapter 4. There it was noted that, although neither of his parents was religious, they had had to undergo ceremonies in 1941 (a document of marriage was needed for the christening of Diman, and a document of christening was needed to enrol him in a school). Diman had had a successful professional career as a geological engineer in which he had travelled a great deal, in China and Mongolia, as well as Mexico and Cuba. After his retirement he continued with what he described as 'a dynamic mode of life'. He had married in 1960 in a civil ceremony, and now lived in Sofia with his wife. During the interview he was very talkative, optimist, and evidently hyperthymic. He said that he was fully satisfied with his life.

> I have lived a good life, and I continue to live … I am not an Orthodox person. I could not accept the hypocrisy of the priests … Man is a biological being. Nature takes priority … I am an Orthodox pagan.

Sometimes he entered the church and lighted a candle. Looking at the flame he imagined that 'good thoughts rise up'.

> We enter into church, light candles. I, for example know that when you light a candle the flame goes up. It guides thought, it guides that which is not material, the flame goes up, somewhere there where the good ones are. That is why we will send them only good thoughts. Do you understand, this is neither pagan nor Christian. I have my own view on the issue. I know that we emit and this is it. [*In what do you believe?*] I don't know. The poet Vaptsarov said "I believe in man". Men are those who make good and evil. To inspire a love for others, for doing good, and to become better oneself.

Diman was puzzled why his daughter had become religious.

> Perhaps this is some counterbalance.

However, as a tolerant person he was avoiding disputes with her about religion.

> We are a highly harmonious family, and my family in childhood was harmonious.

The most important holidays for him now were birthdays and the name days of his children. He also observed the Christmas and Easter festivals, but without giving them a religious meaning.

> At Easter we coloured eggs, but how does that signify a religious holiday? It is not religious, it is a folk custom.

He had avoided church rituals all his life. Once when a priest on the feast of Bogoyavlenie (Epiphany) had knocked on door of his apartment in order to bless it with holy water, he had turned him away. He had not attended the funerals of his grandfather and grandmother because of his work commitments, but spoke openly about caring for his mother until her death. He spoke about the physical and psychological difficulties of tending a close person at the end of life. He also discussed the difficulty of accepting the loss of a beloved person and admitted the lack of a spiritual aspect. However, he said that he did not have a fear of death.

> No, I am an Orthodox pagan. Why think about death? Often friends and colleagues call inviting me to accompany someone to his/her last resting place, but this is not sufficient reason for me to fear death. Cases of death are something normal for people of our age. A person should not convince himself that he or she is ill and is not well. They should control their mood.

As regards the after-life, his answer reflected his scientific interests.

> I could accept ... I don't know what there is on Mars, Venus ... I read a lot.

His most happy moment in life was 'the flight of Gagarin – I was extremely happy'.

> He agreed that social values had changed.

> Earlier we had youth-brigades. It was also pleasant for me to take part in the parades ("manifestatsia") ... I liked it when there were crowds, some waving flags, and others carrying posters. Somehow you feel part of the holiday, of something big, enthusiastic and you become affected. Now they criticise the parades. They say they were imposed forcibly on people. Get lost! It was a natural thing, I really found great pleasure in shouting "Hooray", "Glory", "We live nice lives" ... Now the young people go to discotheques, many of them are not involved, they have not developed ways of working.

On the SET test he answered generally positively but asserted that he was only '53 per cent happy'. When asked what was missing he said:

> Nothing! But simply that man should strive to be better. Because, if you say you are here (at the top of the line) you have to lie down and die.

Similarly in regard to health, he declared that he was:

> A healthy man, perhaps about 80 per cent. When you stand up the morning,
> if there isn't something to hurt, you should think if you are healthy or you are
> already dead.

The roots of Diman's high level of subjective well-being seemed to lie in his
personality structure, his upbringing in a family environment with strong values,
and his rich cultural and professional experience. He was not religious, but he
accepted that there something 'spiritual' about interpersonal relations. He believed
in the spirit of goodness that could '*inspire a love for others, for doing good,
and becoming a better person*'. There was no evidence that there had been any
substantial changes in his personality or well-being since his youth.

Aleko Radev, 81 years old at the interview, was the only other example of a
non-religious man in our Bulgarian sample. In fact he described himself as an
atheist and a communist like his father. His childhood and youth had been difficult.
He had been born in 1929 into a poor rural family with an illiterate mother.
Conflict was often present in the family and Aleko was treated cruelly by his father
when young before their relations improved, but then his father was shot by Greek
partisans while serving with the Bulgarian army during the war.

His early career was also not easy. He proved a good student at school despite
the difficulties he encountered, but suffered from lung disease at university, which
disrupted his law studies. His first years as a practising lawyer were also marked by
frequent interruptions and changes. He began in his youth as a Comsomol worker,
but later became an examining magistrate. The last 10 years of his career, in which
he served as a judge in the Supreme Court, had been successful. The interview
data indicated a man whose psychological well-being had been problematic in his
younger days, but who had achieved stability later in life both in work and in his
family.

Aleko had been widowed only six months before the interview. However
he had two children to whom he was very attached. For him the most important
holidays were the birthdays of his children, but also, to a lesser extent, the socialist
celebrations of the 9 September 'liberation' and 1 May. He did not observe the
religious holidays even though he had learned about church services when young
and had sung in the church choir when at school.

Aleko's case has some similarities with Diman's. Both had followed their
father's beliefs. Both were family oriented and maintained strong socialist
principles. Although very different, communism and Christianity have some ideas
in common, which can offer moral sustenance in later life. Both men had had
successful professional careers and formed strong families. Celebrating family
holidays appeared to contribute strongly to their subjective well-being.

Stability of Religiosity and Personality with Age

There is a consensus in psychogerontological research that a slowing of reactions, a drop in vitality and some related 'introversion' of interests is the most common pattern of change with ageing, but that individual differences surpass differences between age groups. Older people in fact appear as the most psychologically heterogeneous age group. Attitudes, particularly religious and cultural, appear to remain stable with age. However 'positive' and 'negative' changes do occur. Some older persons do show greater tolerance and impartiality, and display greater 'wisdom', often as a result of life reviewing (Coleman and O'Hanlon 2004). Others tend to respond to social changes with insecurity, cautiousness, and – related to this – some rigidity of attitudes. These 'normal' reactions are associated with lower levels of education and cultural formation and ageist attitudes on the part of younger generations. It is possible to imagine that these feelings will diminish in the future if education both improves and becomes lifelong in character. Some gerontologists and psychiatrists also find that depressive reactions also increase at older ages. These are mostly borderline or mild, and are labelled as 'existential' depressions or dysthymias. The predominant opinion is that the prevalence of major depression does not increase with age (Fiske and Jones 2005). However, cases of cognitive decline increase sharply with age, and this is the most important cause of later life mental health problems.

In the course of one human life personality will often remain more stable than the external world. This is more likely to be the case as people live longer and social change accelerates. The past century has been marked by incredible progress in technical sciences, communications, means of travelling and many other changes in mode of life. At the same time they have also been marked by cruel wars, revolutions, sharp political changes and terror. It is admirable, yet often poorly acknowledged, how in such a rapidly changing world individual older persons have been able to preserve and sometimes enhance the positive characteristics of their personality. The cases of Naum, Andon and Diman among others illustrate well this fact. They have resisted serious difficulties and negative stresses while retaining many positive features of their personality.

Religiosity built at an early age seems to remain stable during late life. This is the major finding of the only longitudinal cross-generation study of religious attitudes to date, which was conducted in California (Bengtson with Putney and Harris 2013). Most interviewees in our study declared that their religious beliefs, or their atheistic views of life, had not changed during their life course. Andon said that his strong religious faith had remained unchanged, but thought perhaps that the mystical element in his spirituality had somewhat increased with ageing. Also, as regards observation of rituals and holidays the majority of interviewees, especially in Eastern Europe, did not observe any life-long changes. Those who had observed religious rituals in their youth (before the Second World War) continued to observe them even during the difficult times of Stalinism, albeit in a concealed way, and they observed them again openly after the post-1989 transition. Naum for example, being an acting army officer, organised his civil marriage in 1947 in the town where he served, but immediately after that organised a church ceremony in his native town on the opposite side of the country. He admitted that for a period of several years he ceased to enter a church and prayed at home with an icon-light. Some of the women told how they sent their children for christening to a grandmother or to other relatives, sometimes in distant towns or monasteries.

The Muslims in Bulgaria, along with Greek Catholics in Romania, seem to have suffered the most from communist rule. Although the latter have recovered their practices to a large extent since 1989, the Turkish Muslims appear to have suffered lasting damage from persecution. Their religious beliefs appear to have become weaker since 1944, and with the name-changing repression of the 1980s their sense of identity suffered further blows. This presents a particular social problem for Bulgaria that needs further study.

Well-being and Religion of Older Men in Bulgaria, Romania and the UK

This chapter has focused on older men in Bulgaria and it is worthwhile reflecting in this final discussion whether our major findings on well-being and religion find parallels among those interviewed in Romania and the UK. We suggested that late life subjective well-being is built and supported by a cluster of personality and environmental factors, especially positive experiences in early family life and education, satisfying relationships with closest family members in adult life, and stable social and health conditions. (It was evident from the interviews in this study that past professional activity and interests contributed a relatively greater part to the lifelong satisfaction of older men compared with women, especially in Romania and Bulgaria.) Of the cases we have presented, Naum, Andon and Diman stand out as the strongest examples of this constellation of characteristics. Yet what is the significance of the religious dimension of their lives?

Religious belief may have an essential importance for coping and for subjective well-being in combination with other favourable biographical, personality, family and social factors. All interviews in this study with religious older people confirmed that religious belief and practice helped them. The Romanian sample provided further clear examples. Aurelian Ghelasie appears to have been sustained by a strong family background through the ordeals of his early adult life, in which he was repeatedly imprisoned for membership of a right-wing political movement before the war (his case is analysed in detail in Chapter 10). He himself attributed an overriding importance to religious faith.

> I have noticed ever since I was a pupil how much God has helped me, and I think
> that a man can convince himself personally of this … Many times I think that
> God has a plan for each and every man … Man cannot know his future.

Miron Popescu, whose life was also persistently troubled by fear of religious repression, did not deny the benefits he had received from his religious faith.

> [Religion] builds in you a kind of respect, respect for something that is not material. It's something spiritual. It make you more humble ... I had some moments in life when God gave me two ways. Sometimes I chose good, other times wrong. But I felt His help ... But I made my prayers thinking of the idea that God is helping one.

It is evident from the interviews with religious older people that religious faith was usually acquired in early childhood. Often one of the parents or both had been very religious and had taken the young child with them to church. In most cases this was the mother. In some cases the child had performed some functions within the church services. In other cases religious belief was acquired imperceptibly in the childhood and in most cases it was inseparably linked with the tradition.

Is there some equivalent resource to religious faith that supports the subjective well-being of non-religious persons? In analysing the accounts of the lives of the two Bulgarian non-religious men interviewed in our sample we presume that these two men had assimilated, both from their fathers' communist principles and probably also from their professional and personal experiences, some strong moral principles. Their successful professional development, probably with honest relationships with other people and a stable family life, contributed to their stable personality structures. Diman especially stood out as non-religious person who believed 'in humanity' and 'in goodness'.

There were men of similar stature in the UK sample. An excellent example is Harold Stevenson (whose case has been described in Chapter 7). The religion he had been introduced to in his youth had led him to a strong interest in Christianity and its theology but also to questioning its underlying transcendental dogma and principles. In middle age he developed explicitly humanist principles. His professional development as a teacher was strong. He had a stable family life, good health up to an advanced age, and high subjective well-being. Later in life he became a humanist minister himself undertaking funerals, weddings and baby namings. Yet he was not aggressively anti-religious. He accepted that people had different needs, and was against fundamentalism either from the side of humanists or from the side of religion. For him atheism alone was too negative a conception. A 'positive atheism' was needed, one which comprised working for the good and for a better world. Humanists had a responsibility to live up to their positive outlook for humankind. All positions on the SET test chosen by Harold were on the upper part of the vertical lines. The self-ratings of health and happiness in particular were almost at the top of the respective lines. This level of positive subjective well-being seems to derive from his personality structure, good health, a satisfying family and successful professional life.

In a recent study in the UK, Wilkinson and Coleman (2011) interviewed two matched groups of people over the age of 60, one group with strong atheistic and generally humanist views and the other with strong religious belief. They examined the role of the content of the belief system itself in coping with different negative stresses and losses commonly associated with ageing. The authors found that all the study participants, regardless of their beliefs, were coping well, and that a strong system of owned humanist principles appears to be able to fulfil the same role in people's lives as a strong religious system in terms of the support, explanation, consolation and inspiration it can bring. Further comparative investigation is needed into the origins, formation and support of such 'psychophilosophies' (Sherman, 1981), forms of moral thinking that have constructive effect on personality, whether of a religious or secular character. The benefits they provide perhaps become most clearly evident in late life.

References

Bengtson, Vern L., with Norella M. Putney and Susan C. Harris. 2013. *Families and Faith: Generations and the Transmission of Religion*. New York: Oxford University Press.

Bobak, Martin and Michael Marmot. 1996. East-west mortality divide and its potential explanations: proposed research agenda. *Br. Med. J.* 312: 421–5.

Coleman, Peter G. 2010. "Religion and Age'. In *International Handbook of Social Gerontology*, edited by Dale Dannefer and Chris Phillipson , 164–76. London: Sage.

Coleman, Peter G. and Andrew W. McCulloch. 1990. 'Societal Change, Values and Social Support: Exploratory Studies into Adjustment in Late Life'. *Journal of Aging Studies* 4: 321–32.

Coleman, Peter G. and Ann O'Hanlon. 2004. *Ageing and Development. Theories and Research*. Oxford: Oxford University Press.

Coleman, Peter G., Christine Ivani-Chalian and Maureen Robinson. 2004. 'Religious Attitudes among British Older People: Stability and Change in a 20 Year Longitudinal Study.' *Ageing and Society* 24: 167–88.

Coleman, Peter G., Roxana O. Carare, Ignat C. Petrov, et al. 2011. 'Spiritual Belief, Social Support, Physical Functioning and Depression among Older People in Bulgaria and Romania'. *Aging and Mental Health* 15: 327–33.

Fiske, Amy and Randi S. Jones. 2005. 'Depression'. In *The Cambridge Handbook of Age and Ageing*, edited by Malcolm L. Johnson, Vern L. Bengtson, Peter G. Coleman and Thomas B.L. Kirkwood, 245–51. Cambridge: Cambridge University Press.

Gutmann, David L. 1987. *Reclaimed Powers: Towards a New Psychology of Men and Women in Later Life*. New York: Basic Books [2nd edn, 1994].

Henry, J.P. 1988. 'The Archetypes of Power and Intimacy'. In *Emergent Theories of Aging*, edited by James E. Birren and Vern L. Bengtson, 269–98. New York: Springer.

Hummer, R.A., R.G. Rogers, C.B. Nam and C.G. Ellison. 1999. 'Religious Involvement and U.S. Adult Mortality'. *Demography* 36: 273–85.

Kryspin-Exner, I., E. Lampimayr and A. Felnhofer. 2011. 'Geropsychology: The Gender Gap in Human Aging'. *Gerontology* 57: 539–49.

Levin, J. and L.M. Chatters. 1998. 'Religion, Health, and Psychological Well-being in Older Adults: Finding from Three National Surveys'. *Journal of Aging and Health* 4: 504–31.

Levin, J., K.S. Markides and L.A. Ray. 1996. 'Religious Attendance and Psychological Well-being in Mexican Americans'. *The Gerontologist* 26: 454–63.

Muller, O. 2004. 'Value Systems of the Citizens and Socio-Economic Conditions – Challenges from Democratisation for the EU Enlargement'. Policy Paper Series 'Democratic Values'. Policy Paper 10. East Germany: Democratisation par excellence? Available at: http://www.kulsoz.euv-frankfurt-o.de/EU%20 Project/papers/Pp10.pdf.

Nisbet, P.A., P.R. Duberstein, Y. Conwell and L. Seidlitz. 2000. 'The Effect of Participation in Religious Activities on Suicide versus Natural Death in Adults 50 and older'. *Journal of Nervous and Mental Disease* 188: 543–6.

Nolte E., M. McKee and A. Gilmore. 2004. Morbidity and mortality in transition countries in the European context. Background paper for the session 'Morbidity, mortality and Reproductive Health: Facing Challenges in Transition Countries' at the European Population Forum 2004. Available at: http://www.unece.org/ pan/epf/nolte.pdf.

Petrov, Ignat C. 1976. 'Self-evaluation of Some Personality Aspects of the Aged by the Dembo-Rubinstein test. Experimental–Psychological and Clinical Psychopathological Investigation' ['Самооценката на някои страни на психиката на стария човек според теста на Дембо-Рубинштейн. Експериментално-психологично и клинично-психопатологично изследване']. PhD thesis, Meditsinska Academia, Sofia (in Bulgarian; abstract in English).

Petrov, Ignat C. 1996a. 'Feelings and Attitudes toward the Changes during Social and Economic Transition: A Study of Sofia Autonomous Elderly Subjects'. *Romanian Journal of Gerontology and Geriatrics* 17: 73–82.

Petrov, Ignat C. 1996b 'Feelings and Attitudes Toward the Changes During Social and Economic Transition. Part II. Evolution of the Feelings and Attitudes; Comparison with Health, Personality and Social Variables'. *Romanian Journal of Gerontology and Geriatrics* 18: 76–85.

Rubinstein, S. 1970. *Experimental Methods of Pathopsychology and an Attempt to Use Them in the Clinic. A Practical Guide* [Экспериментальные методы патопсихологии и опыт применения их в клинике. Практическое руководство]. Moscow: Meditsina (in Russian).

Schaie, K. Warner and Glen Elder, G. (eds) 2005. *Historical Influences on Lives and Aging*. New York: Springer.

Seabrook, J. 1980. *The Way We Are*. Mitcham, Surrey: Age Concern England.

Sherman, Edmund. 1981. *Counseling the Aging: An Integrative Approach*. New York: Free Press.

Wilkinson, Peter J. and Peter G. Coleman. 2010. 'Strong Belief and Coping in Old Age: A Case Based Comparison of Atheism and Religion'. *Ageing and Society* 30: 337–61.

Woodhead, Linda. 2004. *Christianity. A Very Short Introduction*. Oxford: Oxford University Press.

Chapter 10

Religiosity and Women's Ageing: Biographical Perspectives

Teodora Karamelska

One of the key effects of modernisation and social transformation in twentieth-century Europe was the broadening of women's access to various social spaces, including the religious ones. Religion was seen by men as deprived of prestige and it was transformed into a natural component of women's social activity. The festive ritual stabilisation of the family community was imagined as mainly 'women's task'. Women's religious activity 'has less to do with false consciousness than with the ways in which religions offer social spaces for articulation and, in some case, the realisation, of women's desires' (Woodhead 2002, 333–4). Thus the processes of secularisation, which practically restricted religion to the private sphere (Martin 2005), resulted in a gradual change of both women's positions in traditional communities and women's subjective experience of religiosity. The increased social mobility of women and their mass presence in the public space corresponded to the new adoption of religion as a valuable resource for constructing meaning and dealing with social insecurity. These two interrelated effects of secularisation have given Linda Woodhead a reason to speak about an overall 'feminization of Christianity' (Woodhead 2002, 176; Woodhead 2007, 249–80).

If the diminishing loyalty to the traditional confessions and the intensifying women's quest for self-expression beyond the family and professional roles after the Second World War stimulated the spread of organisational forms of religiosity, not so strongly dominated by the men's authority,[1] the period 1945–89 in Eastern Europe witnessed the power of antireligious communist ideology. Political control over priests' activities and respectively the decline in their social prestige informally empowered women in the local parishes to maintain ritual-religious life, thus turning them into guardians of particular expert knowledge of the sacred.

The present chapter is focused on *the biographical dimensions* of the above described processes in three European countries – Bulgaria, Romania and the UK – and more precisely on the meanings that women from these countries assign to religious rituals in the course of *ageing*. Here ageing is discussed in terms of narrowing of social inclusion and diminishing physical resources (Hunt 2007).

---

[1] The 'holistic spirituality' which began to boom in the 1970s (Woodhead 2005; Sointu and Woodhead 2008, 259–76).

The following questions are raised: does religiosity increase with age and loss of social stability? In which cases is religiosity sustainably adopted in the process of family socialisation and in which cases does it follow a personal crisis and gather strength in the course of life?

Biographical Narrative Interviewing:
Some Remarks about the Methodological Framework

Unlike quantitative methods, the use of qualitative methods in social studies does not aim to 'measure' or 'describe' religious attitudes, convictions and behaviours, nor to discover 'correlations' among them. While standard questionnaires tend to produce what are mostly static, 'instant photos' of social reality, qualitative methods direct our attention to the *functional* aspects of religion and to the *significance* that social actors ascribe to certain religious practices. These methods enable the researcher to trace the dynamic changes in religiosity occurring as a result of certain subjectively experienced *turning points*. In the concrete case, this means to analyse the significance of religious (and secular) rituals, not only through the prism of the socialisation that characterises the interviewees, but also through the 'limit situations'[2] and intrapsychological processes that are not directly accessible by outside observation (Kelle 2008, 11–31). That is the important reason why the questions I have asked in this study are not only of the type 'how often?' or 'to what degree?', but also 'how and why' certain events and experiences influenced the attitude of ageing women to religiosity. This research perspective allows the broadening of the labels 'religious' or 'non-religious', and the viewing of religiosity in a wider sense as a 'proposed way to deal with the crisis of meaning'. That is why observance of religions will be seen here as a result of certain biographically motivated decisions aimed at routinising everyday life, but also as dealing with the critical situations in life, which become more frequent with advancing age.

One means of access to the subjective reality of individuals is oral in-depth interviewing. This method represents a free, verbal self-thematisation in which the biographer recreates their personal history according to their own experience and self-definition (Schütze 1983; Rosenthal 2005). In the course of the interview, we let the interviewees reveal the depth of their 'value system' and allow them to put their own emphasis on certain aspects of religiosity in their life course. In this way, the accumulated empirical material permits tracing the *dual-aspect* biographical relevance of religion: on one hand, religion is thematised through

---

[2]   Karl Jaspers introduced the notion of the 'limit situation' in 1919 to describe an 'unpredictable situation, in which the individual fails to overcome a crisis by conventional means', thus becoming aware of the ultimate ground of his finite existence. Examples of limit situations are to be found in failure, suffering, guilt and death (see Jaspers 2000, 129–72).

its importance as ritual, that is, its social and normative ordering function; on the other hand, it is placed in the context of life situations, which trigger the process of self-observation and self-knowledge (on occasions of illness, loneliness, widowhood, loss of parents, empty nest syndrome), that is, through its reflexive function (Nassehi 1995, 123–6).

Religious Contexts: Common Sources, Different Pathways

Even though the Judeo-Christian tradition is a main *common source* for all three surveyed cultural contexts, the three countries started out on *different paths*, especially after the Second World War (Davie 2007, 26). As regards the interviews from Bulgaria and Romania, we can see the effects of Marxist–Leninist ideology and the systematic coercive destruction of religiosity in the time of the socialist regime (Metodiev 2010); the interviews from UK depict a complex situation of religious pluralism after the war, with a typical growth of secularisation and weakening of traditional religious communities, with a tendency towards 'believing without belonging' (Davie 2002; Knoblauch 2009; Casanova 2010). In the UK, there has been a model, typical for most Western European countries, of spirituality without institutional engagement. However, this does not signify that British people are anti-clerically inclined, for, although not regularly taking part in religious rituals, they still maintain loyalty to their self-definition as Christians. On this basis, Grace Davie formulates her well-known thesis regarding a transition from a 'hard commitment to church' to 'soft faith' and 'fuzzy fidelity' (Davie 2007, 89–95; Voas 2009; see also Knoblauch 2009, 29–30).

In the period April 2010 to March 2011, a total of 34 in-depth biographical interviews were recorded with women; of these, 12 were conducted in Romania, 10 in Bulgaria and 12 in the UK. The youngest woman was born in 1937, and the eldest in 1915. Among the interviewees there were some with university degrees, and some with secondary vocational and some with primary education. There were widows and divorced women; some women were living with husbands and/or children, with brothers and sisters, or alone, or in old people care homes.

Biographical *Turning Points*

Based on the empirical material, three common *turning points* can be distinguished in these women's lives, which they have usually tried to manage with the help of religious practice. At the first one, those of the interviewees who created a family had to stop or reduce their professional careers owing to childbirth and childcare. In some cases marriage was followed by failure to preserve the family and by divorce, and this affected the social and economic status of those women in the later phases of their lives. At the second one, the biographical trajectory changed at the end of the professional career, when life became enclosed within the home. At that time, a feeling of being useless appeared and grew owing to the absence of children (or grandchildren) within the home. For the women born in the 1920s, the so-called 'post-parental period', the time when children lived outside the family home, was considerably prolonged. In this situation, women were not able to use the important resource of motherhood to achieve social stability and recognition. After they attained the age of 65, the contacts of the interviewed women that had children living with them were mostly characterised by 'inward closeness and outward distance', by intimacy at a distance, and this was something that aggravated the feeling of 'overpowering loneliness' and isolation. The third discontinuity appears with advanced loss of close relatives: in this phase of life there is a highly increased risk of psychological dependence on the presence of other people and the loss of meaning in life (World Health Organization 2002; Kohli 1990).

Camelia Ionescu, Bucharest: 'It's hard, very hard, it's ugly to be on your own'

Camelia was born in 1933 in a relatively well-to-do family and received a good education (high school degree); until her retirement she worked for nearly 30 years in a factory – the Romanian Chemical Factories. Her pension was not enough for her to get by, and, at the age of 77, she was compelled to clean homes in order to supplement her income. In her biographical narrative there are two distinguishable discontinuities: during the time of Ceaucescu (when Camelia enjoyed a good standard of living and was actively employed), and after the revolution with the democratic changes, when her life became difficult and, with ageing, she grew poor. Her mother had died two years previously and from that point on she had felt worse; it took her some time to recover from that death. It was the greatest loss she had undergone in her life, and involved illness and prolonged suffering:

> When my mother died I got sick, I had my third heart attack and a severe pneumonia. Can you imagine?

Her distance from her sister, her impoverishment and her advancing age had made her prepare for death and for her funeral (she had paid for a place in the cemetery). However, she could not reconcile herself to the burden of loneliness:

> It's ugly! Ugly! Especially when you are alone and you don't have anybody. I can say that I don't have anybody here; … You see this cat, in the evening, especially when I was sick she stayed on the radio box and you should have seen how she would caress my hair with her little paws and the dog the same, he stayed on my belly.

She defined herself as a religious person: similar in this to other interviewed women, Camelia regularly attended Sunday liturgy, but without feeling fully a 'church person'. She strived to communicate with other women in the parish, rather than seek social support or spiritual comfort from the clergy:

> Yes, of course, I believe in God … But I don't trust these priests any more. I don't know why, they are not truthful. Especially when my mama was ill I would call a priest all the time and I saw how they were not honest.

Along with this, she devoted time for prayer every evening:

> I never go to sleep without saying a prayer. I ask first and foremost for health, the rest, whatever He might give me. But that's about … and also not to forget I'm here, to prepare a place for me because I'm really lonely.

Dorina Badea, Cluj: 'For it seems to me that my life has been so empty since I stopped working'

Dorina was born in 1934 in Cluj into a family of Hungarians. She graduated from the Pedagogical School for Kindergarten Teachers and worked for 38 years as a teacher in Cluj. Her parents were of different confessions; she was raised in a spirit of tolerance. She went to a Catholic girl's school, taught by nuns, where the pupils were obliged to make confession to the nuns; she has fond memories of the rules and order that prevailed in the school. Dorina defined herself as inter-confessional: being baptised as Greek Catholic, she attended services in the Reformed and Roman Catholic churches as well,

> I liked the sermons both in the Romanian churches and in the Hungarian language.

She pointed out the birth of her daughter as the happiest moment of her life, and caring for her parents the most painful. Her memories of religious holidays were connected mostly with her childhood years. Although they were poor, in the postwar years the family consistently observed the traditions. Later, when the communist regime cracked down on religious activity, Dorina was afraid to go to church services, expecting to be persecuted for this or dismissed from her job. Her daughter was baptised in the Reformed Church, which made it impossible for her to have a church wedding with her husband, who was Orthodox. Her daughter and son-in-law lived in Greece and kept in touch with her mostly by telephone. Dorina described the period after her retirement in such a way that it resembles a 'limit situation':

> For it seems to me that my life has been so empty since I stopped going to work.

Dorina defined her present situation as emotionally unstable – she was afraid of what would happen to her if she were to fall sick, and at the end of the talk she repeated several times that she was not happy. However, despite her growing feeling of loneliness and of being useless, Dorina – similar to Camelia – did not seek stability in engaging with the church community. When she took part in religious services, she did so mostly passively (by listening to sermons or to the Sunday liturgy on the radio). Usually, she prayed only 'on very bad and very hard days', and did it in her own way, without resorting to the mediation of a priest, without a prayer book, and without icons:

> Only when trouble comes to you … only then do you ask for help. You ask for help and you pray. Not in the sense of the prayer in the book, in the sense of a prayer in your own words and from your own heart which pours forth and you ask, you ask for help.

As she got older, Christianity was losing importance for her as an existential support:

> While Cristina [her daughter] was little, indeed, I prayed every night. But after she grew up and I was more tired and more … days went by differently.

Dorina was unable to clearly define her religious attitudes: although she did transform them into a system of ethical rules, this did not actually bring her consolation as her age advanced:

> I don't know what to consider myself … I haven't really had faith, in my own mind or my own heart, that there was somebody who was guiding my footsteps. I can't really say that for certain, but I've felt something like that, and then I knew what my father had said: You should take care in your life, ever since the very first day I went to work: don't lie, don't steal, and give your everything to the job you have chosen.

Functions of Rituals

According to the classical definition of the Belgian anthropologist Van Gennep, religion is one of the basic means for a person's integration into social models of living. It symbolically marks certain transitions by means of 'rites that accompany every change of place, situation, social position, and age' (quoted from Turner 1999, 95). In some of the interviews, the multiplication of women's social roles is linked with taking part in such rituals; regardless of their different features in the different religions, they refer to the same life transitions. Through such rituals the change of social status is legitimised and certain family transitions are sanctified. Moreover, religious rituals make it possible for certain critical situations (such as birth, or the death of someone close) to be stabilised at a *supra-individual* level, that is, at the level of family or parish. In some of the women's biographical narratives transition rituals are not related to an experience of the transcendent or the sacred, or to *emotional appurtenance* to a religious community. In other cases, however, ritual practice and religious representations exist together in a *systematic and consistent unity*. To illustrate this correspondence of practice and representation, I will present interviews with two women who never married, never built a family of their own and for whom religiosity is an important constituent of their identity building. In their cases we see the function of religiosity to stabilise everyday life through participation in religious services.

Doreen Potter, London: 'Ours is not to reason why'

Doreen, born in 1930, was not married and had resided all her life in the same area of London. When she was a child she attended a Methodist Church with her family, but now she was a member of the Congregational Church. Doreen received her religious education and connection with the church from her family – her father was the Sunday School superintendent:

> Morning church, afternoon Sunday School, evening church and then most often there was things after church, meetings and like.

Even now, she attended religious services at least once a week and prayed in the evening before going to bed. One of the basic themes in her biographic narrative was the change that took place in the religious context in UK during the 1970s: the number of parishioners declined during that time so much that many church buildings closed down, parishes were merged; religious education was becoming increasingly superficial, and rituals were gradually becoming traditions without depth or religious meaning; the number of christenings was also decreasing:

> Different life these days in all respects of anything … But it's the way things change a lot.

Doreen was constantly looking back with nostalgia to those past times – the rituals were no longer an occasion for social contacts, for recreation and games, as they were in the poor years just after the war. In 1976 Doreen became a church secretary and even at the time of the interview she was still engaged in administrative activity, taking care of the church building and organising church picnics and festivals. As she had not made a family of her own, Doreen found support in active engagement in parish life:

> Well and you're together praying, you know, you can get a lift from everybody, you know by being together, you know … Well you don't feel alone in, you know, troubles and sickness and, you know, things. But, as I say, we haven't got that many there so, and the age group is all getting older, so we just keep on praying for someone to come, you know.

Despite this, she found retirement and advancing old age hard to bear:

> *How did you feel when you retired?*

> Bit sad. And afterwards it was strange because I was sitting, at three o clock I was sitting in the armchair, I thought "I shouldn't be sitting down this time of day". It took a lot – a friend of mine said "Don't go and join too many things at once" you know, because in time you find that you want more time to yourself, you know, you just want to be with people to start with.

Asked to define herself, Doreen answered:

> Well, I hung round the religious but I'm not over religious where I'm spouting out like some people all the time every time you pass them.

For Doreen, religiousness did not consist simply in an abstract system of values or in belonging nominally to a parish community, but was an orientation for conduct:

> Just going to church and listening and believing and trying to do what you, you know, what you learn to live a good life.

Her traditionalism found expression, among other things, in the enthusiasm with which she celebrated national holidays such as Empire Day and Coronation of the Queen.

Eleonora Moldovan, Cluj: 'For indeed, faith in God helped me get over everything'[3]

Eleonora, born in 1934, was a former professor of foreign languages, especially proficient in many Romance languages, and also in English and German. Although retired, she was the volunteer curator of the Italian Library at the university. She had never married and had no children.

The main part of Eleonora's narrative was filled with recollections of her parents, whom she depicted with great respect as professionals, selfless people and good neighbours, even though they were Romanians living among a Hungarian population; they had raised her in the spirit of Christian humility:

> Exactly in the Biblical spirit and like St Paul – that we should accept what comes, that somewhere a sign has been given that this is coming from above and by the will of God.

---

[3]   See also chapters 5 and 8 for this case.

Her mother was a doctor and her father a judge. They decided to send Eleonora to a German kindergarten and to a school in which religious education played an important part:

> I had religious education from the beginning, … we would sing the Lord's Prayer and after that we entered the classrooms.

The first 'limit situation' she faced was the fear of military operations during the Second World War in Romania, when her mother survived a bombing attack as if by a miracle:

> We actually forgot that that was a real bombing. Well, and here I felt for the first time, let's say, and I realised what God's power meant … we must say: "We believe in one Lord", and then we won't have to fear anything. … And, as I say, it was here that I felt, that I even realised a little, when I was a small girl, the power of God.

Her second 'limit situation' was when her father was spared during the repressions in the first years of the communist regime, even though he had refused to become a member of the Romanian Workers' Party. In fact, her father was a leading figure in her biographical narrative. Eleonora constantly mentioned his high reputation as a respected judge, his being impervious to bribes, despite the poverty in which they lived, and the respect he enjoyed in the eyes of the clergy:

> God helped and he was kept alive […].

> I had once done some prank there, in the house, and, like that, as small a child as I was, … but my father, very seriously, he took my hand – there was an icon of the Virgin Mary – "Well, look, ask the Virgin for forgiveness". Yes, and that was our religious education.

The severe poverty of the family in the postwar period prevented them from holding feasts on religious holidays:

> No, no, we didn't mark Christmas or Easter in any way, except by going to church.

The death of her parents intensified her religiousness:

> If I still want to be in spiritual communion, of mind, with my parents, all I had to do was to start my day with the Holy Liturgy. And since then, since August 1, '72 until today, I've started my day by … going to church, to the cathedral, so, and as I pray … I do not know if it's happened once or twice, I don't know, if I was sick and I couldn't … Yes, exactly, for 38 years.

The second predominant theme in Eleonora's biographical narrative is related to her efforts to master foreign languages as rapidly and as well as she could. After graduating in Romance languages, for about two years she worked at the Institute of Linguistics as an external collaborator, and after that was appointed in the Department of Romance languages. She regularly attended church services, which got her into trouble in the mid 1970s with the dean of the Faculty of Law, who was Communist Party secretary of the university. She was transferred to the Central Library, where working hours began at 7 in the morning, and Eleonora could no longer attend liturgy. Hence she started to attend services at 6 in the morning at St Michael's Roman Catholic church:

> It is still God, it is still in the Holy Church.

After she was laid off from the library, she was employed for many years in the Archdiocese in bureaucratic and administrative work. It was then that she became personally acquainted with high-ranking clergymen. Eleonora described faith as:

> the scaffolding which my whole life was built on, which has helped me overcome even the difficult times. And I've also been through some very difficult moments, but with God's help everything turned out well.

She prayed every day, for about one hour, not only with her own, personal prayers, but also using prayer book texts. In fact, Eleonora linked her surmounting all 'limit situations' to the power of prayer and faith in God, to the principle of non-resistance to evil:

> That I never felt how powerful God is except when it was most difficult for me.

Despite declaring several times how strongly connected she was with the Orthodox tradition, Eleonora did not go to confession often, nor have a personal confessor:

> I resolved them myself, directly with God.

This is a frequently encountered attitude among people from the former socialist countries, from the generation born between the two world wars; they explain that they refrain from confession out of a habitual fear of disclosure. Even though Eleonora's financial situation today is very difficult – she does not have a home of her own and has very small income – she finds existential support in Christianity and continues to apply religious, transcendental based strategy in everyday coping with loneliness and ageing.

Women as 'Experts in the Sacred'

In some of the biographical narratives the women's desire to be part of religious communities is linked to their need for a social confirmation of their religious representations and worldview, within *collective structures*. Usually this confirmation is provided by participation in activities of the church parishes (in the Sunday service or in deacon activity). Active participation in parish events has given some of the interviewed women, especially from Bulgaria and Romania, the opportunity to accumulate specialised knowledge about rituals, and to become real 'experts in the sacred'. For them religiousness is mainly *ecclesiastically–hierarchically* defined; it is a community practice that has its canons and rules, and which must be integrated systematically into everyday life, and which gives a unified meaning of life, including suffering as part of life (Bourdieu 2009, 14–15). In the cases given below, the religious women are not only actively and permanently a part of the parish, but are somehow *active* in it. They experience their religiousness as willingness for social cooperation (Weber 2005, 39).

Ivanka Grozdeva, Targovishte: 'It's God who supports me.
It's probably God who gives me happiness in life too'[4]

Ivanka was an educated 73-year-old woman, who graduated in 1958 from the Library Institute in Sofia, but even during the times of the socialist regime did not make it a secret that she attended Orthodox church liturgy:

> I was in charge of the Atheism department of the library book collection; it was called department Atheism 2. But this didn't stop me from going to those three churches.

Ivanka's narrative was rich in events that show her good knowledge not only of the traditional rituals for marriage, baptism and funeral service, but also of other rites, such as blessing with 'holy water':

> I went to the children's library ... and I said, "Please, let us sanctify this building". So the children's department was sanctified. Holy water. The priest from "St. Nikola" came with candles, with everything. So we had the sanctification, the transfer of children's literature in the Party House.

Her motives for refusing to become a Communist Party member were also related to her self-definition as a Christian believer:

> It's not in accordance with my beliefs to carry the red party card in my pocket and to go to church.

---

[4]   See also chapters 7 and 8 for this case.

Ivanka gave a picture of herself as active and socially engaged during the time of the communist regime; she had both her daughters baptised at that time. Her religiousness grew stronger after the death of her first husband, when she became a widow at the age of 28. Attendance of Sunday liturgy became a stable habitus for her, and to this she gradually added trips to monasteries, participation in blessings with holy water, memorial services and collective prayer with friends and relatives:

> That was my hobby, that's what my second husband used to say. Churches, memorial services, yes, monasteries [...];

> This one falls ill, the other one ... – I constantly pay for holy liturgies, holy 40-days memorial service, as soon as I hear that someone has died. I know they'd never think of it themselves. But I go there and I pay for holy 40-days memorial service for the dead. Because it is the dead who are in greatest need of us, the living – to mention them in our prayers. Not everybody leaves this world having confessed all their sins, not everybody fasted and received Holy Communion or was allowed to receive it. So the living have to help the dead and to pray for their sins.

Ivanka had a strong commitment to the church as a hierocratic community – in the course of her narrative she showed on many occasions that she knew how to behave towards the clergy:

> This morning I met Father Biser ... He is a pearl indeed[5] among Christians in Bulgaria ... And I bent to kiss his right hand.

After 1990, with the change of the religious situation in Bulgaria, her religiosity found new fields of expression: Ivanka began to care for the preservation of antique icons and co-founded the charitable organisation 'Orthodoxy'. Moreover, her Orthodox religiousness was not rigidly limited to ritual, but served to structure her everyday life and her holidays:

> We get together every year in Varna – the four grandchildren, two daughters, the sons-in-law. And we gather for Christmas Eve ... First we begin with the prayer "Our Father", then purification with incense, etc. [...];

> I was 9 years old when I asked my grandfather Valko to give me the Bible to read ... I'm in my 74th year, but when I read from the Bible I sometimes feel as if I was reading something completely new. Every single day I read a chapter from it and I also read the Psalms [...];

> *Do you make time to pray at home?*

---

5   'Biser' in Bulgarian means 'pearl'.

It's in the morning and in the evening. I have to admit, though, that in the evening I often feel very tired and all these prayers that I read in the morning – I read them from the prayer book, the icon lamp is still lit at home, it's lit day and night, and I read prayers.

Dimana Dimova, Varna: 'You have to receive communion,
it is for forgiveness of your sins '[6]

Dimana, born in 1919, was one of the oldest women among the interviewees; for her, religiosity signifies strict observance of rituals and a rational systematisation of her way of life. She worked as a sexton at the Orthodox cathedral in Varna even in the time of socialism:

The church with the priests, what can I tell you, everything was wonderful, it was clean everywhere in the altar. And then, I'd first go to the altar in the morning and in the afternoon I'd stay at the cash desk because they couldn't find people to work there. People were afraid to work for the church.

The long years she worked at the church had made her an expert and many people turned to her with questions about the rules of church ritual; she was the godmother of more than 70 persons:

I'm 91 years old but the whole city knows me, they greet me – "you told me this, you taught me that". I teach these people how to prepare "the five loaves", they do it almost every Sunday. The five loaves, blessings. And they'd ask, "Auntie, what is this for?" – it is for good health and blessing for your homes, that's why the five loaves are prepared. Whenever I could, I explained. And people respect me and look up to me when they see me.

Similar in this to Ivanka, Dimana not only observed all the 'transition rituals' herself but made them a rule for her relatives as well.

Oh, unwed and unbaptised people could not enter our home – on the whole, this was the situation in the village, all the people there would say – the unbaptised and unwed is not to enter your home ... Well, I was baptised on the 6th day – that's why I've lived so long. The sooner you are baptised, the sooner you'll get your guardian angel. That's how our grandmothers and mothers interpreted it [...];

If a person dies, we pay for the 40-days service, so that the person gets inside right after his death and till the 40th day, when the soul appears before the Last Judgment.

---

[6]   See also Chapter 11 for this case.

Her everyday life was structured by a series of prayers and ascetic practices, such as making the sign of the cross over the bed and in front of the icon, as well as by strict observance of the Orthodox fasts:

> When we were schoolchildren they'd take us to church to receive communion. I do it till this very day, you have to fast during all the fasts, you have to receive communion.

Dimana was the only one of the interviewed women to give detailed description of the ceremony she planned for her funeral:

> So I have prepared for my death – a blanket, a sheet, basil, incense, everything. My candles are ready, before leaving work I bought two packets of candles to have for my death, so as not to bother them … I hope that angels and not devils will welcome me. I hope that the Good Lord will forgive me. I hope, but what will happen, I don't know … I've written everything that needs to be done. The incense, the candles, how to bathe the body. And to anoint the body with wine and basil. And you spread a white piece of cloth in front and behind. That's how a person appears on Judgment Day.

Suffering as a 'Conditio Humana'

Turning to the second dimension of religiousness – not as a system of rituals but as an intimate order of being, as a *temper that penetrates one's whole life* (Simmel 1995; Krech 1999), we see that this dimension is often thematised in the life narratives in connection with *suffering*.[7] The issue of theodicy is raised by interviewed women in connection with the death of parents, illnesses of friends and relatives, or the experience of the Second World War. This religiously coloured reflection on pain and suffering usually becomes more intense with age, when loneliness, physical helplessness and financial insecurity grow stronger. In one of the cases the respondent rejected the explanations of institutional religion, which proved unable to give a satisfactory explanation of Divine justice – 'How can God let that happen?' – especially in connection with the death of loved ones. In other interviews, the suffering that increases with age enforces the conviction in traditional church doctrine about the salvation of the soul, while biographical self-reflection about past sufferings – whether this is done in confession before a priest or simply by confiding in people – makes them easier to bear (Wohlrab-Sahr 1995, 9–13).

---

[7]   Biographical interviewing makes it possible to analyse the experiencing of *passive states* that cannot be reached through standardised questionnaires.

*Rumyana Dimitrova, Varna: 'After Pencho died, I've been living
by what the priest says'*

Rumyana's narrative began with recollections of the time before the Second World
War (she was born in 1925), about the high authority that Orthodox priests had
then in Bulgaria and the obligatory study of religion in school, and she expresses
nostalgia for the social solidarity of the past, now lost:

> The old priest that we had … he was very good. He'd find a way, with this
> audience – my grandmother and grandfather, the parents, the church was always
> full.

Rumyana emphasised that for many years she had been observing the 'transition
rituals' of the church: despite the restrictive policy of the communist state in this
respect, both of her children were baptised:

> When Anna was born, her godmother was a fervent communist. But she was
> also a very agreeable woman.

> I judge people by their deeds. I didn't dare tell her, not to offend her. But she
> herself proposed it when the child was a year or two: "Why don't we baptise
> Anni?" Well, I say, godmother … Well, I'm religious, she said, I might be a
> communist, but I'm religious, let's baptise her.

The main 'significant other' in her narrative was her husband, for whom Rumyana
was still grieving:

> But why, why did he leave? Let me tell you again – it was very hard for me at
> the beginning.

For seven years she attended church together with him in the parish of one of the
best known and charismatic priests in Bulgaria, Father Lyubomir Popov in Varna:

> The other thing I want to tell you – may he have a long and healthy life – the
> priest. I respect him because he is a holy man, but I respect him even more
> because he opens the souls of many, many people […];

> When the priest started talking, you could see light streaming from the speech, I
> can't explain to you what light it was.

With advancing age and being a widow, attendance at Sunday services had become
one of the basic ways for Rumyana to satisfy the need for social contacts, and there
she could discuss important existential questions like the meaning of pain and
suffering. After her retirement her interest in religious literature grew stronger,

as did her desire to build a consistent picture of the world through talks with the priest and the other parishioners:

> What actually is the human organism? I read about other doctrines that say "there's no God" but only matter, light, energy, and they were somehow transformed and formed protons, electrons and cells … What they say is true, but who created this light? It's God. God created it.

Sylvia Jones, Southampton: 'Well I think it's something that deepens all through life'

Sylvia was born in 1931 into a family of Catholics, and her mother was Irish. One of the first 'limit situations' she experienced, which she narrates, was the bombings during the Second World War, when she would hide with her family in bomb shelters:

> I can just remember my mother splashing us all with holy water. And praying really, because the noise was absolutely tremendous.

An intense experience from her childhood was connected with the mood of prayer around her, and the hope for an end to the war:

> I was quite used to seeing people praying from a very early age, because it was cold in those days, back in the war and so on, so people very often said their prayers down in front of the fire.

Sylvia described her mother as a woman of strong faith who found it hard to get over the death of her husband, and as a person who not only strictly observed religious rituals herself but also insisted on the whole family taking part and aligning their conduct with the rituals:

> But I can always remember when my mother was praying I knew instinctively that there was somebody much more important than I … And they always gave tremendous example, when you went on holiday the first thing my father always did was see where the local church was and what time Mass was. He went to Mass every day when he retired.

Her parents' religiosity was displayed in individual and collective praying ('We always say grace before meals') and attendance of church services, as well as in frequently making the sign of the cross, in reading the Bible and in the wish to 'give the day to God', in the consciousness that every family member is standing before God, 'that Christ was a person. You were following a person'. Sylvia has preserved unchanged all elements of the Christian worldview that she assimilated through family socialisation:

Hard though it is, how people live without faith, you know, I just can't fathom.

One of the key social-political events that influenced her attitude to the church was the Second Vatican Council (1962–65) and the so-called *aggiornamento*. The reforms that took place in the Catholic world in the 1970s took up a major part of her biographical narrative. She dwelled in detail on the separate changes: the changed language of religious service, the falling into disuse of Latin, the new arrangement of the church interior, and in the change the attitude towards ecumenism and interreligious cooperation (with people of other faiths):

> Tremendous change, tremendous change. It was just like an earthquake really; the big milestone.

Although she assessed the influence of these changes positively as regards the modernising of life in the Catholic parishes, Sylvia expressed nostalgia for the time in which the churches were also a place for social life, for intense communication and meetings, for prayers together and spiritual instruction given by the clergy. Despite all the changes, she said the number of parishioners was gradually decreasing; secularisation was growing in influence, one of the symptoms of which was that even religious people were turning more often to individual meditative practices. Unlike them, Sylvia felt that participation in religious rituals, especially in Mass, and the acknowledgement of the authority of priests, was an obligatory condition for being part of the community of faithful Catholics:

> Because without the Mass the Catholic faith is nothing.

The second 'limit situation' that marked a dramatic biographical discontinuity for her was her falling into a clinical depression after the death of her mother:

> Tremendous depression and I didn't know what had happened to me, you know, it was absolutely awful. Panic attacks … You feel outside of everything. You can't eat anything. I mean literally nothing. And at night you get this, you know, these awful shakes, absolutely like that … You feel outside. It's very difficult to describe.

With advancing age and approaching death, the religious feelings that penetrate her life were growing deeper, yet Sylvia did not experience ageing as a 'limit situation'. Her Christian disposition was to accept what life brings with 'joy and enthusiasm, they're the sort of hallmarks, or should be, the hallmarks of a Christian'; this shows through in her stable conviction that life does not end with death, but simply changes. She explains her satisfaction with life as being a result of Christian personalism:

Well, because happiness I think is accepting yourself as you are with all your faults and strengths, that's the way God made me, he knows me, he understands me through and through. And I do accept myself as I am with all my failings and so on and I know that he accepts me as I am. And I've always been in a family that's accepted me. So I feel, well, I've been very privileged.

Intellectual Sovereignty versus Church Affiliation

As early as 1967 Thomas Luckmann wrote in *The Invisible Religion* that religiosity must not be thought of mostly in sociological terms or only as church-related, but may appear in a great variety of individual dimensions. Luckmann shows that Judeo-Christian contents increasingly assume social forms that are unrecognisable as religious *per se* (Luckmann 1991, 1996). He believes that, even assuming that modern (European) society is secularised and that church traditions are no longer able to operationalise values into habitus, individuals still continue to experience anxiety. In this sense, the radical secularisation that took place in Europe after Second World War did not lead to the disappearance of religiosity (Oevermann and Franzmann 2006, 53); on the contrary – the greater the possibility of choosing between various religious communities or worldviews, the more reflective women become. They continue to ask themselves, 'who am I, where do I come from, what do I believe in, where am I going?', and these questions have a universal structure inasmuch as they concern everyone, regardless of their concrete life destiny. Such questions mirror the universal human need for integrating one's fragmented existence, for a solid support against the backdrop of transience and for justice.

Such issues are introduced into the interviewees' narratives in some cases by means of contrast: by rejecting the authority of church institutions and of the clergy (Bourdieu 2009, 21–9). In these cases the emphasis is placed on the *individual* formation of religious ideas, on guarding one's intellectual sovereignty. Yet those interviewed women who show mistrust in the public presentation of religion do not reject the idea of a transcendent reality and are not indifferent to religion. For them the transcendent does exist, independently of its empirical concrete manifestations and the symbols, rituals and performatives related to it, and is expressed best in the ritual of *personal prayer*. The contemplative-mystic attitude of these women mostly implies a depersonalised and immanent divine force (Weber 2005, 232). If at all inclined to overcome their mistrust in traditional religions, these women seek temporary affiliation to partially structured, non-hierarchic *communitas* (Turner 1999, 132–66), such as pilgrimages or visits to monasteries. In the analysed biographic material, the following causes may be indicated for this distanced attitude: (1) insurmountable mistrust in the clergy, usually inherited from the parents; and (2) the new scale of complexity of social life after the Second World War and the existing pluralism of worldviews, which stimulate critical attitudes and intellectual reflection. When traditional religious content no longer gives sufficiently firm answers to the questions of suffering and death, women seek those answers in a subjective turning inward and by inscribing essentially religious representations into their personal model of interpretation of the world (Berger 1992, 32–3).

Margareta Calinescu, Bucharest: 'I lost my faith when my mother fell ill, I didn't believe anymore'

Margareta was born in 1928. She was baptised in the Orthodox confession, but was among the few women in the project who were inclined to call themselves atheists (see Chapter 3). Margareta had a very clear idea that she wanted to be cremated, and why; she was very critical of the Orthodox clergy and their wealth. Two main reasons can be distinguished for her anti-clerical attitude: on one hand, she had been influenced by her father's attitude – he nominally observed church holidays ('Easter, with red eggs, and everything'), but did not conceal his negative attitude to the ministers of the church:

> Because he knew, he used to say that they were thieves and that they take money from the people for their own use.

Similar in this to her coevals, as a schoolchild Margareta was obliged to attend liturgy twice a week, but after the educational reform in 1948, she ceased to do so. The other reason for her distancing from the church as institution was the suffering she underwent as a child – the bombings of Galati, the great famine after the war, the sight of people dying in the streets, the poverty and inflation:

> This God, why doesn't he look upon us? And I think that was the moment when I became an atheist. Because I don't believe, believe in a superior force, you see?; I don't have faith.

Margareta described in detail the sufferings of her mother, and sickness holds an important place in her story. Both her parents died in the first years after the war, in 1946 and 1947. Margareta was 18 then and experienced an emotional breakdown:

> I used to say, why does God do this?

After the death of her mother, she stopped praying, but her rejection of Christianity was not radical, since she had a rosary and a Bible:

> Yes, of course, even today I respect the religious ceremony, how couldn't I? I am married to the son of a dean.

Margareta's father had an influence over the formation of her value system, in which willingness to work hard was most important. Ambition and the striving for self-fulfilment, for a good social position and prestige, were features she inherited from him:

> I think I inherited it from my father, that I have always been a hard working person and a, how do you say, an ambitious nerd, to be the first, and I have worked very hard for this.

Margareta's marriage proved difficult. She adopted a child because she was physically unable to have one of her own, and her husband took to drinking and had growing problems with drugs and gambling:

> He was religious enough to eat red eggs for Easter, but that was all, he didn't fast or anything … to sing "O Tanenbaum", he liked those things, it was a tradition and he was doing it in a non-religious way, but it was something superficial, he wasn't much of a believer.

An interesting point was that Margareta's self-definition as 'not much of a religious person' was not sustained consistently. She believed in the existence of a

> higher power that created this world, but I don't think that God helps Margareta just because I went to the church today, or because I gave money.

She defined her own religiosity basically through the prism of her anti-clericalism and anti-institutionalism. She did not like Orthodox priests because they do not articulate their words clearly, because of the long rituals and the way in which they collect funds:

> The church is the most corrupt and the priests are the most venal.

Margareta was convinced that the church should stop publicly demonstrating its riches, and that Christian ethics should be operationalised as socially responsible behaviour:

> Loving each other, that's what Jesus Christ taught, he didn't teach religious service with expensive clothes, but to love each other, love thy neighbour just as you love yourself, do no harm, if you are not doing any good.

At the end of the interview, in answer to the European Values Study questions,[8] she responded: 'I consider myself an Orthodox, all my life I have been an Orthodox'. Her 'believing without belonging' is confirmed by the fact that she did not attend religious services but at the same time was willing to be part of a flexible, temporary 'communitas':

---

[8]   European Values Study, 2008, http://www.europeanvaluesstudy.eu.

Sometimes I go visit a monastery … I go in just to watch the people, how the priest reads, and I sit there, it doesn't mean that I attend the ceremony. I observe the church, if it has the three books … but I don't stay and pray. Often I'm ashamed so I make the sign of the cross, because the people would notice, so they wouldn't say … but I know that this cross doesn't have. I don't know, that I believe.

She found questionable not only the political and economic side to the church (both Orthodox and Roman Catholic), but also its dogmatic interpretation of certain notions about human nature, about the soul and salvation. Her wish to be cremated after her death (which is entirely contrary to the Orthodox canon) may be interpreted as an expression of opposition to the *institutional* religious doctrines. Margareta did not limit her religious picture of the world to Christianity, and she showed that she could choose on her own those images that corresponded to her interest in the supernatural:

I believe in a higher force that created the Universe; I believe in evolutionism, I think that I'm an atheist.

Barbara Morris, London: 'Practising Jewish but not very religious'

Barbara was an 80-year-old resident of North London, married for 56 years, who defined herself as Jewish but declared several times in her biographical narrative that she was not very religious ('Very much Jewish but not religious'). For Barbara, being religious meant strict observance of the Shabbat, preparing kosher food with all the accompanying rituals and prayers, etc.:

Keeping everything exactly to – very difficult to explain to someone about another religion – for example, if you were having, if you were a very religious person you'd pray before you have a meal, you'd pray after the meal. But that is really extreme, you know.

She grew up in a family in which going to synagogue was not a usual practice, and Judaism was perceived mostly as a normative mark of ethnic appurtenance:

You married somebody that was Jewish?

Yes, oh wouldn't even think about anything like this … The religious bit, no, we didn't go to synagogue. My father didn't go to synagogue.

Her family observed Judaic rules as far as observing the traditional Jewish transition rituals, such as bar mitzvah (for her brother) or marriage ceremony in synagogue:

> Now the interesting thing about this is – you say about religion – whatever
> happens, however irreligious you are, you still got married in a synagogue.

Together with this, Barbara had never attended religious courses as a child, nor
did she observe the purification prayer ritual in Mikveh after the birth of her
children. However, that was when her interest arose in synagogue meetings: this
was mostly due to her lack of sufficient social contacts. That was why in Barbara's
biographical narrative one may trace a dividing line between this knowledge of
Judaic religious practices, such as funeral ceremonies, lamentation for the dead,
Shabbat, etc., on one hand, and a distanced personal attitude to orthodox Judaism
on the other:

> There are lots of – in the Jewish religion, I suppose in other religions – there are
> lots of procedures that one needs to know and if you don't know them – I don't
> know it all.

Barbara regularly attended prayer meetings in the synagogue, but she stressed that
she was motivated mostly by the need for social contact and by interest in certain
existential questions and the various interpretations of the Torah offered during the
thematic lectures (Shuir) given apart from the religious service:

> I'm not very religious. I like, I go to the synagogue, I like the meeting of people.
> I don't understand it all but I read;
>
> And if you read the English of the Torah it makes, you can relate it to, it makes
> sense. It does.

An expression of this reflexive attitude was the practice of contemplation and
meditation in a way that did not strictly have the character of prayer. Barbara's
reflective attitude to Judaism was evident in her insistence on tolerance and respect
for religious differences:

> I have very mixed feelings because, as I explained to you, I'm sure it's the
> same in other religions but the Jewish religion there's a lot of diversity. And
> sometimes one group is intolerant of the other. And of course it creates personal
> problems, it does create, you know, it's around all sorts of things. Dietary laws,
> slaughter of animals, you've seen that in the press, things like that all come
> under the umbrella of religion.

One mark of this was her respect for Christian holidays such as Christmas, which
she interpreted as an occasion for relatives and friends to get together, as well as
the secular celebration of her golden wedding.

Conclusion

Regardless of the socio-cultural and confessional particularities and differences between the three countries I have studied, the gathered biographical material gives me reasons to assert that, for the generation of women born before and between the two world wars, religion was a significant factor for their initial socialisation and had biographical relevance throughout the interviewees' later lives. Even when the religious content of Judeo-Christian origin is *metaphysically neutralised*, it continues in some form or other to be a part of the construction of the interviewees' values system and their picture of the world. However, their religiosity manifests itself in different ways in their biographies, and is incorporated with different intensities in their habituses. In the course of ageing it can really assume an actively rational character, become interwoven with the everyday way of life, become disciplined and rationalised in the form of a practical ethic and a collective ritual. In these cases religiosity is connected with the need for a legitimate collective strategy for dealing with biographical crises and 'limit situations' in life. On the other hand, religiosity is thematised by the biographers also as a passive experience, while the rituals related to it are presented in the form of self-reflection. In this case the women reject or partially question the clerical monopoly on the interpretation of the world and religious public presentations, and prefer the field of socially 'invisible' religion. They then become oriented not to the ritual but to their own personal spiritual experience, and with advancing age they build individual strategies for dealing with suffering and insecurity.

Translated by Vladimir Vladov

References

Berger, Peter L. 1992. *Der Zwang zur Häresie. Religion in der pluralistischen Gesellschaft*. Freiburg: Herder.
Bourdieu, Pierre. 2009. *Religion. Studien zur Kultursoziologie 5*. Konstanz: UVK.
Casanova, Jose. 2010. 'Religion in Modernity as Global Challenge'. In *Religion und die umstrittene Moderne*, edited by M. Reder and M. Rugel, 1–21. Stuttgart: W. Kohlhammer.
Davie, Grace. 2002. *Europe: The Exceptional Case. Parameters of Faith in the Modern World*. London: Darton, Longman and Tod.
Davie, Grace. 2007. *Sociology of Religion*. London: Sage.
Hunt, Stephen. 2007. 'Religion as a Factor in Life and Death Through the Life-course'. In *Sage Handbook of Sociology of Religion*, edited by James Beckford and N.J. Demerath III, 609–29. London: Sage.
Jaspers, Karl. 2000. 'Die Grenzsituationen als conditio humana', 'Die Frage nach der Transzendenz'. In *Was ist der Mensch? Philosophisches Denken für alle*, 129–72. München: Pieper.

Kelle, Udo. 2008. 'Alter und Altern'. In *Handbuch Soziologie*, edited by N. Baur, H. Korte, M. Löw and M. Schroer, 11–31. Wiesbaden: VS Verlag für Sozialwissenschaften.

Knoblauch, Hubert. 2009. *Populäre Religion. Auf dem Weg in die spirituelle Gesellschaft*. Frankfurt am Main: Campus Verlag.

Kohli, Martin. 1990. 'Das Alter als Herausforderung für die Theorie sozialer Ungleichheit'. In *Lebenslagen, Lebensläufen, Lebensstile*, edited by P.A. Berger and S. Hradil, 387–406. Göttingen: Schwartz.

Krech, Volkhard. 1999. *Religionssoziologie*. Bielefeld: transcript.

Luckmann, Thomas. 1991. *Die unsichtbare Religion*. Frankfurt am Main: Suhrkamp.

Luckmann, Thomas. 1996. 'Religion – Gesellschaft – Transzendenz'. In *Krise der Immanenz. Die Religion an den Grenzen der Moderne*. Frankfurt am Main: Fischer Taschenbuch.

Martin, David. 2005. *On Secularization: Towards a Revised General Theory*. Aldershot: Ashgate.

Metodiev, Momchil. 2010. *Between Faith and Compromise. The Orthodox Church and the Communist Regime in Bulgaria (1944–1989)*. Sofia: Siela (in Bulgarian).

Nassehi, Armin. 1995. 'Religion und Biographie. Zum Bezugsproblem religiöser Kommunikation in der Moderne'. In *Biographie und Religion. Zwischen Ritual und Selbstsuche*, 103–26. Frankfurt am Main: Campus.

Oevermann, Ulrich and Manuel Franzmann. 2006. 'Strukturelle Religiosität auf dem Wege zur religiösen Indifferenz'. In *Religiosität in der säkularisierten Welt. Theoretische und empirische Beiträge zur Säkularisierungsdebatte in der Religionssoziologie*, 49–82. Wiesbaden: VS Verlag für Sozialwissenschaften.

Rosenthal, Gabriele. 2005. *Interpretative Sozialforschung: Eine Einführung*. München: Juventa.

Schütze, Fritz. 1983. 'Biographieforschung und narratives Interview'. *Neue Praxis* 1(3): 283–93.

Simmel, Georg. 1995. 'Religion'. In *Gesammtausgabe*, Vol. 10, 39–118. Frankfurt am Main: Suhrkamp.

Sointu, Eeva and Linda Woodhead. 2008. 'Spirituality, Gender and Expressive Selfhood'. *Journal for the Scientific Study of Religion* 47(2): 259–76.

Turner, Victor. 1999. *The Ritual Process*. Sofia: Lik (in Bulgarian).

Voas, David. 2009. 'The Rise and Fall of Fuzzy Fidelity in Europe'. *European Sociological Review* 25(2): 155–68.

Weber, Max. 2005. *Wirtschaft und Gesellschaft. Religiöse Gemeinschaften*. Tübingen: J.C.B. Mohr (Paul Siebeck).

Wohlrab-Sahr, Monika. 1995. 'Einleitung'. In *Biographie und Religion. Zwischen Ritual und Selbstsuche*, edited by M. Wohlrab-Sahr, 9–23. Frankfurt am Main: Campus.

Woodhead, Linda. 2002. 'Christianity' and 'Women and Religion'. In *Religions in the Modern World: Traditions and Transformations*, 153–82 and 332–56. London: Routledge.

Woodhead, Linda. 2005. *The Spiritual Revolution. Why Religion is Giving Way to Spirituality* (with Paul Heelas). Oxford: Blackwell.

Woodhead, Linda. 2007. *Christianity. A Very Short Introduction*. Sofia: Zaharij Stojanov (in Bulgarian).

World Health Organization. 2002. 'Health and Ageing. A Discussion Paper'. Available at: http://whqlibdoc.who.int/hq/2001/WHO_NMH_HPS_01.1.pdf.

PART V
Review and Conclusions

Chapter 11

Ritual in the Changing Lives of the Very Old

Peter G. Coleman, Sidonia Grama and Ignat C. Petrov

In this first of two concluding chapters we focus on what we have learned from our interviews about the role of ritual in older people's lives in Eastern and Western Europe. We re-iterate a number of the points that have been made in previous chapters, for example about the formative influence of early life experience, especially within the family, about persons' capacity to resist external influences during adulthood, and about the continuing importance of ritual in later life. Indeed there is evidence that ritual practice, and especially private prayer, may become a more significant part of people's lives as they become very old, and we begin this chapter by reviewing the oldest and frailest persons in our sample.

Research findings on the associations between religious belief and well-being are consistent with the hypothesis that strength of belief confers greater benefits as frailty increases (Kirby, Coleman and Daley 2004). Indeed, one of the concerns expressed, as a result of the decline in religious affiliation in Western Europe, is that the alternative non-religious and secular cultures and meaning systems that have developed within later twentieth-century society do not provide equivalent spiritual sustenance to people as they age (Howse 1999). If religion is one of the major cultural 'friends' of ageing, that allows the self to transcend bodily decline and the threat of impending death, one might expect that the oldest would be able to provide the most considered and authentic account of the place of religious belief and practice in their life story, both past and present (Pargament, van Haitsma and Ensing 1995).

There is a further reason for focusing on the very old in this penultimate chapter. All of those we interviewed in their later 80s and 90s had already reached adulthood, and formed their initial identities, at the time of the transition to a more secular society in the postwar years. Social change in matters of religion is likely to have come as a surprise for them and therefore their comments are likely to be of particular interest. Participants over 85 years of age in Eastern Europe were socialised pre-war within a strongly religious culture. They were young adults when, after 1944–45, they were required, at least in certain sectors of life, to conform to new secular norms of behaviour. Those in the equivalent age group in Western Europe experienced a more gradual change towards secularisation, especially from the 1960s onwards, when they would have been in early middle age.

The next section thus provides portraits of the oldest and frailest persons in the samples in each of our three countries. As the numbers are small, we have included everyone we interviewed over the age of 87 years, and those of our participants between 85 and 87 years who were in evident ill health at the time of the interview. We briefly mention their significant memories and experience of religion throughout the course of their lives. However, we focus on their current attitudes to religious belief and practice, particularly in relation to their present health and social situation. We draw some comparisons between the cases in the three countries, but leave major consideration of the implications to the following discussion sections.

The Oldest and Frailest in Our Sample

In Romania

We interviewed four very old Romanian persons with failing health, Ioana Georgescu, Ecaterina Florea, and Aurelian and Teodora Ghelasie. Their physical status was sufficiently precarious to justify a description as frail. All four expressed a strong religious faith and were able to speak in detail about the importance of religious faith in their lives both in the past and in the present.

Aurelian and Teodora Ghelasie (96 and 85 years respectively) have been discussed in detail in Chapter 5 (and Aurelian also in Chapter 2). Aurelian gave a remarkably detailed interview just before his 97th birthday in which he stressed the importance of his religious faith throughout his life, particularly in some of the important choices he had made, including the 'fateful' decision to join the nationalist movement, the Iron Guard, in pre-war Romania. Although mentally alert for his age, he was physically frail, still mobile inside the house but not outside, and spent much of the day lying down. He had to be very careful walking, having already fallen and fractured his leg twice. His sight was very poor and he was unable to read. He could only attend religious services by listening to the television or radio. His attitude to his present health condition was marked by religious faith, consistent with the rest of his life story: 'I know that nothing happens without the will of God, and if God let this happen, then we shall bear it.'

Their situation, childless as they were, seemed extremely vulnerable. Teodora was more than 10 years Aurelian's junior, but also frail, and he was concerned how she would manage without him. However he had been reassured by a monk that they would not be separated for long. He stressed how they were 'dependent spiritually upon one another'. Night was a particularly difficult time, feeling how 'powerless' their situation was, but night was also the time when he repeated phrases from memory, poems and prayers. He began to recite to interviewer: 'May Your gaze descend upon us, O most pure and eternally virgin Mother Mary.'

In her own interview Teodora described her early life, her meeting with her husband after the war, his subsequent persecution at the hands of the communist authorities and her own suffering and bravery in very difficult circumstances.

Throughout all of the difficulties she encountered she ascribed great importance to her faith as a source of coping, especially in the time after her husband was arrested.

She had come from a strongly religious background and when young had wanted to become a nun. She had already witnessed the results of postwar political persecution within her own family before she met her husband, and had learned to avoid politics as a result. Her health had not been strong, and probably the greatest sadness of her life, which still caused her emotional pain, was her inability to give her husband a child (she had incurred three miscarriages).

Her health problems had multiplied. She had retired at 55 years because her eyesight was deteriorating and she now could hardly see. One eye should have been operated on earlier but she had not felt able to leave her husband on his own in his frail state. She was also suffering from cardiac problems and sporadic seizures with headaches and numbness in the limbs, which would last for days and keep her in bed. However, still she would not rate her health as bad, and expressed herself content with what she had. Her life was suffused with religious images, real and imagined, from the icons around the apartment to visions in her dreams. Like her husband, she also expressed strong devotion to the Mother of Christ.

> I'm more with the Holy Mother. Yesterday night I dreamed that … a dream … I
> told my husband. I've been dreaming of my sister, who's dead! She's been dead
> for three years. I saw her by the chandelier. I say, "But why are you dressed like
> that?" And she says, "I'm the Lord's Mother now". Then she vanished. She was
> very religious too.

Ioana, a widow of 86 years described herself as a happy person, pleased especially with her children. She bore well the health problems she experienced. Heart problems had led her to retire from work at 44 years, and she was now awaiting her tenth hospital operation. For the last two years she had been unable to walk outside. Heavy or difficult housework was out of the question and even simple cooking, like making a soup, took her a long time. Yet she did not complain.

> Health is … you know something? I am very sick, but still I am very healthy …
> I have to have all sorts of tests done, but as long as you don't complain, "Oh my
> God what is happening to me", and you take life as it is … I think it's normal
> when you are 86 years old and you don't have the strength you used to have or
> the health you used to have.

Ioana described to the interviewer in great detail the sad events of her life, from her mother's death when she was only 12 to her guardian brother's early death in a motorcycle accident, and yet the memories were not suffused with sorrow. Most remarkable was her response to her husband's desertion of her and their two children when she was aged 37 years. She had remained living with her mother-in-law. However, 16 years later her husband's new house was irreparably damaged in an earthquake and she accepted him and his second wife back in the old house living with her. They lived together for 26 years. Her husband's second wife died of breast cancer the year after his own death, and in that last year Ioana and the second wife cared for each other.

Ioana herself made the connection between her serenity, despite her difficult life experiences, and her religious practice. Her adaptation to bereavement has already been discussed in Chapter 8. She described the 'inner peace' she felt also as an old person when she was in church, and especially in the monasteries she had visited. At the time of the interview she was intending to ask again for the priest to come to perform the Prayers of St Basil, which were:

> a special religious service carried out to protect the house, for breaking spells, bad things and that sort of stuff. Last time I did it was three years ago. I believe in this, that I need a protector who watches over this house.

She had strong beliefs in a life beyond death and that throughout her life she could call on the help not only of God but also of loved ones, especially her mother and her brother. At the same time, and despite her deep knowledge of religious-related ritual, she taught a balanced approach to its use. For example alms-giving, also required by the Orthodox tradition she belonged to, was for her the most important ritual following a death.

Ecaterina, also a widow, aged 85 years, lived with her daughter's family, had been house-bound for the last two years, and at the time of interview had been lying in bed for many weeks. She found it especially hard not to be able to walk, and she could only read with a magnifying glass. However, she was pleased that 'her head was still functioning' and above all grateful that her family were well. She hoped for a quick death and that she should not burden people.

Ecaterina, like Teodora, had worked as a nurse and had also encountered health problems throughout most of her life. After childbirth she suffered from serious haemorrhaging, and remembered the concerns she had felt that she might leave her child without a mother. She said that her faith 'kept her going' in that period of her life. Although considering her own religious practice to be 'mediocre', she stated that God 'has helped me all the time':

> I do have faith in God and also in the Holy Mother … It has never happened to me to pray and not get what I prayed for, there are some things nobody would imagine you could do something like that and lo and behold I have thought the thought and God has helped me.

Following the teaching of her uncle, who had been a Greek Catholic priest, she had confessed regularly throughout her life, once a month, but less often now as she was house-bound and depended on the priest visiting her. She prayed regularly in the morning, evening and throughout the day 'whenever anything happens':

Not a day goes by, thank you God for everything you have given me. Prayer books say that even saying that little is good and I'm telling you God has helped me from all points of view, my daughter is grown up, she's a darling, she has beautiful, healthy children and a good husband, so I'm very content, a happy grandmother, mother.

In Bulgaria

Our Bulgarian sample provided fewer examples of older people in very poor health. The most evident was Alexandra Koleva, aged 93 years, a widow who lived with her son. She felt her poor health and dependency strongly. With deteriorated eyesight, hearing and mobility, she had been house-bound for a number of years and experienced little enjoyment in life:

I'm 93 now, and I'm good for nothing. I can't help Dima [her son] much, I am just doing the dishes from time to time. He is taking care of everything, he is shopping, cooking. He used to take me to the doctor's, but now I can't do this either, since I can't walk. Old age has overtaken me, and I am a burden to Dima, I am a great burden to him, but what can I do. So it is.

She had also been bereaved not only of her husband but also of her older son. This latest loss was weighing heavily upon her at the time of the interview. Her conversation stressed the hardships of her life, the many bereavements, in particular the death of her brother, killed by Serbian partisans during the war, and the difficulties of life under communism, which had destroyed the relative affluence of small businesses like her own family's.

Alexandra's upbringing had not been particularly religious. She said that her parents only went to church once in a while, and her mother had died when she was only 12 years old. Therefore it was not surprising that she converted to a Protestant Christian faith when she married into a pastor's family in 1944. She then began attending church and appreciated the sermons that were given. However, she continued to describe herself as 'not very religious'.

She was now ready to die, and wished for it:

I've been thinking a lot about it lately. I am already praying to God to take me, but he wouldn't. Here I am already 93 years old. I've become such a great burden to Dima … Old age is so hard, I am just watching TV, with earphones on.

She had prepared her laying out clothes and given instructions to her son, also for the funeral: a Protestant service, cremation and interment of the ashes next to her son and husband. She was unsure about her belief in an after-life but did pray every night for her deceased son.

Dimana Dimova, at 91 years, provided a marked contrast to Alexandra, in terms of both her personal well-being and her religious enthusiasm. She had been fortunate in her health for most of her life and was still very active for her age. Her remarkable role in serving in the church during the period of communist persecution has already been described in Chapter 10. Dressed in simple clothes and thin because of her ascetic life style, she still kept the Orthodox fasts on Wednesdays and Fridays and also in addition on Mondays. In fact her daughter attributed her active brain to this way of life.

Her sight and hearing were now deteriorated, but she remained fixed on the example her mother and her mother-in-law had given her:

> Whatever I've asked God has always given me it ... That's how my mother used to teach us. Those who ask God for help and go to church, God helps in all enterprises and now I'm thankful. I worked in the church, I baptised my children, and I wed them.

Her life was organised around prayer and ritual:

> Every morning when I get up, the first thing I do is to cross myself in front of the icon, I wash and I say my prayer and then, "Dear Lord, you first, I follow". Now that I can't see so well and I can't hear I say, "Dear Lord, send me guidance". There's always a person and they'd tell me where to go – come on, my girl, my boy, no one has refused to take me to the other side [of the road].

She had also prepared instructions for all that needed to be done after her death:

> the incense, the candles, how to bathe the body. And to anoint the body with wine and basil. And you spread a white piece of clothing at the front and behind. That's how a person appears on Judgement Day.

The oldest Bulgarian man in our sample was Andon Igov, 87 years of age and living in Sofia at the time of his interview. His life has been described already in chapters 6 and 9. At the time of the interview he was recovering from a major operation carried out earlier in the year, and now had to use a walking stick. Nevertheless he attended church every Sunday, and visited his wife's grave afterwards, so he could not be considered particularly frail.

He had come from a strongly religious background. His grandfather on his father's side was a priest and as his mother was also very religious he grew up in a strictly practising setting. Although he thought that problems that arise in life, including within the churches, would benefit from more a more rational approach, he realised that not everything can be explained, and that in fact 'mysticism intensifies' in him as he grew older, and that there was a meaning in God's will for him. He had thought a lot on theological issues, on what God was for him and how he experienced God in his life:

> He cannot be described, he can only be felt, sensed, I can feel Him – all the
> questions I can't explain to myself, the entire existence, the circle of life, all this
> is a kind of power – be it God, be it Lord, be it Allah. The realisation of these
> things leads to different attitudes. I can feel He's with me, I can feel it.

He graphically described the daily life trials of a very old person like himself, for
example waiting for a bus, and the way he used religious coping to deal with the
situation:

> Sometimes it's cold, I say, "Dear Lord, when will the bus come?" And in a
> minute it comes. He helps me, it's again God that helps me. Thank you Lord!
> I'm on the bus! Besides, every morning I wake up, I believe it's the first day of
> the rest of my life, it's the first day, the next day – again it'll be the first day of
> the rest of my life, my life that belongs to God. That's the truth.

In the UK

Within the UK sample only one person, Sarah Hazelwood (aged 95 years), could
be considered significantly disabled. Kitty Howard was also very old (96 years),
but had only very recently begun to encounter some major health worries. Of the
older men, Derek Cousens (aged 89 years) had been diagnosed with a significant
health problem, but was still in relatively good health for his age.

At the time of interview Sarah rated her health poorly. She had just returned
from hospital but thought she needed more help with rehabilitation. She
complained about her balance, and in fact had fallen again a few days previous to
the interview, despite having a support frame to get around her house. Previously
she had enjoyed good health but now she said that life was all a 'struggle'. She
found the physical therapists who visited her insufficiently sympathetic:

> She says "It's all in the mind, of course you can do it" you know. But they don't
> know how you feel when you're old, when your balance has gone, you know. It's
> just awful. No, I just feel I've lived long enough for now.

As she could not go to church anymore, the local minister visited her to administer
Eucharist.

She ascribed her own religiousness to her stepfather, who was a retired army
chaplain who took over as a minister of a rural church. She received a thorough
education at a church school that also required religious lessons on a Saturday
morning. She was confirmed at the age of 14 years in the local cathedral in a
ceremony that made a big impression on her. Like her stepfather, she liked high
church Anglican ritual with 'candles, incense', 'marvellous music' and a sense of
'reverence'. She lamented the changes in church practice in England, listing all
the churches that had closed in her home city of Southampton, and criticising the
ordination of women priests because they 'didn't look the part' to take the place of

Christ in the Eucharistic service. She had experienced a 'downhill process' within the church, also within her own family, remembering her own nephew, who had been christened but was now a 'non-believer' and had not christened his own daughter:

> I don't know what is going to happen really. It's very sad I think. You see that old church we had (where her stepfather was minister) I think was joined up to another parish. There's no rector now. They sold the rectory which we lived in ... I don't think England is a Christian country, not basically.

Kitty's health had been remarkably good but had in recent weeks she begun to experience 'horrible turns', including pains in her head, which her doctor had not been able to diagnose. This situation meant that she no longer was confident about going outside her home.

Although she had been introduced to Christianity at Sunday school, for most of her life religion had played only a minor role. It was only after the death of her mother when Kitty was aged 60 years that she began attending the church near her home. Neither her father nor her mother had attended church regularly when Kitty was young. In fact her mother was hostile from her experience of 'Christian people' while working in service as a cook. Nevertheless she had memories of things her father had said that indicated he was religious, for example disapproving of her dress-making on Good Friday. He had also taken her as a child to visit St Paul's Cathedral in the City of London, which had remained for her an important memory.

However it was Sunday school that had made the biggest impression. Kitty had enjoyed it immensely and what she had been taught had made a lasting influence:

> Well I wouldn't say I was a religious person ... but I do believe in what our religion is. I do believe that. Even when I didn't go to church, it was there, what I'd been taught in Sunday school. That, you know, was so deeply put into me though, as I say, I didn't go to church.

She had found her way back to church, after her mother died, on the invitation of a friend, and she had been a regular attender since. A day trip to St Paul's had awakened her interests in the cathedral and the possibility of offering to serve as a volunteer behind the shop counter there. She was sad that the cathedral was getting so commercialised, that the 'friends of St Paul's' were now less involved. She wished that more people would attend church and, in particular, that families would go as in the past – although her own family had not.

Derek had been operated on for testicular cancer four years ago and was now taking hormone injections for his condition. His hearing had deteriorated as well and despite having a hearing aid could not hear church services well anymore. His interview took place in stages as he needed breaks.

As in Kitty's case, attending Sunday school in childhood had been particularly important to his religious formation. He described his becoming a Christian as a gradual development. His growing religious interests had influenced his parents, and after his confirmation they began attending church again, even taking on roles in the church community. After war service (in which he was in prisoner of war camp for some years) Derek became a Sunday school teacher himself and took an active role in church services, singing in the choir. Finally at the age of 29 years he became a 'lay reader'.

He said that his main beliefs had remained stable since then. He prayed every morning and evening and read the Bible every day following guidelines. Also on occasions, when the vicar was not there during the week, he officiated at services in the same local church in which he had been christened. However, he had chosen to attend a different church on Sundays, one that was 'high church' with more ceremony, including more elaborate use of robes, incense and bells.

Like Sarah, Kitty and a number of the other British sample interviewed, Derek had experienced substantial change in religious services during his time as a lay minister, and had clearly reflected a great deal on this. In his case this was the result of a shifting population, with in- and out-migration, in his area of North London:

> Our minister, our vicar, is a Nigerian and he has got, I mean on the whole we've only got two or three white people left in the church now. Now I've nothing against coloureds, it's not that, but it's they love this happy clappy stuff. They wave their arms and they move up and down. And they go on and on with this, and to me that puts me off. I go to church, to a communion service, to say my prayers and to sing a few hymns and all the rest of it. But all this – and it goes on and on and on – and what put me off was we had a harvest festival service which went on for four hours. I mean a normal service is an hour, an hour and a half at the most and this went on for four hours. And what infuriated me was that our vicar – he's got three churches to look after ... and he wasn't [at our church] he was at one of the other churches, well he came in after this service had been going on about a couple of hours or so and he said "Oh well we haven't got time for the communion, we'll cut that out". And that's, I mean I couldn't believe it, because that is a communion service, the Eucharist is what you go to it for.

Nevertheless Derek seemed to have coped well with ongoing change in the Church of England, showing a willingness to accommodate to the different needs of the present day, including the movement towards ordaining women priests and bishops.

Ritual, the Lifespan and Ageing

Before we attempt to draw some conclusions from our study on the role of ritual in older people's lives, the limitations of our sample need to be acknowledged. Our interviews involved a substantial demand, not only on participants' time, but also on their capacity to engage in the effort of articulating personal and often very sensitive memories of trauma and loss. As we have indicated in Chapter 9, those willing to agree to these interviews were predominantly extroverted in personality, non-depressed and in relatively good health for their age. Therefore they cannot be considered representative of their respective age groups. In particular, we interviewed hardly anyone with noticeable signs of mental impairment, despite the fact that the prevalence of dementia increases markedly in the 80s and 90s.

Nevertheless the data we collected on memories of ritual practice over the lifespan are very rich and some general conclusions seem justified. In general, participants seem to have remained with the same level of religiosity they acquired during childhood (see especially Chapter 8). Those with religious parents tend to have become religious themselves. Other religious influences when young – including attending Sunday school – also seem to have had lasting effects. At the same time there appear to be few if any examples of religious conversion in adulthood, although there are some striking examples of conversion from a religious to a non-religious humanist viewpoint on life. Moreover, as the cases of the persons already described in this chapter suggest, the oldest members of our sample in all three countries seem both to have been and to continue to be more religious in their behaviour than the somewhat younger cohorts.

These results are consistent with those of substantial longitudinal cohort studies on religious attitudes in the USA, which have found both significant cohort differences in religiosity and stability of religious attitudes with age (Bengtson with Putney and Harris 2013). They do not seem to bear out the oft cited thesis that the process of ageing itself makes people more religious. Rather ageing provides the setting for a person's final commitments, whether to a religious, non-religious, or as we have seen earlier in this book (for example, chapters 3, 5 and 6), a sometimes seemingly paradoxical commitment to both religious and non-religious meanings. Changes in religious attitudes in later life when they occur are striking because they are unusual.

Particularly telling was the further evidence our study provided on the resistance to secular pressure among many religious believers in Eastern Europe (see especially Chapter 5). All of our oldest Bulgarian and Romanian participants had arrived at adulthood as religiously practising individuals and therefore were liable to encounter potential problems under the new communist regime. Aurelian Ghelasie is an extreme example of a man who endured long years of imprisonment, but Miron Popescu and others endured dismissal from employment or had to hide their religious affiliation in order to maintain employment. The women, such as Aurelian's wife Teodora and Eleonora Moldovan, also behaved heroically, or were called by the circumstances of the time to undertake unusual tasks, such as Dimana

Dimova in her service to her church alongside the priest within the sacred liturgy. It is perhaps significant that the one person in the oldest age group (Ion Cotescu), whose faith was never strong, and who perhaps never had to demonstrate it, said that he personally did not witness persecution.

What do our interviews contribute to our initial question of the psychological value to very old people of religious belief and particularly ritual as they encounter increased difficulties with health? In line with previous research, our observations suggested certainly no lessening of commitment to religious faith and personal practice (i.e. prayer), despite physical frailty leading to decreased attendance at religious worship and religious reading. Our religious participants appeared to keep up their religious activities as best they could, for example, the Orthodox continuing to confess, receive communion and fast where appropriate.

There was strong evidence for the consoling value of religious practice. Aurelian Ghelasie and his wife Teodora articulated in some detail the frailty of their situation, particularly their powerlessness at night. Their belief that 'nothing happens without the will of God' sustained them. They were content that they could still walk. All Aurelian asked for was that he would not go blind completely.[1]

The study of religious coping is now a well-developed field of research that has left behind the legacy of Freud's dismissive attitude (Pargament 1997). The particular salience of religious modes of coping to the experience of ageing has also been identified (Emery and Pargament 2004; Coleman 2010). Among the types of religious coping that have been identified are religious reframing (seeing, for example, apparently negative events as part of God's plan for the person), collaborative religious coping (in which God may be seen as a partner in dealing with stress, particularly important for older people as social networks decline) and religious focusing (involving prayers of entreaty and thanksgiving in regard to particular objectives). Not surprisingly, religious coping appears more effective when practised by people with stronger levels of belief.

An important theme in the developmental psychological literature of later life, already referred to in Chapter 7, is 'life review', in which past experience is consciously surveyed, evaluated and integrated (Coleman and O'Hanlon 2004). A valuable potential spiritual outcome is forgiveness, both of self and others. Forgiveness is increasingly demonstrated to have important positive health benefits, affecting both physical and mental health (McCullough et al. 2009). Our sample contained examples of spiritually strong elders, such as Ioana Georgescu, described earlier in this chapter, who seemed very much at peace with themselves and others, despite the hardships they had encountered. They were looked at by those around as examples of wisdom in late life. The high level of wisdom they had reached appeared a product both of the suffering they had experienced and the way they had responded to it without hatred and resentment.

---

[1]   After eye surgery, Aurelian has been able to read again.

Differences between Eastern and Western Europe

Although we began this project with an equal focus on contrasts between our two Eastern European countries and on those with the UK, in the end the latter comparison has proved more striking. There seemed to be noticeable differences between attitudes to ritual practice in our Eastern European and Western participants. This is a point which has already been emphasised in Chapter 8 The participants from both our Eastern European countries appear to have engaged more with and to be currently more respectful of religious ritual than our UK ones. This can be largely accounted for by their different historical experience, in particular the stigma attributed to secular ritual by its encouragement during communist rule in Eastern Europe. However, as we have seen in Chapter 9, communist rule was not perceived negatively by everyone. Indeed the older population of Eastern Europe has tended to be nostalgic for the greater material securities of their society before the return to capitalism in the 1990s. Yet the attempt on the part of communist authorities to replace traditional religious rituals, especially for life transitions such as births, marriages and death, appears to have been deeply unpopular (Chapter 6). The continuing sense of resentment affects even present day attitudes to secular, as opposed to religious, ritual.

The earlier roots of secularism in Western Europe also need to be considered. The differences in religiosity are even evident among the very old in our sample. All those of 85 years and over we interviewed in Bulgaria and Romania – who thus grew to adulthood during or just before the Second World War – appear to have been a traditionally religious generation (Alexandra Koleva and Ion Cotescu are the only possible exceptions and neither of them is definitely non-religious). They have kept to the religious norms with which they were socialised. This is much less true of our oldest British participants. In fact we interviewed some explicitly non-religious persons among the oldest age group in the UK sample, including Evelyn Everett and Jennifer Renwick (see chapters 2 and 4), as well as Lewis Farrow and Harold Stevenson (chapters 5 and 7).

Nevertheless there do seem to be other factors that need to be taken into account in explaining the greater apparent religiosity of older Eastern Europeans. Much of the discussion on differences in religiosity between Western and Eastern Europe has focused on the greater influence on the former of questioning of religious beliefs begun at the Protestant Reformation with its rebuttal of the Roman Church's authority and the later Enlightenment challenge to all religious authority. However there has been less discussion on the different character of religious transmission across Europe. Our interview data suggest interesting differences in modes of religious socialisation in childhood between our samples that may have contributed to the greater durability of religious commitment in the oldest participants in Romania and Bulgaria.

Early religious experience provides the emotional basis for the subsequent interpretation of religious experience. One of the most enduring theories of psychological development is the theory of attachment, which postulates the need for a secure base with a parental figure on which to rely for stability of emotional well-being, also in the absence of the attachment figure (Bowlby, 1969). This expresses itself first strongly in early infancy but remains evident throughout the vicissitudes of life, especially in the subsequent building of intimate relationships but also in late life attitudes to care and dependency. Early life variations in parental experience lead to differences in attachment style which appear to distinguish persons until the end of their lives. As religion is one of the main cultural providers of emotional security, it is no surprise that attachment theory has also been applied to the psychology of religious development (Kirkpatrick 2004). Religious socialisation often occurs in the context of family life, in which concepts and images of parental and divine love and authority are often juxtaposed and intermingled.

Recent studies on the more successful transmission of Islam compared with Christianity in the UK emphasise the habitus of the Muslim family and community and how children do not just learn what it is to be religious but become religious by actively copying their parents and others (Scourfield et al. 2013). Similarly our Romanian and Bulgarian elders' memories of religion are richly intertwined with the religious practices of their parents, grandparents and other members of their extended families, which sometimes included priests. The family appears to have remained the main source of religious socialisation throughout the pre-war and war period, and indeed even more so after the removal of religious education from schools and the limitations on the teaching function of religious organisations imposed during the communist period. This may help explain why the emotional ties with their faith of our Eastern European participants appear somewhat stronger than those of their UK counterparts. In our UK sample, strong attachments, such as Derek Cousens and Sylvia Jones expressed towards respectively their Anglican and Roman Catholic churches of origin, appear rarer.

It is noteworthy that the roles of the Sunday school and subsequent formal religious education appear to be more significant features of religious socialisation in our British sample. The importance to British culture of the twentieth century of children attending separate classes of religious education away from their parents, typically on a Sunday late morning or afternoon, often as a preparation for receiving sacraments of initiation as Eucharist and Confirmation, has been pointed out by others. Davies (2004) for example has argued it to be a major source in the making of the British moral character. The institution was widespread up to the 1950s and often led to young people attending church two or even three times a day on Sunday.

Mention of Sunday school comes up frequently in interviews with British older people in regard to their religious history (Coleman et al. 2011). It was an important institution in the country and there is an oral history literature on the subject (e.g. Roberts 1985, 1995). Sunday school is often remembered positively and could have lasting influence (as in the cases of Kitty Howard and Derek Cousens), but this is not always so. As the sole or principal basis of religious education its discursive and rationalistic character could also lead to questioning of paradoxical, illogical and poorly represented doctrines of Christian faith. This also applies to religious teaching received in schools and later. Harold Stevenson went through a long process of religious education first at a Catholic then at a Quaker school and finally at university. He was captivated by Christian moral teaching but finally could not accept its transcendental claims. Similarly Lewis Farrow, when he did begin to pay close attention to religious doctrine, at Catholic Teaching Training College where he was expected to learn to teach religious education, he found unacceptable the responses he received to his questioning of church doctrine.

It is interesting that, also in the British sample, associations with the faith of parents and other members of the family were often seen as especially significant, as for example in Kitty Howard's belief in her father's intrinsic religiosity despite his lack of church-going. Even among the non-religious and atheists, the more affective ties with religion could leave a lasting impression, as with Jennifer Renwick's happy memories of Catholic processions in her childhood in the poor East End of London. Also, Lewis Farrow, whose mother was, in his own words, a 'non-thinking Catholic', appeared to regret the loss of the Latin mass and remembered how in war service in France in 1944 it had made him 'feel part of something'. However family religiosity could also be a detrimental influence if communicated coldly. It may not be merely coincidental that Harold Stevenson, who in his long searching of Christian doctrine could not find a God to trust, had negative experiences as a child, first of his parents' rejection of him and then of the kneeling prayers at night time that his foster parents enforced on him.

Among other factors that need to be considered in explaining these differences between Western and Eastern Europe are some of the particular distinguishing ritual characteristics of Eastern and particularly Orthodox Christianity, the dominant form of religion in both Bulgarian and Romanian culture. These include the earlier involvement of children in communal, including sacramental ritual (children receive priority at communion and are brought to receive it from baptism onwards) and lay members' generally greater knowledge of and involvement in ritual practice within the church (including the kissing of icons, the lighting of candles and preparation of communion bread ('prosphora') and related prayer intentions both before and during the liturgy).

Another possibly important diverging factor in Orthodoxy is the considerable importance given to visits to spiritual elders, usually living in monasteries, which can act as a counterweight to temper the authority of the institutional church (Paert 2010). This may help explain why rejection of the spiritual authority of the church hierarchy has been less evident in Eastern than in Western Europe. Perhaps most importantly, the cultural and family ties associated with religious ritual are deeper and stronger in the former as well as the feeling of belonging to a tradition of spiritual and ritual practice. This creates a sense both of responsibility for and also ownership of this tradition. A number of the people we interviewed in Eastern Europe indicated such close attachment to ritual. Ioana Georgescu (Chapter 8) and Dimana Dimova (Chapter 10) are strong examples of such attitudes. Such conditions strengthen the position of older people as both witnesses to and custodians of tradition.

Ageing and the Future of Ritual

Particular attention has been given in chapters 5 and 6 to the analysis of the meanings of engagement in ritual, particularly its performative meaning. As an outward form of behaviour, ritual expresses a communally shared belief or attitude. Of course it is possible to imitate ritual, to act as if one held such a religious or secular belief, while in fact not holding to such belief. However, the ritual would soon become empty of meaning if few or no people held to the underlying belief expressed. In reality there is likely to be a large variation in the extent to which a person's ritual actions are consonant with their inner disposition to believe what is expressed. The presence of strong believers ensures the continuation of the tradition.

As a number of our case studies indicated (for example Ivanka Grozdeva in chapters 7, 8 and 10, Ioana Georgescu in chapters 8 and 11, and Dimana Dimova in chapters 10 and 11), membership of such a ritual tradition appears to be of great benefit to many people as they age. Older people are given the opportunity not only to be part of the continuation of this tradition, but perhaps most importantly to teach younger generations how to maintain the tradition into the future. This contributes greatly to a person's sense of generativity, the ability to be able to transmit valuable cultural products to the next generation, an important concept in the developmental psychology of ageing (Coleman and O'Hanlon 2004).

However, the practice of tradition also changes and develops throughout time, and this brings with it inevitable tensions, especially if the change is abrupt and inadequately introduced. To live a long life is to experience much change in the world around. Adaptation is required of every person as they age, but successful adjustment (in the sense of acceptance) can be especially difficult if the changes also affect a person's sense of continuity of society moving forward into the future.

In the West imposed religious change has mainly been liturgical in character. Surprisingly little investigation has been carried out into older people's experience of the sometimes disruptive reforms that have occurred, for example the sudden abolition, following the Second Vatican Council in the 1960s, of the centuries-old Tridentine form of the Roman Catholic Mass. Some echoes of this are found in our interviews, not only in Lewis Farrow's comments previously cited, but also in Molly Stevens's preference for attending the revived form of the old Latin Mass (see Chapter 8). However it should be noted that Sylvia Jones (see Chapter 10) welcomed the reforms of the Second Vatican Council because they inaugurated a greater openness in the Roman Catholic Church.

More significant than liturgical change for older people in the UK and much of Western Europe has been their experience of declining attendance at acts of worship, the closure of churches and diminishing respect for Christian culture within society as a whole. Failure of transmission of faith was a painful aspect of interviews with older people in the UK. Kitty Howard, Sarah Hazelwood and Derek Cousens also regretted the various changes in their Anglican parishes in London, especially the declining numbers at church. Derek described himself as 'bitterly disappointed' that his goddaughter never decided to become confirmed as a Christian. Although participants who had been brought up religiously in the UK had mostly maintained their religion, often their expressions of faith were accompanied by regret at the extent of the falling away of faith within the succeeding generation.

In this respect our Eastern Europeans religious elders' situation was better. Particularly the members of the oldest generation were likely to see their own faith reflected in their children. However, there had been some gradual failure of faith transmission during the long period of communism. Moreover, some, including Miron Popescu, were aware that further challenges lay ahead for religious faith in their countries as a result of European integration. In a world of increased globalisation and migration influences are likely to be multi-directional (Coleman et al. 2011), and as some of our interviews in both Eastern and Western Europe have shown, generational movement has not been all in a secular direction. Miron Popescu's, Diman Vasilev's and Evelyn Everett's children display stronger religiosity than their parents.

However, it would be wrong to think that older people are also not capable of change. Indeed, even within a religious context, prophecy – reading the signs of the time – is associated with age, experience and wisdom. Faithfulness to a tradition is compatible with, and can be argued to require readiness to accept, new insights into that tradition's meaning. It is often older people who have the necessary maturity of mind to integrate the tension between tradition and change (Sinnott 1998). Hence Christianity and other world religions have the tradition of spiritual elders.

Although we did not find examples in our samples of persons whose faith had changed during later life, we did interview some older people who had developed during adulthood different perspectives on the faith they had been introduced to as children. There were examples even in the Eastern European samples. Although remaining critical of priests and of religious teaching, Diman Vasilev described himself now as an 'Orthodox Pagan' (Chapter 9). He sometimes entered churches and lit a candle and imagined that 'good thoughts rise up'. He accepted that there was a spiritual reality which he associated with positive human relationships.

The strongest examples though were from the UK. Both Lewis Farrow and Harold Stevenson had both followed careers as teachers and left their churches of origin to become humanists. Political beliefs were important to Lewis and these were the issues, rather than religious beliefs, that he spoke about with his children. The Catholic teaching he had been brought up with he found inconsistent. He was impressed by the way the British Humanist Association held funerals and contrasted this with the 'insult to his intelligence' of the talk of a past colleague's husband 'waiting for her' that he had heard recently at a Catholic funeral he attended.

Harold in fact had trained to hold humanist funerals himself. He was not anti-religious, and preferred to emphasise the positive qualities of humanism. He was prepared to allow some religiouscontent to funeral services he conducted if specifically requested, and before the period of silence that he always introduced into the service, would say words to the effect that 'this is an opportunity for those with religious faith to have a few moments of silent prayer'. He could accept that people varied in their needs for ritual and ceremony. He seemed very much at peace with his beliefs and had reconciled his early interest in a vocation to be a Christian minister with his later humanism:

> Sometimes I've said to the family "Let's have both the crucifix and the humanist symbol side by side". Because humanism is one side of Christianity … It's the human side of Christianity … the man, the human side … rather than the divine.

Harold's integration of religious and humanist symbols may offer a suitable solution for increasing numbers of Europeans in the future as they are faced with the need to design ritual services in an ever more pluralistic society.

References

Bengtson, Vern L. with Norella M. Putney and Susan C. Harris. 2013. *Families and Faith: Generations and the Transmission of Religion*. New York: Oxford University Press.

Bowlby, John. 1969. *Attachment and Loss. Volume 1, Attachment*. London: Hogarth Press.

Coleman, Peter G. 2010. 'Religion and Age'. In *International Handbook of Social Gerontology*, edited by Dale Dannefer and Chris Phillipson, 164–76. London: Sage.

Coleman, Peter G. and Ann O'Hanlon. 2004. *Ageing and Development: Theories and Research*. London: Edward Arnold.

Coleman, Peter G. et al. 2011. *Belief and Ageing: Spiritual Pathways in Later Life*. Bristol: Policy Press.

Davies, C. 2004. *The Strange Death of Moral Britain*. New Brunswick, NJ: Transaction.

Emery, E.E. and Kenneth I. Pargament. 2004. 'The Many Faces of Religious Coping in Late Life: Conceptualization, Measurement and Links to Well-being'. *Ageing International* 29(1): 3–27.

Howse, Kenneth. 1999. *Religion and Spirituality in Later Life: A Review*. London: Centre for Policy on Ageing.

Kirby, Sarah E., Peter G. Coleman and David Daley. 2004. 'Spirituality and Well-being in Frail and Non-frail Older Adults'. *Journal of Gerontology: Psychological Sciences* 59B: P123–9.

Kirkpatrick, L.A. 2004. *Attachment, Evolution and the Psychology of Religion.* New York: Guilford Press.

McCullough, M.E., L.M. Root, B. Tabak and C. v.O. Witvliet. 2009. 'Forgiveness'. In *Handbook of Positive Psychology*, 2nd edn, edited by S.J. Lopez, 427–35. New York: Oxford University Press.

Paert, Irina. 2010. *Spiritual Elders: Charisma and Tradition in Russian Orthodoxy.* DeKalb, IL: Northern Illinois University Press.

Pargament, Kenneth I. 1997. *The Psychology of Religion and Coping: Theory, Research, Practice.* New York: Guilford Press.

Pargament, Kenneth I., K. van Haitsma and D.S. Ensing. 1995. 'When Age Meets Adversity: Religion and Coping in the Later Years'. In *Ageing, Spirituality and Religion: A Handbook*, edited by M. Kimble, S. McFadden, J. Ellor and J. Seeber, 47–67. Minneapolis, MI: Fortress Press.

Roberts, E. 1985. *A Woman's Place: An Oral History of Working Class Women 1890–1940.* Oxford: Blackwell.

Roberts, E. 1995. *Women and Families: An Oral History, 1940–1970.* Oxford: Blackwell.

Scourfield, Jonathan, Sophie Gilliat-Ray, A. Khan and S. Otri. 2013. *Muslim Childhood.* Oxford: Oxford University Press.

Sinnott, John D. 1998. *The Development of Logic in Adulthood: Postformal Thought and Its Applications.* New York: Plenum Press.

Chapter 12

Reflections on the Study:
Why are there No Simple Answers?

Joanna Bornat and Daniela Koleva

In this concluding chapter, we cast a contemplative glance back on the two and a half years of working together on the RASC project and on this volume. We summarise what has been learned from a multidisciplinary approach to a comparative oral history in the area of religion and ageing. In a project such as our own, crossing national boundaries which encompass very different histories and cultures, it was inevitable that we would be researching and writing with many voices, as well as languages. In this final chapter, we address the difficult issue of competing interpretations of interview material, and especially, in regard to conducting research on religion, reconciling the sometimes diverse perspectives of religious and non-religious researchers. We conclude with some pointers for future research while suggesting possible rewards from our findings with regards to policies addressing the lives of older people.

From the start we were aware that we had undertaken an ambitious project, but as the months progressed we grew increasingly aware of how difficult it was, yet also how revealing and rewarding at the same time. We came from the West and the East of Europe, and from different research fields: social gerontology, oral history, social anthropology and psychology. Each of us was motivated by some deficit we had identified in our respective fields, or was interested in the topic. Gerontology has only recently begun to produce insights on religion and its impact on ageing; oral history's engagement with religion is perhaps even less. The anthropology of post-socialism had barely touched on our areas of interest. So each of us had to leave the comfort of their own field with its consensuses and prepare for challenges and learning. The comparative design of the project, calling for attention to the complexity of three national contexts, was a further challenge. Added to this was the need to keep together the two thematic axes – ageing and (non-)religiosity. Thus we set out to explore the secular alternatives to religious belief and practice, while not losing from sight the plurality of religious denominations in the three countries. Aiming to produce psychologically responsible accounts, our approach privileged subjectivity and experience over institutions. We focused on practices and emotions rather than statements of belief, and on participation in collective rituals as much as individual practices. In this way our interest lay in rites of passage as links in the individual life course with the public/social aspects of religious or secular activity.

There was something particularly challenging about religiosity as a topic which, for the most part, tends to be treated as something private and personal and therefore at some level beyond critical evaluation. At the same time, and contrastingly, in all three countries, religious belief and non-religion have historically and in present times been a focus for fierce debate and public position-taking. This elision between the personal, the political and the topic of research meant that some aspects of our own subjective and opposing perspectives were moderated during discussion in the interests of reaching our goal. We come back to this point later, with comments from members of the team. As for the participants, some appeared initially uneasy on being invited to talk about what they had been accustomed to regard as a strictly private matter. Finding interviewees for this project, either religious or non-religious, was always going to be a challenge and so it proved, although the 60 people whose interviews we drew on provided us with accounts that were rich in empirical detail and highly expressive of emotion and feelings.

In summarising what we feel are the key points we have learned from the project and from the chapters preceding us here, we highlight: the importance of historical context; the significance and enduring role of ritual at various life transitions; the role of beliefs and meaning in late life; and the contribution of a focus on gender. In what follows we provide a brief summary of our findings in relation to each of these points.

We begin with the importance of historical context, present in the argument of each of the preceding chapters. The participants in the RASC project are a unique generation having lived not only through war and major societal changes in the twentieth century but also through a reversal of the normative assumptions about religion and secularism. They spent a good deal of their lives in social settings where the norm was to be religious (until the mid twentieth century). Now as they engage in reflective conversation about their experiences of religiosity and non-religiosity, this norm has long since changed, statistically at least (except in Romania). This change has had an impact on the ways older people remember and make sense of their experiences of religion. In the UK, to talk about religion (even less to adhere to it) is not among dominant social expectations. In Bulgaria and Romania, the historical situations have been more complex than general statements of 'persecution of religion' may suggest. First, politics was different with respect to different denominations: a ban on Greek Catholicism in Romania; trials against Catholic priests in 1950s in Bulgaria; and subsequent attempts to eradicate the Muslim religion and culture which peaked in the 1980s. Second, the regimes' attitudes towards Orthodoxy changed with time as both slid into nationalism. In Romania, Orthodoxy was deemed an inextricable part of national identity, in Bulgaria of cultural heritage (chapters 3 and 6).[1] Therefore, in post-

---

[1]   It can be hypothesised that in both countries these politics were part of the attempts to deal with significant ethno-religious minorities (Hungarians and Muslims respectively) in the course of building homogeneous and monolithic 'socialist nations'.

communist Bulgaria and Romania adherence to Orthodoxy can be both a way to state one's anti-communism and to affirm one's national identity. Conversely, participants with no religious commitment tended not to have felt or 'noticed' any religiously based discrimination. Thus, taking national historical contexts into account reveals responses to cultural memory, helping to differentiate what might be regarded as systematic distortions from biases and aberrations of memory and to deepen understanding rather than discard these as background noise.

Interviewing people over the age of 75 in the three countries meant that inevitably we drew on multiple temporalities. We needed to have a sense of the times our interviewees had lived through as well as the timing of our project and the experience we drew from our own individual life histories. While there were some generational similarities, in terms of interviewee's individual life transitions and personal histories, the framing which political events and broad social change provides, and the different ways in which these were recalled and presented in the interviews, has been an essential part of understanding and analysing the accounts we were given.

Our second key point is the significance and enduring role of ritual at various life transitions. Perhaps surprisingly from the point of view of the thesis of the individualisation of religion, famously put by Grace Davie as 'believing without belonging' (Davie 1994), the RASC project found out that rites of passage did not seem to have waned during the life course of the participants. In all three countries, but especially in Bulgaria and Romania, family life has proven to be closely bound up with the use of religious ritual and very important for the successful transmitting of religious knowledge and practices (chapters 4, 6 and 7). A possible explanation is that rituals are behaviourally salient, merging belief with practice and belonging. On the other hand, even participants who did not identify themselves as religious stressed the importance of rites of passage (Chapter 6). This is in line with Davie's (2006) thesis about the 'vicariousness' of religion, implying that for large segments of the population it is enough to have religious ritual as a resource on which to draw when needed. Furthermore, the popularity of rituals probably has to do with the productive ambiguity of symbols allowing various meanings to be read into them. In addition, the performative and aesthetic dimension of rituals seems to be increasingly important (chapters 5, 7 and 8). The attempt to replace religious with secular rituals at key transition points as births, marriages and deaths does not appear to have been successful in either Bulgaria or Romania. More examples of successful secular ritual were given in the UK, where secularisation has occurred independently of government intervention, and where attachment to traditional religious rituals appears less strong. Ritual, whether religious or non-religious, still appears to play an important role at points in people's lives when transitions introduce feelings of uncertainty and loss. How ritual is then drawn on or elaborated was described in various ways with individual choice and meaning predominating in, for example, accounts of recalling and communicating with deceased relatives or making plans for interviewees' own funerals. Taking responsibility for the organisation and performance of rituals rather than entrusting them to ministers has brought about a greater ownership of Orthodox rituals in Bulgaria and Romania (Chapter 11), which can to some extent account for their endurance. However, this tendency does not seem to be specific to Orthodoxy only, as it is also found in the interviews of UK secular humanists.

From the perspective of ageing, it seems that rituals and other forms of religious practice connected with places of worship provide social roles for older people (chapters 5, 8 and 10). Where these are accompanied by volunteer work there is overlap with secular alternatives reinforcing the well attested role of the older generation in maintaining social networks and markers of transition and time passing (van Tilburg and Thomése 2010; Bytheway 2011, 128ff). The continuing performance of religious rituals at life transitions cautions against too rigorous dichotomies of 'the religious' and 'the secular' and sensitises to various hybrid and entangled forms. Interviews with secular humanists provided further evidence for questioning dichotomies with regard to rituals testifying to the elaboration of their own rituals for life transitions (Chapter 7), sometimes with striking parallels in form to religious ones. Research into ritual raises intriguing methodological issues, including the difficulties of assessing the depth of individual involvement in religious ceremonies and accounting for self-presentation biases in the course of interview.

A focus of particular interest for any research on religion and ageing has been the part played by religious beliefs and practices in later life. Religion has traditionally been seen as a friend of ageing. Indeed religiosity has been expected to increase with advanced age as existential security[2] decreases, with religion being argued as providing psychological (security, meaning, belonging in the face of decline and death) and social benefits (e.g. transmitting belief and ritual across generations) (Coleman 2010). Therefore, where religion is in decline, one might expect the well-being of older people to be detrimentally affected while those belonging to religious communities would be advantaged. However, while curtailing some of their functions throughout the twentieth century, churches have kept their core role in pastoral care, which has been most relevant from the point of view of this research. The project did find religious coping to be a beneficial factor in many older people's lives (chapters 5 and 7–11). However the research also uncovered evidence for the benefits of strong secular commitments on well-being and coping throughout life (chapters 4, 6, 7 and 9). It seems that transcendence of the self – whether this-worldly or directed to God – contributes to older people's emotional and mental well-being.

The project did not find indisputable evidence in support of the thesis of growth of religiosity with age. Participants who identified themselves as religious tended to state that they had always been so, having acquired their religious habitus through their family with some early attachments still playing a strong part in the expression of some of the very old. Religious belief and/or practice seem to have been amplified by particular events, most often the loss of significant

---

[2]   The belief that one's survival and well-being can be taken for granted.

others (parent, spouse) rather than age. In one or two cases, however, traumatic experience was reported to have led to loss of faith. On the whole, bereavement emerged as a key testing time for religious belief in which the value of well-conducted and meaningful ritual was highlighted (chapters 7, 8 and 10). Death rituals turned out to be important for non-religious participants as well. However, while elderly Bulgarians and Romanians tend to stick to church rituals and disapprove of 'communist' ones, UK participants are of varying opinions, with some of them actively seeking new rituals and new meanings (chapters 6 and 7). For the generation that survived the Second World War, it seems that the need for belonging has not decreased while the essence of 'belonging' might have changed: belonging (being together with and useful for others) is more important than authenticity (being true to oneself).

For many of these older men and women church membership and ritual, most especially for the religious, has a particular significance in relation to belonging. Several of our interviewees were without close family members, either as survivors of a generation and without descendants of their own, or because their children lived abroad. The social benefit of inclusion or association with a place of worship appeared to play an important part in the lives of such people, giving 'belonging' a particular significance for late life (Chapter 10), even for those without strong religious convictions (chapters 3 and 4). The role of such associations and practices in combating loneliness, now an acknowledged aspect of many older people's lives (Yang and Victor 2011; Ye et al. 2012; Khaleeli 2012) is also worth remarking.

The research revealed specific gendered ways of being religious. Older Bulgarian and Romanian men often saw their own religiosity as part of a national identity, a patriotic ethos, a traditional morality or an anti-communist orientation that they had managed to preserve over the years. Thus their religiosity appeared not only to be a source of support in later life (chapters 5 and 9) but also to acquire a kind of publicity, a wider relevance. The particular significance of religion for women was highlighted as well. In a large number of cases, belief in God and mourning rituals was instrumental for coping with hardship in life and with bereavement in particular (chapters 5, 8 and 10). However, in some instances religion turned out to be a means of empowerment for women who became informal experts in rituals (chapters 7, 8 and 10), thus acquiring a real albeit not always explicitly acknowledged authority in their communities. Communal religious ritual gives older women in particular opportunities for social presence which they otherwise do not have (Woodhead 2002). This turned out to be particularly important for participants in Bulgaria and Romania, where opportunities for public activities for older women outside church communities are not numerous. Again, commitments to parish life provided them with a chance to belong and a purpose and meaning in later life other than family and (grand)children. Non-religious people, especially in UK, found alternative venues for public activities such as volunteering in adult education and social work; some with a more openly expressed commitment to non-religion had developed a particular expertise and were in demand with respect to the development of secular rituals and gatherings (chapters 3 and 7).

For the future it will be interesting to see to what role gender plays in the generations that follow. Brown (2012), for example, argues that there is a correlation between the decline of religion in the West and shifts towards more liberal attitudes with respect to marriage and the family. Dating this change to the 1960s using statistical as well as oral history evidence, he sees women as having played a key role in initiating this trend. Several of the RASC participants' children and grandchildren, and in one case a god child, were described as having weak or no religious affiliation. In one case the roles were however reversed, with a religious daughter of non-religious parents. Longitudinal studies would provide further insight and perhaps reveal the extent to which religiosity is gendered, generational or indeed a mix of both in very late life.

Our chosen method was oral history. We knew that it promised much and that, having spent time discussing our interview schedule, samples and recruitment and how we would share the ensuing data, we would be presented with rich and illuminating accounts of rituals and ceremonies from religious and non-religious people whose memories stretched back over more than 60 years. So it proved. We were rewarded with thoughtful and personal accounts linked to events in national histories and to the repercussions of changing ideologies and social trends within individual life histories. We were able to hear how people accounted for their personal beliefs and how they marked changes in their own and other people's lives with shared activity, sometimes of their own making, but more often in customary ways. Participants responded with engagement and seemed to need little prompting to talk about a topic that is often considered personal and internal to an individual. We were aware of the many ways in which oral historians have worked with accounts they are given (Abrams 2010, 29–31).

Working across three countries when not one person amongst us could speak or understand all three of the languages we were hearing meant that we were going to have to place a great deal of emphasis on developing shared interpretive skills, but also rely on trust amongst ourselves. For example, as pointed out in Chapter 5, the significance of silences in all the interviews we accepted as specific to each encounter without drawing broader inferences. Contrastingly we were more confident in our conclusions regarding the significance of ritual in late life in all three countries and in relation to all persuasions, religious and non-religious. The immediacy of the recording and the recognition of the force and quality of recall is at the heart of the oral history endeavour. We hope that the voices of participants come through clearly in all the chapters, although we are aware that working across language barriers has meant that more in-depth engagement with linguistic nuance, dialect and imagery remains to be developed by researchers interested in reusing our data.

As we have pointed out (chapters 1 and 2), this was always going to be a challenging undertaking. For one thing ours was a very small sample from which to draw out conclusions. In fact working comparatively, from only 60 interviews, brought many rewards. Perhaps most important to the spirit of the whole project were the common threads that soon emerged as we heard interviewees' accounts of universal existential issues: life transitions, partnering, bereavements and awareness of finitude. Exchanges at the three seminars were open and informative, particularly as we were able very quickly to share narratives with each other, and where familiarity with contexts was lacking this stimulated discussion and the development of ideas. Explaining differences and making connections across time and national boundaries made for a privileged learning experience.

Even so, some unresolved aspects persisted. A reviewer of the manuscript asked, 'how were biased and unbiased interpretations discriminated between … and was the dilemma of competing interpretations ever resolved for this project?' The answer to both these questions is that they were not, as readers working through all the chapters assembled here will have noticed. Attitudes for and against religion ranged across the spectrum amongst project members and remained as we came to write up our findings, following continuing research interests as well as newly kindled ideas. The view evolved that, so long as we made our personal commitments clear, we would each be free to draw the conclusions that we felt were appropriate. We were never going to be able to speak with one voice and by making differences clear we were inviting readers to decide for themselves how they would make sense of what they were reading. This is not such an unusual stance, although it tends to happen more often between publications rather than, as in our case, within the covers of one book. Aware that these differences in personal philosophy and in world outlook were a feature of the team's composition, we asked members to send us their views of how they had dealt with this and what they had learned from the experience. In the paragraphs that follow we have edited these personal accounts into a brief anthology of anonymised contributions:

> I believe working on the project has broadened my personal development. For example I found it very useful to listen to the subjective thoughts and feelings about religious and secular belief and practice of other members of the group and this made me think and reflect more deeply about the development and path of my own personal belief and practice and at times challenged my thinking or what I thought I knew. In particular discussion about secularism and humanism heightened my awareness and appreciation for the potential benefits associated with secular behavioural and psychological processes. Indeed, the project allowed me to interview humanists for the first time.

> As I reflect more I realise the profound dissatisfaction – the alienation – I feel of living a double life of moving between religious and secular understanding according to context. I have also found conducting this research more uncomfortable than I expected. At best it leads one to be honest with oneself and others about what can be truthfully said. At worst it leads to falling back on security in the faith of fellow believers. Nevertheless one part of me wants to continue such investigation but in a more focused and historical study of the past

(for example I am particularly interested in the struggles for personal religious liberty of expression in the later medieval period).

I was attracted by the opportunity to explore personal testimonies of people from other countries in order to challenge my own understanding of oral history practice. For the Bulgarian and Romanian interviewers to interview in their own language and then share their research findings in English must have been tiring and testing but always amazed me. However, I often felt twice-removed when reading the Bulgarian and Romanian interviews – possibly because they were conducted by other people therefore I needed to read more closely in order to sense the context but I sometimes felt that some of the texture of the interview situations and relationships between the interviewer and interviewee were lost in translation or that I needed a deeper knowledge of the history.

Somehow I assumed one has to be an affirmed atheist in order to study religion. I was not. I am not. I am not a firm believer either. I know now, after our research reached its results, that I am probably a typical Eastern Orthodox, attached to a tradition that gives one a sense of belonging. I know I dreaded the moment when someone from the team would ask if I am religious or not. After all, this was one of the basic questions we were going to ask all our interviewees. But then, during an evening walk through Sofia, [name] told me about his becoming an Orthodox. A few months later, [name] had a humanist wedding whose story and script she shared with us. [Name] baptised her child Orthodox and sent us beautiful images of the ceremony. I baptised my second child as the project was unfolding. The subject of religious ceremonies and religious (non-)attachments has never been in our group just an academic subject. It was part of our lives and the group dynamics. It reminded me that we are not studying life on Mars but we are always, in some way, studying ourselves.

The discussions at our methodological workshops were very useful for me, especially the joint work with the British colleagues. Their attitudes to religion were as a whole similar to those of German colleagues with whom I have been working for years, so it was not difficult to communicate and discuss with them but rather interesting (especially with regard to the new secular rituals). In addition, I myself have taken interest in Christianity for 15 years, … I remember well my own steps of gradual acquaintance with it, confronting my own notions and church authorities, so I understand both colleagues who do not share my Christian outlook …, and colleagues … on the other hand [who do].

The fact that I am religious and am a regular church goer was an advantage rather than an obstacle or difficulty in the course of the interviewing, as well as at a later stage during the analysis of the interviews. My modest stock of theological knowledge in the field of Orthodoxy for instance was important in my attempts to win the confidence of those respondents who identified themselves as believers

... In so far as I touched on the question of secular humanists in my study, I can't help acknowledging ... extremely inspiring and fruitful discussion ... where we could together negotiate and clarify the working hypotheses and terminology.

Working with people on a research who have strongly held views which I don't share is a new experience for me. I kept trying to think of any parallel endeavour, but couldn't. For example even members of a group investigating experiences of poverty or racism would expect to share a common outlook. Did the differences we experienced get in the way, or did they give us more of an edge? I'd like to think the latter and from my own perspective I feel much more confident in claiming ritual and feelings of spirituality for the non-religious, seeing these as shared human practices and traits.

Within each of the three countries we encountered multiple ways of growing old and being old. Differences lie not only across but also within national borders. Nevertheless, a comparative perspective helps to make sense of them and to gain deeper understanding of the situation in one's own country. Our study serves as a reminder that subjectivities and individual biographies are intrinsic to understanding the position of older people in society and their role in sustaining and representing continuities between past, present and future. How older people make sense of their lives plays a central role in this. As von Stuckrad has noted, '*pluralism* and *pluralization* are linked to a process of contestation, in which thinking about religion becomes *reflexive*' (von Stuckrad, 2013, 3, emphases in the original). Such reflexivity is worthy of research in its own right, particularly with respect to the promotion of intergenerational solidarities and the development of appropriate welfare policies. Older people's well-being depends on a range of factors, such as health and physical condition, material circumstances, family ties and social contacts. Our study demonstrated the importance of spirituality, which has often been overlooked in the design of welfare policies. If the latter are to be responsible, they have to respond to such needs in open and flexible ways. As succeeding generations age in societies that are becoming more secular and where ritual and belief become more personalised and diverse, psychologists of old age and oral historians will doubtless continue to ask new questions and find simple answers elusive as they seek to explain and understand the view from later life.

References

Abrams, L. 2010. *Oral History Theory*. London: Routledge.

Brown, Callum. 2012. *Religion and the Demographic Revolution: Women and Secularisation in Canada, Ireland, UK and USA since the 1960s*. London: Boydell & Brewer.

Bytheway, Bill. 2011. *Unmasking Age: The Significance of Age for Social Research*. Bristol: Policy Press.

Coleman, Peter G. 2010. 'Religion and Age'. In *International Handbook of Social Gerontology*, edited by Dale Dannefer and Chris Phillipson, 164–76. London: Sage.

Davie, Grace. 1994. *Religion in Britain since 1945: Believing without Belonging*. Oxford: Blackwell.

Davie, Grace. 2006. 'Religion in Europe in the 21st Century: The Factors to Take into Account'. *Archives Européennes de Sociologie/European Journal of Sociology* 47(2): 271–96.

Khaleeli, H. 2012. 'The Loneliness Epidemic'. *Guardian*, 23 January, 8–11.

Van Tilburg, Theo and Fleur Thomése. 2010. 'Societal Dynamics in Personal Networks'. In *International Handbook of Social Gerontology*, edited by Dale Dannefer and Chris Phillipson, 215–25. London: Sage.

Von Stuckrad, Kocku. 2013. 'Secular Religion: A Discourse-historical Approach to Religion in Contemporary Western Europe'. *Journal of Contemporary Religion* 28(1): 1–14.

Woodhead, Linda. 2002. 'Women and Religion'. In *Religions in the Modern World: Traditions and Transformations*, 2nd edn, edited by Linda Woodhead, Christopher Partridge and Hiroko Kawanami, 332–56. Routledge: London.

Yang, K. and C. Victor. 2011. 'Age and Loneliness in 25 European Nations'. *Ageing and Society* 31: 1368–88.

Ye, L., C. Hawkley, L. Waite and J. Cacioppo. 2012. 'Loneliness, Health and Mortality in Old Age: A National Longitudinal Study'. *Social Science and Medicine* 74: 907–14.

Appendix I: Research Team

Simina Bădică – Researcher, Romanian Peasant Museum, Bucharest, Romania

Dr Ileana Benga – Principal Researcher at the Folklore Archive of the Romanian Academy Institute in Cluj-Napoca, Romania

Dr Joanna Bornat – Emeritus Professor of Oral History, The Open University, Milton Keynes, UK

Dr Peter Coleman – Professor of Psychogerontology, Faculties of Social and Human Sciences and of Medicine, University of Southampton, UK

Vanya Elenkova – Historian, Sofia University St Kliment Ohridski, Bulgaria

Dr Galina Goncharova – Assistant Professor of Modern and Contemporary History, Sofia University St Kliment Ohridski, Bulgaria

Dr Sidonia Grama – Independent Researcher in Oral History and Social Anthropology, Cluj-Napoca, Romania

Anamaria Iuga – Researcher, Romanian Peasant Museum, Bucharest, Romania

Dr Teodora Karamelska – Assistant Professor of Sociology, New Bulgarian University and Bulgarian Academy of Sciences, Sofia, Bulgaria

Dr Daniela Koleva – Associate Professor of Theory of Culture and Cultural Anthropology, Sofia University St Kliment Ohridski, Bulgaria

Dr Ignat Petrov – Consultant Psychiatrist and Associate Professor of Gerontology and Geriatrics, Medical University of Sofia, Bulgaria

Dr John Spreadbury – Research Psychologist, Faculty of Social and Human Sciences, University of Southampton, UK

Dr Hilary Young – Oral Historian, Museum of London, London, UK

Appendix II: List of Participants

['Pseudonym', gender, year of birth, main occupation, marital status, living circumstances, religious belief.]

In Bulgaria

'Evlogi Anastasov', male, born 1926, journalist, divorced, living alone in Sofia, Orthodox Christian

'Aydan Berber', male, born 1933, barber, married, living with wife and son in Shumen, Muslim

'Milena Chakalova', female, born 1929, jeweller/teacher, single, living alone in Sofia, Evangelical Christian

'Rumyana Dimitrova', female, born 1925, economist, widowed, living alone in Varna, Orthodox Christian

'Dimana Dimova', female, born 1919, assistant in church, widowed, living with daughter in Varna, Orthodox Christian

'Lidia Emilova', female, born 1929, shop assistant, widowed, living alone in Sofia, Orthodox Christian

'Ivanka Grozdeva', female, born 1937, librarian, widowed, living alone in Targovishte, Orthodox Christian

'Demir Hamidov', male, born 1937, teacher, married, living with wife in Targovishte, Muslim

'Andon Igov', male, born 1923, marine officer, married, living with son and daughter-in-law in Sofia, Orthodox Christian

'Alexandra Koleva', female, born 1918, tailor, widowed, living with son in Sofia, Protestant Christian

'Malina Marinova', female, born 1931, widowed, bank official, living with daughter in Targovishte, Orthodox Christian

'Aleko Radev', male, born 1929, jurist, widowed, living with daughter in Sofia, atheist

'Naum Ruskov', male, born 1926, military officer/engineer, widowed, living with daughter in Sofia, Orthodox Christian

'Murad Sezgin', male, born before 1930, farmer/labourer, divorced, living alone in Targovishte, Muslim

'Tanya Teneva', female, born 1934, teacher, widowed, living in Sofia with son's family, Orthodox Christian

'Anna Tosheva', female, born 1924, economist, widowed, living alone in Sofia, Orthodox Christian

'Nayden Usunov', male, born 1935, journalist, married, living with wife in Varna, Orthodox Christian

'Diman Vasilev', male, born 1935, geologist, married, living with wife in Sofia, non-religious

'Valentina Vassileva', female, born 1934, fabric worker, married, living with daughter in Shumen, Orthodox Christian

'Zahari Zaimov', male, born 1934, teacher, married, living with wife in Shumen, Orthodox Christian

In Romania

'Dorina Badea', female, born 1934, kindergarten teacher, divorced, living alone in Cluj-Napoca, Greek Catholic Christian

'Dinu Bunescu', male, born 1930, engineer, widowed, living alone in Bucharest, Orthodox Christian

'Mihail Calan', male, born 1930, school inspector/opera soloist, widowed, living alone in Cluj-Napoca, Orthodox Christian

'Margareta Calinescu', female, born 1928, engineer/tourist guide, divorced, living alone in Bucharest, atheist

'Florina Campeanu', female, born 1928, teacher/school director, widowed, living alone in Bucharest, Orthodox Christian

'Ion Cotescu', male, born 1924, engineer, widowed, living alone in Bucharest, non-religious

'Stefan Cotrus', male, born 1926, priest, married, living with wife in Cluj-Napoca, Orthodox Christian

'Mirela Dinescu', female, born 1930, tailor, widowed, living alone in Bucharest, Orthodox Christian

'Ecaterina Florea', female, born 1925, nurse, widowed, living with daughter's family in Cluj-Napoca, Orthodox Christian

'Ioana Georgescu', female, born 1924, pharmacist, divorced, living with daughter in Bucharest, Orthodox Christian

'Aurelian Ghelasie', male, born 1914, economist, married, living with wife in Cluj-Napoca, Orthodox Christian

'Teodora Ghelasie', female, born 1925, nurse, married, living with wife in Cluj-Napoca, Orthodox Christian

'Camelia Ionescu', female, born 1933, worker, widowed, living alone in Bucharest, Orthodox Christian

'Viorel Ionescu', male, born 1927, university professor, married, living with wife and son in Bucharest, Orthodox Christian

'Laura Levi', female, born 1927, nurse, widowed, living alone in Bucharest, Jewish

'Eleonora Moldovan', female, born 1935, university lecturer, single, living with sister's family in Cluj-Napoca, Orthodox Christian

'Miron Popescu', male, born 1924, military officer, living with wife and two daughters in Bucharest, Orthodox Christian

'Emil Tatu', male, born 1932, physician, married, living with wife in Cluj-Napoca, Greek Catholic Christian

'Claudia Voiculescu', female, born 1935, economist, widowed, living with daughter and family in Cluj-Napoca, Orthodox Christian

'Eduard Vornic', male, born 1927, engineer, widowed, living alone in Cluj-Napoca, Orthodox Christian

In the UK

'Derek Cousens', male, born 1921, sales office manager, single, living alone in Hackney, Church of England Christian

'John Cruikshank', male, born 1926, general labourer, widower, living alone in Hackney, Church of England Christian

'Kevin Drake', male, born 1930, probation officer, married, living with wife in Southampton, Church of England Christian

'Evelyn Everett', female, born 1925, administrator, married, living with husband in Hackney, non-believer

'Lewis Farrow', male, born 1925, teacher, married, living with wife in Southampton, atheist

'Rita Gardner', female, born 1935, primary school teacher, married, living with husband in Hackney, Church of England Christian

'Matilda Hastings', female, born 1932, music teacher, married, living with husband in Southampton, Church of England Christian

'Sarah Hazelwood', female, born 1915, secretary, single, living alone in Southampton, Church of England Christian

'Kitty Howard', female, born 1916, dress maker/insurance clerk, single, living alone in Hackney, Church of England Christian

'Sylvia Jones', female, born 1931, secondary school teacher, single, living with sister and brother in Southampton, Roman Catholic Christian

'Barbara Morris', female, born 1931, secretary, married, living with husband in Hackney, Jewish

'George Newberry', male, born 1932, secondary school teacher, single, living alone in Southampton, Church of England Christian

'Kate Osborne', female, born 1925, doctor, widowed, living alone in Southampton, Church of England Christian

'Doreen Potter', female, born 1930, office worker, single, living alone in Hackney, Methodist Christian

'Jennifer Renwick', female, born 1924, school assistant, divorced, living alone in Hackney, non-believer

'Len Robeson', male, born 1931, dress designer, married, living with wife in Hackney, Jewish

'Polly Rutherford', female, born 1931, teacher/headmistress, divorced, living alone in Hackney, humanist

'Sunjay Sarwar', male, born 1933, lawyer, married, living with wife in Hackney, Muslim

'Molly Stevens', female, born 1926, housewife, widowed, living alone in Hackney, Roman Catholic Christian

'Harold Stevenson', male, born 1925, teacher, married, living with wife in Southampton, atheist/humanist

Appendix III: Interview Guide Instructions

I. *Preliminary conversation.* It will frame interviewees' thinking so it is important how we present the project and the themes of the conversation to follow. The UK team is required to work out an information sheet that we can then adapt and translate. The following applies maybe more to Bulgarian and Romanian contexts:

> We are interested in: how people lived their everyday lives, the most important events and the turning points in individuals' lives and how these were marked in the course of their own lives/families of origin and their grand/children's lives; how they see their life now in retrospect; which have been the happiest and the most difficult situations they have had to cope with; what has been most important and what is most important now.

> We work together with colleagues from other countries to see what was/is similar and what was/is different in peoples' lives and ways of thinking in these countries. Anonymity guaranteed.

II. *Interview.* Our interviewees are likely to get tired easily, so two to three-session interviews are recommended if possible (also, bearing in mind that people usually go on thinking after the interview, this approach will let us obtain richer information):

> II.1 Interviewer briefly presents the project (see I. above). Record, transcribe and translate this so we can later think about how we have prompted certain replies/associations. Please add a couple of sentences about the interview situation at the beginning of the transcript: where the interview is conducted, how the interviewee behaves and other impressions. If you are at the interviewee's home, look around for items related to belief (icons, calendars, etc.); you may wish to ask about them later.

> II.2 Interviewee's life story ('Tell me about yourself, your life ...'). The idea is to (a) set the conversation partner at ease; (b) learn about their background and situation; and (c) see if our topics of interest emerge in a more or less spontaneous narrative.

II.3 Additional questions. These will depend on what has already been said in the life story. Here are some thematic nodes that seem important:

- *Tell me more about* [life passages mentioned in the interview]. Try to develop both the 'objective' (ceremonial) and the 'subjective' (how people felt) aspects. Some interviewees might find it easier to talk about others' experiences, not their own. It would be good if they compared the marking of life passages in their own lives and in those of their parents and children ('before–after').
- *What about* [life passages not mentioned, including army, graduation ball, retirement, becoming a parent, birth of grandchildren (if appropriate), etc.]. Same as above.
- *Happiest moments in life? Crossroads/key moments in life? Most difficult moments in life?* (accidents, illnesses, bereavement). How did they cope – a story of coping is easier to tell than one of loss. *Experiences of death – the first one, a recent one?* Try to develop the theme of death: how people prepare, rituals (also those of mourning), beliefs.
- *Most important holidays for you/your family?* It might be telling if the person mentions private (e.g. birthdays, wedding anniversaries) or public (May Day) or religious (Christmas) ones. Some might have both religious and secular meanings attached to them. Ask about all in detail: their public and private/family aspects, what they meant, etc. Try to find out if the interviewee foregrounds religion/ belief or tradition as in cases of 'belonging without believing' (saints' days and church holidays re-branded as folklore/cultural heritage). Ask the 'before–after' questions – about change in rituals/ holidays but also what was celebrated before communism (e.g. old people in Bulgaria sometimes speak about the celebration of the crown prince's birth in 1937).
- *Religion and communism.* Religious holidays before 1989 – how people celebrated, etc. What is known about restrictions on religion, persecutions, etc.; how people reacted; own experience and that of others. Please beware of suggestive questions, i.e. ones that in advance presuppose that there were repressions. *The theme of death may re-appear here* in a discussion of religious and secular funeral/ mourning rituals.
- *What do you believe in*? (Not only God, but maybe human soul, destiny, evil forces, supreme justice, life after death, progress of mankind.) *Have your beliefs changed in the course of your life?* Comparison with grand/parents and grand/children. We are interested in 'faith', i.e. religiosity (or lack of it), but also in related symbolic practices, such as lighting a candle – what do they mean? Try to encourage the interviewee's opinion and reflections.

• [For active religious persons] Ask more about the nature and intensity of their engagement: how often they go to church, if they go alone or with friends, how they engage, if they perform related rituals at home, the role of the priests before communism and now, the role of the church nowadays. Religious education – through which sources (family, priest, school, etc.); whether there was any personal effort as well. Religious literacy – how they interpret the rituals.

III. *Structured interview section*

III.1 European Values Survey questions (see pdf file 'masterquestionnaire', Q 22–41). You may find it convenient to have this section printed out and mark the answers with the interviewee's help. Leave the recorder on to record any explanations they might wish to give.

Where I have not given possible answers (Q 27, 29, 38, 40), they are Yes/ No/Don't know.

Q 25 *Apart from weddings, funerals and christenings, about how often do you attend religious services these days?*

1. more than once week
2. once a week
3. once a month
4. only on specific holy days
5. once a year
6. less often
7. never, practically never

Q 26 *Apart from weddings, funerals and christenings, about how often did you attend religious services when you were 12 years old?*

1. more than once week
2. once a week
3. once a month
4. only on specific holy days
5. once a year
6. less often
7. never, practically never

Q 27 *Do you personally think it is important to hold a religious service for any of the following events?*

birth
marriage
death

Q 28 *Independently of whether you go to church or not, would you say you are ...*

1. a religious person
2. not a religious person
3. a convinced atheist
4. don't know (spontaneous)
5. no answer (spontaneous)

Q 29 *Generally speaking, do you think that the churches are giving, in your country, adequate answers to ...*

the moral problems and needs of the individual
the problems of family life
people's spiritual needs
the social problems facing our country today

Q 34 *Whether or not you think of yourself as a religious person, how spiritual would you say you are, that is, how strongly are you interested in the sacred or the supernatural?*

1. very interested
2. somewhat interested
3. not very interested
4. not at all interested
5. don't know (spontaneous)
6. no answer (spontaneous)

Q 38 *Do you take some moments of prayer, meditation or contemplation or something like that?*

Q 40: *Do you believe that a lucky charm as a mascot or talisman can protect or help you?*

III.2 *Self-evaluation test (SET)*. Ignat Petrov developed this some years ago; he and Peter Coleman have applied it and have found it works well with older people, even if they are not very articulate. On a blank sheet of paper, draw a vertical line c. 10 cm long and ask the interviewee to mark their health condition on it, with the top end being best health, and the bottom end the worst. Follow the same procedure with four other lines: for intellect, character, others' attitudes and happiness (strictly in this order). Leave the recorder on to capture comments. Then ask the interviewee to explain their choice, starting with happiness, then health, intellect, character and others' attitudes.

This bit should not necessarily be the last. Ignat advised starting with it as an 'ice-breaker' for 10–15 min. You can try this, if the interviewee is not very talkative. Otherwise, Joanna Bornat and Daniela Koleva thought we would prefer less control at the beginning, i.e. start with the life story.

IV. *Thanks and release form.*

Index